Palgrave Studies in the History of Subcultures and Popular Music

Series Editors
Keith Gildart
University of Wolverhampton
Wolverhampton, UK

Anna Gough-Yates
University of Roehampton, London, UK

Sian Lincoln
Liverpool John Moores University, Liverpool, UK

Bill Osgerby
London Metropolitan University, London, UK

Lucy Robinson
University of Sussex, Brighton, UK

John Street
University of East Anglia, Norwich, UK

Peter Webb
University of the West of England
Bristol, UK

Matthew Worley
University of Reading, Reading, UK

From 1940s zoot-suiters and hepcats through 1950s rock 'n' rollers, beat-niks and Teddy boys; 1960s surfers, rude boys, mods, hippies and bikers; 1970s skinheads, soul boys, rastas, glam rockers, funksters and punks; on to the heavy metal, hip-hop, casual, goth, rave and clubber styles of the 1980s, 90s, noughties and beyond, distinctive blends of fashion and music have become a defining feature of the cultural landscape. The Subcultures Network series is international in scope and designed to explore the social and political implications of subcultural forms. Youth and subcultures will be located in their historical, socio-economic and cultural context; the motivations and meanings applied to the aesthetics, actions and manifesta-tions of youth and subculture will be assessed. The objective is to facilitate a genuinely cross-disciplinary and transnational outlet for a burgeoning area of academic study.

More information about this series at
http://www.palgrave.com/gp/series/14579

Nick Bentley • Beth Johnson
Andrzej Zieleniec
Editors

Youth Subcultures in Fiction, Film and Other Media

Teenage Dreams

palgrave
macmillan

Editors
Nick Bentley
Keele University
Keele, UK

Beth Johnson
University of Leeds
Leeds, UK

Andrzej Zieleniec
Keele University
Keele, UK

Palgrave Studies in the History of Subcultures and Popular Music
ISBN 978-3-319-73188-9   ISBN 978-3-319-73189-6   (eBook)
https://doi.org/10.1007/978-3-319-73189-6

Library of Congress Control Number: 2018934859

Cover illustration: © Paul Salmon/ EyeEm

Printed on acid-free paper

This Palgrave Macmillan imprint is published by Springer Nature
The registered company is Springer International Publishing AG
The registered company address is: Gewerbestrasse 11, 6330 Cham, Switzerland

To all our friends, family and colleagues—you know who you are.

Acknowledgements

Our thanks go to a number of people who have assisted and helped us in various ways. First, Bill Osgerby, who provided support and encouragement both in organising the conference at Keele, was crucial in providing advice and support for our proposal to have this collection included within the *Palgrave Studies in the History of Subcultures and Popular Music* book series. Secondly, this is a collective endeavour and is much more than the sum of its parts. It would not exist without the dedication, support and expertise that the contributors brought to this volume. Thirdly, Carmel Kennedy and Emily Russell at Palgrave Macmillan provided advice, support and patience as we worked through various stages and hurdles to bring this book to fruition. Fourthly, thanks to Matt Worley for reading our submitted manuscript. Fifthly, thanks to Keele Research Institute for the Social Sciences and Humanities, who sponsored and supported the Teenage Dreams conference held in July 2013; to the Subcultures Network who were also very supportive in organising the conference; and to Courttia Newland, Tina Townshend and Don Letts who added their expertise and insights but who did not make it into this volume, for various (good) reasons. Finally, to all our families who provide encouragement, support and the space and time to work on projects such as these when we should perhaps offer more love and attention to them.

CONTENTS

NOTES ON CONTRIBUTORS

Nick Bentley is Senior Lecturer in English at Keele University, UK. He is author of *Contemporary British Fiction: A Reader's Guide to the Essential Criticism* (Palgrave, 2018), *Martin Amis* (2015), *Contemporary British Fiction* (2008), and *Radical Fictions: The English Novel in the 1950s* (2007). He is editor of *British Fiction of the 1990s* (2005) and co-editor of *The 2000s: A Decade of Contemporary British Fiction* (2015). He has also published journal articles and book chapters on Martin Amis, Julian Barnes, Kazuo Ishiguro, Doris Lessing, Colin MacInnes, Ian McEwan, Zadie Smith, Sam Selvon, the city in postmodern fiction, fictional representations of youth subcultures, and working-class writing. He is currently working on a monograph: *Making a Scene: Youth Subcultures in Postwar and Contemporary Fiction* (Palgrave, 2018).

Andy R. Brown DPhil (London) is Senior Lecturer in Media Communications at Bath Spa University. He was part of a nucleus of scholars that got together to imagine the idea of 'metal studies' and out of which arose the International Society for Metal Music Studies (ISMMS). His recent publications include (with C. Griffin) 'A Cockroach Preserved in Amber', *The Sociological Review* (2014); 'Explaining the Naming of Heavy Metal from Rock's "Back Pages"', *Metal Music Studies* (2015); '"Everything Louder than Everyone Else"' in *The SAGE Handbook of Popular Music* (2015); 'The Ballad of Heavy Metal' in *Heavy Metal Studies and Popular Culture* (2016); '"Girls like Metal, too"' in *Heavy Metal, Gender and Sexuality* (2016); and *Global Metal Music and Culture: Current Directions in Metal Studies* (co-editor, 2016).

Matthew Cheeseman is Senior Lecturer in Creative Writing at University of Derby. He works with fiction, non-fiction and art writing, drawing on English literature, film and cultural studies. He runs Spirit Duplicator, a small press (spiritduplicator.org). @eine on Twitter.

Jo Croft is a Senior Lecturer in English Literature at Liverpool John Moores University, specialising in psychoanalysis, spatial theory, and eco-criticism. She completed her PhD, 'Adolescence and Writing: Locating the Borderline', at Sussex University, and borderline subjectivity continues to be axiomatic in her research. Since publishing *Our House: The Representation of Domestic Space in Modern Culture* in 2006 (edited, with Gerry Smyth) Croft's research has centred on forms of mobility associated with 'stuff' (especially those suggested by 'hoarding' and 'gleaning'), and she is currently writing a monograph entitled *Dreaming on Car Park Beach: The Eco-poetics of Matter and Movement.* Croft has also recently been developing her research using audio-visual formats, including two short films about 'swimming and dreaming'.

Dave Ellis is Associate Dean for Student Experience at Oxford Brookes University. He continues to write and teach on contemporary fiction and theory and on the growth of black British writing from the 1950s to the present day. He is also concerned with issues of widening participation and inclusive curriculum design. He published *Writing Home: Black British Writing since the War* in 2007.

David Forrest is Senior Lecturer in Film Studies at the University of Sheffield. His work explores representations of class and region in British film, television and literature. His recent books include *Barry Hines: 'Kes', 'Threads' and Beyond* (co-written with Sue Vice), and he is currently at work on a monograph entitled *New Realisms: Contemporary British Cinema.*

Stephen Glynn is an Associate Research Fellow at De Montfort University and an assiduous follower of the Mod movement. His studies of academic life include *The British School Film: From Tom Brown to Harry Potter* (Palgrave, 2016), while his investigations of youth subcultures range from the general, *The British Pop Music Film: The Beatles and Beyond* (Palgrave, 2013), to the particular, the Beatlemania of *A Hard Day's Night* (2005) and the acme of Mod movies, *Quadrophenia* (2014). He is currently completing a 'hat trick' of Palgrave monographs with a study of the representations of association football in British cinema.

Nedim Hassan is a Senior Lecturer in Media and Cultural Studies at Liverpool John Moores University. His research interests include the roles of music in everyday domestic life, 1980s' rock and metal music culture, as well as contemporary metal music cultures. He has conducted extensive ethnographic research that has examined domestic musical practice, community music-making and metal music culture. Previous published work focuses upon domestic and public musical performing as a resource for social interaction and the articulation of self-identity, the politics of leisure for adults with learning disabilities and the representation of hard rock and metal music of the 1980s. He is currently engaged in an ethnographic project that examines rock and metal music scenes in Merseyside, UK.

Keely Hughes is a Teaching Fellow in Education Studies at Keele University, Staffordshire. She is currently completing her PhD in Sociology at Keele. Her PhD research focuses on the constructions of subjectivity within the relationship between capitalism and education in the city of Stoke-on-Trent.

Rehan Hyder is Senior Lecturer in Media and Cultural Studies at the University of the West of England and author of *Brimful of Asia: Negotiating Ethnicity on the UK Music Scene* (2004). He is co-founder of BLIMA (Bristol Live Independent Music Archive), which documents the everyday experiences of nightlife and musical culture in Bristol. Recent publications have focused on black music in Bristol and also explored the notion of the so-called 'Bristol Sound'. He has also a contributor to Goethe Institute's *Ten Cities* project (http://blog.goethe.de/ten-cities/), and he is currently working as content developer on the *Bristol Music* exhibition to be hosted by the MShed in Bristol during the summer of 2018.

Beth Johnson is Associate Professor of Media and Film at the University of Leeds. Her research interests include class, place, gender and sex as represented on-screen. Beth is the author of *Paul Abbott* (2013), and is co-editor of *Television, Sex and Society: Analyzing Contemporary Representations* (2012), and *Social Class and Television Drama in Contemporary Britain* (2017, Palgrave) with David Forrest (University of Sheffield). She has published in *Screen, Critical Studies in Television*, the *Journal of Popular Television* and the *Journal of British Cinema and Television*.

Ben Jones is a lecturer in modern British history at University of East Anglia with particular interests in class formation, political economy, urban change and the politics of 'race', migration and collective memory. He has published on the working class, housing policy, the British Left, and the community publishing movement. He is currently working on two projects: on race, community development & New Left activism in Notting Hill in the 1960s and on deindustrialisation in England after 1945.

Bill Osgerby is Professor of Media, Culture and Communications at London Metropolitan University. He has published widely on twentieth-century British and American cultural history. His books include *Youth in Britain Since 1945*; *Playboys in Paradise: Youth, Masculinity and Leisure-Style in Modern America*; and

Youth Media and *Biker: Style and Subculture on Hell's Highway*. He has also co-edited numerous anthologies, including *Action TV: 'Tough Guys, Smooth Operators and Foxy Chicks'* and *Subcultures, Popular Music and Social Change*.

Lucy Robinson is Professor of Collaborative History at the University of Sussex. She writes on popular music, politics and identity, feminism and punk pedagogy. Including *Gay Men and the Left in Post-war Britain: how the personal became political*. Since then she has worked on the Falklands War, charity singles, music videos, zine cultures, digital memory, protest and the politics of popular culture. As well as co-ordinating the Subcultures Network, and the open access digital project Observing the 1980s, she has recently advised on an exhibition on Jersey in the 1980s and on a new documentary project funded by the BFI, *Queerama*.

Scott Wilson is Professor of Media and Communication at Kingston University, London. He is the co-editor with Michael Dillon of *The Journal for Cultural Research* and co-editor with Eleni Ikoniadou of the series 'Media Philosophy'. He is the editor of *Melancology: Black Metal and Ecology*. 2014. His most recent book was *Stop Making Sense: Music from the Perspective of the Real* (2015). He is currently writing a book on Scott Walker and existentialism.

Andzrej Zieleniec is an interdisciplinary lecturer at Keele University. His background is primarily in sociology, but he also makes contributions in research and teaching in media, communication and culture, geography, education studies and criminology.

His research and teaching interests focus on the interface between space, society and culture, particularly in the way in which our lived environment is moulded and shaped by social practices, either those imposed by power or those challenged or colonised by the everyday practices of a range of social groups. He has used aspects of spatial theory in research on urban greenspace, leisure spaces, landscape and tourism, youth and space, graffiti and street art, popular music, planning and urban regeneration. He has published two monographs *Space and Social Theory* (2007) and *Park Spaces: Leisure Culture and Modernity* (2013). He is currently Programme Director for the new degree programmes of Liberal Arts.

LIST OF FIGURES

INTRODUCTION

The origins and inspiration for this edited collection was the staging of a conference held at Keele University in July 2013. The aim of the conference was to provide an interdisciplinary open forum to present, discuss and analyse a broad range of texts, contexts, perspectives and approaches extant in the field of contemporary subcultural studies. The conference was an attempt to bring together a variety of perspectives and approaches to readdress both contemporary and historical examples, representations, realities, constructions and case studies of subcultures. It included contributions from researchers and academics working on subcultures from cultural studies, criminology, geography, literary studies, screen studies and sociology, as well as film-makers, novelists and visual artists. The chapters in this collection stem both from papers given at the conference itself and others specially commissioned. The process underlying both the conference and this edition was based on a collective and collegiate endeavour. The aims were to allow and encourage not only a snapshot of current research but an example of social and critical solidarity in which, we hope, the sum is greater than the parts, and the many voices reflect the non-hierarchical and progressive sprit of supportive scholarship in the field.

While there has been a long tradition of analysing youth subcultures in various disciplines, there has been no book-length study of how youth subcultures have been portrayed in fiction, on screen and other media. This edited collection provides a critical discussion and analysis of the representation, articulation and construction of youth subcultures that contributes to filling a gap in the current research into their literary, filmic and visual depictions. The collection brings together scholars working in literary studies, film studies, social and cultural studies whose research interests lie in the aesthetics and cultural politics of youth cultures. The book also contributes to, and enhances, theoretical perspectives and approaches on the ways in which subcultures are (and have been historically) understood in the public consciousness as well as in academic discourse. It addresses examples that perhaps have been less widely covered in research and literature and, where they have, offers new insights and approaches. One of the intentions of the book is to stress that the powerful narrative construction of individual subcultures, and subcultural affiliation more broadly, is in part an imaginative and fictive construction. The study of how fiction, film, TV and other cultural media have contributed to this construction is therefore an important and timely intervention in subcultural studies.

In bringing together these different and sometimes disparate critical voices we have not attempted to impose a universal narrative or suppress diverse voices and perspectives. Our text deliberately aims to bring out the contemporary multiplicity of research in youth subcultures in fiction, film and other media. Subcultures is an amorphous term and notoriously difficult to define, and the contributors to this collection draw on a range of theoretical perspectives that reflect the ways that subcultural analysis has evolved since its inception in the Chicago School and the CCCS (Contemporary Centre for Cultural Studies) at Birmingham, to current manifestations that include post-subcultural theory. However, there is a clear sense in this collection of the continuing importance of identity formation, representation and affirmation. Therefore the changing landscape of subcultural analysis and theoretical approaches in this collection is reflected in the individual chapters that convey and cover a range not only of subjects and fields from a multiplicity of perspectives and analyses of various genres and narrative texts, but also critically address the contributions of seminal subcultural scholars and theorists. The collection identifies developments and differences in the ways in which subcultural studies has evolved and expanded the range of topics, groups, scenes, genres and media. One area for future exploration is perhaps the role of digital and virtual-world experiences. The use and misuse of online existence can be a means to foster and promulgate (un)healthy subcultural allegiances and identities. This seems clear in the worlds of contemporary political processes. However, this is beyond the scope of this collection but is something that could and should be explored and analysed in future research.

The book is divided into three parts with sections on fiction, film and finally new theoretical ideas and perspectives through reference to 'other media'—creative representations, fictional and/or filmic examples and the creative representation of identity. However, whilst the sections are organised as discreet delineations, a clear crossover and connection between chapters is to be found in each section. We anticipate that the reader will find the individual chapters of interest in and of themselves but will enjoy the discovery of similarities and differences in approaches, genres, examples and illustrations between contributions as well as across sections. We hope this contribution to the field explores and expands the work already published in the series *Palgrave's Studies in the History of Subcultures and Popular Music*.

SECTION 1: SUBCULTURAL FICTIONS

The first section of the book examines the ways in which youth subcultures have been represented, constructed and articulated in literary fiction. It follows a broadly chronological approach and begins with Bill Osgerby's analysis of the subgenre of 'bad girl' fiction in 1950s America. Osgerby discusses the way in which these texts contributed to popular anxieties about youth delinquency, crime and gang violence, and identifies how this moral panic was exploited by writers and publishers. The chapter goes on to identify the way in which the success of bad girl fiction can be attributed to wider shifts in the fields of production, demand, reception and regulation.

In the second chapter, Lucy Robinson and Ben Jones also take us back to the 1950s by identifying Colin MacInnes as a key player in the development of subcultural fiction. They begin by identifying MacInnes's 1959 novel *Absolute Beginners* as crucial in establishing the iconic figure of the teenager as slick, cool and creative. They argue that 'the Boy' identity he establishes in that novel is far more than simply a desire for perpetual youth and becomes an autonomous, queer political agent that reoccurs across MacInnes's fiction and non-fiction. The chapter also identifies the inspiration for 'the Boy' as the real life Ray Gosling, and the chapter goes on to discuss Gosling's negotiation of class differences and changing discourses of sexuality in post-war Britain. By analysing Gosling's journalism and unpublished work, Robinson and Jones show how class and sexuality intersected to shape Gosling's activism and his historical construction of selfhood as the political optimism of the 1960s and 1970s gave way to the gloom of AIDS in the 1980s. The chapter argues that the figure of the teenager has always been inflected through queer masculinity and that, in turn, experiences and stories of post-war social mobility impacted the gay activism that followed.

The third chapter in this section moves to the 1970s as Nick Bentley discusses the representation and construction of punk in literary fiction. This chapter pursues two main themes: firstly, it analyses how literary techniques are used in fiction and writing about punk to reflect similar styles, approaches and practices in other cultural manifestations such as in music and fashion. Secondly, it examines the way in which the emergence of punk has been used in selected fiction to indicate a transition or rupture in social, political and cultural discourses in Britain in the 1970s, especially the move in politics from consensus to confrontation. It discusses novels by several writers, including Richard Allen's *Punk Rock* (1977), Jonathan Coe's *The Rotters' Club* (2002), Hanif Kureishi's *The Buddha of Suburbia* (1991) and Gideon Sams's *The Punk* (1977).

In the final chapter in this section Dave Ellis analyses fiction by Courttia Newland and Alex Wheatley in order to explore the links between identity and postcode boundaries in the depiction of black British youth subcultures. Ellis develops Homi Bhabha's concept of New Cosmopolitanism identifying what he posits as a 'new parochialism' being represented in Newland and Wheatle's fiction. This way of looking at these works suggests that established codes of affiliation based on cultural styles and formal and family histories are supplemented (rather than replaced) by new, local histories. Ellis makes the point that if social identities are being reconfigured in this new parochialism then social signifiers of style and affiliation remain strong and can potentially result in violence. Several novels are discussed including Newland's *A Book of Blues* (2011), and Wheatle's *Brixton Rock* (1999), *East of Acre Lane* (2006), *The Dirty South* (2008) and *Brenton Brown* (2011).

SECTION 2: SUBCULTURAL REPRESENTATIONS ON SCREEN

Our second section is concerned with subcultural representations on screen, more specifically, on film. Stephen Glynn's chapter opens with an investigation of the representation of the Mod subculture on film, providing a contextual summary of the development of this essentially British youth movement. His analysis focuses largely on a case study of the 'ace face' of 'Mod at the Movies', Franc Roddam's *Quadrophenia* (1979).

Noting how subcultural leaders are inevitably challenged, a comparative reading is made with Rowan Joffe's younger rival *Brighton Rock* (2010), a bold relocation to 1964 of Graham Greene's catholic noir. Matthew Cheeseman and David Forrest's chapter uses the 1960s as a starting point to analyse representations of nightclub dance floors in British cinema. Focusing on club culture films, including *Human Traffic* (Justin Kerrigan, 1999), *Sorted* (Alexander Jovy, 2000), *Soul Boy* (Shimmy Marcus, 2010), *Everywhere and Nowhere* (Menhaj Huda, 2011), *Northern Soul* (Elaine Constantaine, 2014), and a contrasting French example, *Eden* (Mia Hansen-Løve, 2015), Cheeseman and Forrest propose that British film tends to use the dance floor as a narrative device that occludes or disturbs notions of youth culture, turning it into a problem to be solved. The notion of the problem of/in subculture and its mediation also occupies the work of Adam R. Brown whose chapter on heavy metal subcultural tropes, from *Bill & Ted's Excellent Adventure* (1989) to *Wayne's World* (1992), explores the contradiction that a youth subculture at the centre of a mass-mediated moral panic was also the inspiration for a string of Hollywood movies. Noting the significance of the male-teen-buddy 'met-alhead' experience at the centre of the narrative, Brown looks to issues of genre, in particular the comedy labelling of these texts, to consider the ways in which they both soften heavy metal tropes and, simultaneously, articulate a form of 'protest masculinity' that subverts both plot and narrative. Authored by Beth Johnson, the last chapter in this section provides an analysis of two recent rockumentary texts—*The Stone Roses: Made of Stone* (2013), directed by Shane Meadows, and *Oasis: Supersonic* (2016), directed by Mat Whitecross. Thinking through both the form and structure of their visual and sonic compositions, as well as the content, Johnson's chapter considers the ways in which both texts use the revival culture of the present to look back at the past (1980s and 1990s), and situate the bands at their heart as authentic, Mancunian creatives. Addressing issues of subcultural and generic labelling, Johnson also considers the female-centred stories, the socio-cultural alignments between the bands and the directors, and the significance of place—Manchester—in order to more accurately key out the cultural and identity work of these documentary texts, and consider their contemporary relevance.

SECTION 3: CRITICAL THEORY AND SUBCULTURAL REPRESENTATIONS IN OTHER MEDIA

The chapters in this final section provide an exploration and analysis of a variety of critical offerings that reflect the interconnection between identity and their representation in a variety of other media, as symbol and artefact as well as practice. The scope of these essays demonstrates a vibrant engagement with a range of material, examples and genres. The approaches and perspectives applied in this section reflect the diversity of contemporary subcultural research and analysis. They include a philosophical and historical exegesis of a musical genre underrepresented in subcultural studies, followed by a comparative analysis of how it is represented in film. The following chapter considers the role and significance of film in the depiction of the pop music industry. A photoessay on graffiti and street art argues for and illustrates the use of the urban landscape as a canvas for the self-representation and practices of an activity that is increasingly universal in the urban landscape. The link between public and private space is discussed and addressed in the subsequent essay linking youthful practices in the street with dreams, desires and hopes manifest in the private experience of the home and bedroom. The final chapter seeks to address the similarities and differences in two film representations of youth, bringing a contemporary and critical analysis of the social and cultural context of their production and reception.

In the first chapter of this section, 'Figures in black: Metal and the void of working-class culture', Scott Wilson looks at the subculture of heavy metal. It notes metal's longstanding lack of academic attention, particularly from cultural studies. This is ironic given cultural studies' association with Birmingham, UK, the birthplace of metal in the late 1960s. The chapter argues that Black Sabbath's initial template for heavy metal offers the form and structure for a work of mourning for the deindustrialisation and destruction of traditional working-class culture in the UK. Looking initially at Sabbath, then at Bolt Thrower, the essay suggests that metal's work of mourning introduces a process of subcultural identification, supplanted through states of sonic ecstasy, that allows something to be made out of 'an inferred experience of loss', to create 'out of chaos and destruction.'

Nedim Hassan in the chapter 'Shock Rock Horror! The representation and reception of heavy metal horror films in the 1980s' argues that though existing academic work has examined moral panics surrounding heavy metal music in the USA during the mid-to-late 1980s, previous studies have not assessed the impact they have had on popular film. Hassan's chapter focuses upon horror films released in this period that directly engage with and satirise debates about metal music's alleged corrupting influence. Drawing upon genre analysis and assessing the audience reception of *Trick or Treat* (1986) in particular, the chapter contends that these films articulated anxieties about the social control of youth during this crucial period. Hassan argues that the films addressed youth audiences in ways that fostered potential opportunities to reflect upon their experiences of metal music culture and to counteract wider media discourses that constructed such culture as deviant.

Rehan Hyder in his chapter 'Youth, hysteria and control in Peter Watkins' Privilege' explores how the ideas of standardisation and conformity are reflected in the near-future narrative of Peter Watkins' 1967 feature film *Privilege*, and considers how such concepts have informed the post-war tradition of British cinema focusing on the machinations of the music industry. Watkins' explicit linking of the popular music industry with the dominant ideologies of the state (including politics, consumer culture and religion) draws on the ideas of the Frankfurt School, particularly Adorno's work on popular music and conformity. The chapter will consider how this critique of the music industry focused around the manipulation of the pop superstar is informed by more recent debates about cultural agency and fandom.

In 'Representing subcultural identity: A photoessay of Spanish graffiti and street art', Andrzej Zieleniec presents graffiti as a universal and ubiquitous feature of the modern urban experience, both signifier and material object of a creative street culture. The chapter, using the author's own photographs from visual ethnographic research, explores and analyses the ways in which graffiti writers and street artists represent themselves and their identities, the methods and practices they use, the meanings and values associated with their sense of belonging to a subcultural community of shared interests and experiences. These are both individual and collective responses to and engagement with the urban as a lived experience and practice that reflects a commitment to know, colonise, decorate and adorn the public arena of cities' streets, places and spaces with an alternative urban aesthetic.

Jo Croft's chapter, '"Destruction after all is a form of creation": Donnie Darko, and the spatial dynamics of the teenage dreamer', explores the teenage dreamer's liminal terrain, focusing upon states of borderline consciousness rather than upon more familiar aspects of subcultural identity. Beginning with the premise that 'youth', 'teenage' and 'adolescence' have distinct but overlapping discursive resonances, Croft argues that teenage dreamers occupy a uniquely borderline position: caught between bedroom and street, they straddle the divide between (threatening) public space and (introspective) private space. The chapter traces continuities between different inscriptions of liminal subcultural identity, from August Aichhorn's 'wayward youths' and 'juvenile delinquents', to Frederick Thrasher's 'susceptible gang-boys' and Ian Hacking's 'fugueurs'. Highlighting the relationship between borderline spatiality and ambivalent mobility, Croft concludes with an intertextual reading of Graham Greene's *The Destructors* and Richard Kelly's *Donnie Darko*, foregrounding the teenage dreamer's ambiguous creative potential.

The final chapter by Keely Hughes, 'From exaltation to abjection: Positive and negative subcultures in *Quadrophenia* and *Ill Manors*', explores the veracity and accuracy of defining and describing subculture in contemporary society. Using an analysis of the films *Quadrophenia* (1979) by Franc Roddam and *Ill Manors* (2012) by Ben Drew, the chapter provides a critical discussion of the constructions of subcultural affiliations in light of the role and representation of class relations and 'symbolic styles' (Hebdige 1979). She argues that there has been a shift in the construction of subcultural movements and affiliations from a form of self-othering in *Quadrophenia* to external-othering in *Ill Manors* which is largely connected to changes within the capitalist system and the increasing desperation of the working classes to survive as an entity under contemporary neoliberal policies.

PART I

'Subcultural Fictions'

Girls on the Rampage: 'Bad Girl' Fiction in 1950s America

Bill Osgerby

'BAD GIRL' FICTION AND THE 'CIRCUIT OF CULTURE'

Billed on its front cover as 'a shocking novel of teen-age gang life in the slums of Manhattan', *Tomboy* was a hit in 1950 for American author Hal Ellson. The previous year Ellson had scooped success with *Duke*, a hard-hitting bestseller depicting the lifestyle of New York's violent, teenage gangs. And in *Tomboy* Ellson's attention switched to the female of the species; with a narrative that focused on a teenage girl's life in a street gang and her journey into a world of ruthless turf wars, audacious heists and torrid sleaze. The novel was another Ellson winner, earning plaudits from critics and quickly running to a succession of paperback editions. Other authors soon followed his lead, contributing to a prolific genre of 'bad girl' popular fiction that graced American bookstands throughout the 1950s. Albert Quandt's *Zip-Gun Angels* (1952), for example, profiled the 'leader of a new kind of street gang ... a gang of tough and beautiful girls', while Wenzell Brown's *Gang Girl* (1954) recounted the exploits of Rita, a fifteen-year-old hellion from New York's Lower East Side who 'knew

---

B. Osgerby (✉)
London Metropolitan University, London, UK

© The Author(s) 2018
N. Bentley et al. (eds.), *Youth Subcultures in Fiction, Film and Other Media*, Palgrave Studies in the History of Subcultures and Popular Music, https://doi.org/10.1007/978-3-319-73189-6_1

how to fight with her knees, her elbows, her teeth, how to hold a black-jack, how to spot a cop, how to roll marijuana, how to lure a man into a dark hallway'.[1] And, in the same vein, Joseph Hilton's *Angels In The Gutter* (1955), Harry Whittington's *Halfway to Hell* (1959), Leo Margulies' short story collection *Bad Girls* (1958) and Wenzell Brown's 'gang girl' reprise, *Girls on the Rampage* (1961), all offered gritty tales of young vixens prowling the backstreets of 1950s America.

This 'bad girl' fiction was a subgenre in a broader flood of cheap and lurid 'juvenile delinquency' novels that traded on contemporary anxieties about youth crime and gang violence.[2] For the most part, 1950s teen crime was characterised as a male problem—the stock delinquent por-trayed as a swaggering, leather-jacketed hoodlum with a duck-tail haircut and a bad attitude. But the belief that girls were becoming 'tougher', 'harder' and 'more vicious' was also widespread; and novels such as *Tomboy*, *Zip-Gun Angels* and *Gang Girl* rode the wave of these concerns. Successfully exploiting contemporary angst surrounding girls, morality and crime, 'bad girl' fiction took the febrile newspaper headlines and con-densed them into potboilers of sensational sex and violence.

The rise of 'bad girl' literature, however, was not solely indebted to con-temporary anxieties about miscreant femininity. Like any media configura-tion of youth subculture, 'bad girl' fiction of the 1950s was the product of a confluence of mutually constitutive processes—a 'circuit of culture'—in which social and cultural influences *were* important; but *also* decisive was the way these factors interacted with developments in other realms, espe-cially the fields of production, demand, reception and regulation.

The concept of a 'circuit of culture' was originally developed in the mid-1980s by Richard Johnson. According to Johnson, to understand the way media forms develop, circulate and generate meaning, attention must be given to the way they move through a 'circuit' consisting of three main stages—production, textuality and reception. Each stage, he argued, was distinct and involved 'characteristic changes of form', but were linked together in processes of interdependence and interaction so that '[e]ach moment or aspect depends upon the others and is indispensable to the whole' (Johnson 1997, 83). Analytic perspectives that failed to acknowl-edge each stage of the circuit and its relation to the others, Johnson con-tended, could not adequately account for the form and meaning of media texts. In these terms, then, approaches that dwelt exclusively on issues of (for example) authorial intent or textual character were insufficient. Instead, other aspects of the cultural circuit—for instance, the organisation of production and the readings generated by audiences—also demanded attention, along with the dimensions of influence and interplay that invariably existed between the various points of the circuit.

Since Johnson's original model, various configurations of the cultural circuit have featured in a diversity of studies. Versions of the cultural circuit have, for example, underpinned analyses of product design (Julier 2000) and the development of technologies such as the Sony Walkman (Du Gay et al. 1997) and mobile phones (Goggin 2006), as well as in case studies of textual forms such as the British 'lads' magazines of the 1990s (Jackson et al. 2001). And ideas of a cultural circuit can also be usefully applied to media forms associated with youth cultures and subcultures. American 'bad girl' fiction of the 1950s is exemplary. The rise of the genre can be seen as the outcome of an interlinked circuit of culture in which the social and cultural controversies of the period undoubtedly played an important role, but crucial was the way these influences interacted with other contemporary developments—most obviously the shifts in business organisation, markets and censorship that transformed US publishing after the Second World War.

THE PAPERBACK BOOM AND A MARKET FOR THE 'THREE SS'

Issues of production always play a key role in a circuit of culture, and they were fundamental to the rise of 'bad girl' fiction. The success of the 1950s 'bad girl' novels was indebted to the wider boom in paperback books. Of course, paperbound books were hardly new. The commercial possibilities of paperbacks had already been demonstrated in Germany during the 1930s, where Albatross Books had successfully produced a range of mass-market paperbacks whose innovations in size, typography and layout became the industry standard. And in Britain the Albatross format was imitated by Allen Lane's launch of Penguin Books in 1935, which revolutionised British publishing through the introduction of high quality, inexpensive paperbacks. But American talent was also quick to appreciate the paperback's potential.[3]

Leading the way, entrepreneur Robert de Graff joined forces with publishers Richard Simon and Max Schuster in 1939 to found Pocket Books, which soon became a market leader with its paperback reprints of classics, light novels and popular non-fiction. The company's success was partly indebted to its books' low price (25 cents) and attractive presentation, but it was also indebted to the firm's innovative distribution. Whereas hardback sales traditionally relied on bookshops, de Graff (a seasoned pressman) saw how a much broader market could be reached via the distribution systems used for newspapers and magazines. Hence Pocket Books were racked-up on newsstands and in drugstores, a strategic masterstroke that, within a year, had clocked up sales of more than 1.5 million.

Following Pocket Books' success, rivals soon appeared. For instance, Avon Books (publisher of *Gang Girl* and *Halfway to Hell*) had started out as a magazine publisher—J.S. Ogilvie Publications—but was bought up by the newspaper distributor American News Company (ANC) and relaunched in 1941 as Avon, a paperback imprint that closely imitated Pocket Books. And more competition quickly followed. Dell was launched in 1942, then Popular Library in 1943; in 1945 Ian Ballantine (formerly director of Penguin's American operations) set up Bantam Books (publisher of the paperback edition of *Tomboy*), followed by Ballantine Books, launched in 1952. And in 1948 Kurt Enoch (who had fled Nazi Germany after launching Albatross Books) established New American Library, initially publishing paperback reprints of classics, then a few original mysteries, romances and adventure stories.

But the key pioneer in the production of paperback originals was Fawcett, a major magazine publisher and leading newsstand distributor. Handling the distribution of New American Library's Mentor and Signet imprints, Fawcett soon saw the potential of paperback sales, and in 1950 the firm launched the industry's first major line of original paperback novels—Gold Medal Books (publisher of *Angels in the Gutter* and *Girls on the Rampage*). Specialising in westerns, mysteries and thrillers, Gold Medal had churned out over nine million books by the end of 1951, with many novels quickly going to three or four editions. By 1953, then, the paperback trade was burgeoning and the business magazine *Fortune* could trumpet 'The Boom in Paper Bound Books', estimating that the previous year had seen national paperback sales of 243 million in a market worth over $69 million (*Fortune*, September, 1953, 122).

The paperback bonanza, however, was itself indebted to another link in the 'cultural circuit'—the shifts in markets and consumer demand engendered by America's economic upturn. After the Second World War disposable incomes and living standards rose across the board, and publishers rode the tide of consumer affluence. But one market was especially attractive—teenagers and young adults. The post-war 'baby boom' ensured a 'bulge' in the US teenage population throughout the 1950s and 1960s; and this, combined with buoyant levels of youth employment and a growth in parental allowances, ensured a sustained growth in young people's spending power.[4] In 1956, for example, *Time* magazine estimated that 'allowances and earnings give the teenage boy an average weekly income of $8.96, compared to only $2.41 a dozen years ago' (*Time*, 13 August, 1956, 72); and by 1959 an awestruck *Life* magazine was observing that American youth had 'emerged as a big-time consumer in the US economy', with teen wallets reckoned to be worth around $10 billion per year (*Life*, 31 August, 1959, 78). Industries scrambled to stake a claim in the teenage goldmine, with everything from rock 'n' roll records to 'brothel-creeper' shoes pitched to young consumers. And publishers, too, were keen to cash-in.

While paperbacks enjoyed a diverse readership, teenagers and young adults were squarely in the book trade's sights. In 1946, for example, Pocket Books launched the Teen-Age Book Show, a touring exhibition that pitched paperbacks to young readers, while throughout the 1950s New American Library had an educational sales department geared to penetrating the classroom market. Largely based on paperback reprints of classic titles, such initiatives were promoted as offering young readers easy access to literature deemed worthy and educational. But, alongside this earnest fare, there also lurked a legion of paperback books with less high-minded sensibilities.

During the early 1950s the flourishing paperback trade was regularly decried by critics who argued the market was dominated by what they dubbed 'the three Ss'—'sex, sadism and the smoking gun' (Schick 1958, 96). The point was not without foundation. Many paperbacks were noir-*esque* tales of hard-boiled tough guys and hot-blooded dames; their scorching narratives matched by covers that bristled with sneering hoodlums and their improbably buxom molls. The formula had its roots in the traditions of pulp magazine publishers, many of whom had become major players in the new paperback business.

The 'pulps'—so-called because of the low-cost, wood pulp paper they were originally printed on—were cheap fiction magazines renowned for their gripping themes and racy cover art. The genre's heyday was during the 1920s and 1930s when US newsstands were thronged with cheap, visually striking pulp titles such as *Argosy*, *Amazing Stories* and *Dime Detective*, all proffering thrilling tales of mystery, crime and adventure. Paper shortages during the Second World War brought a steady rise in costs and a decline in the pulps' circulation and, in peacetime, the pulps' sales were hit further by competition from television, comics and the boom in paperbacks. But, like mainstream magazine publishers, many pulp publishers survived by, themselves, shifting into the paperback trade. Pulp magazine specialists Leo Margulies (editor of *Bad Girls*) and Ned Pines were quick off the mark, launching their paperback imprint, Popular Library, in 1942. Others soon followed. Founded in 1949, Pyramid Books was an offshoot of the pulp firm Almat Magazines, while Ace Books was established in 1952 by A.A. Wyn, owner of the pulp publishing house Ace Magazines. Like Pocket Books and Fawcett, the pulp publishers exploited their established systems of magazine distribution and sales, and their new paperbacks did a brisk trade in newsstands and drugstores. And, as the companies' writers, artists and editors shifted from producing magazines to paperbacks, the pulps' sensational themes, styles and subject matter were reincarnated.

Like the original pulp magazines, their paperback progeny traded in the thrilling and the taboo. They were home to ruthless gangsters, hard-bitten detectives and shameless hussies. And, like the earlier pulps, the 1950s paperbacks were adept at exploiting contemporary controversies, appropriating their concerns and motifs for narratives calculated to shock and sensationalise. It was a strategy to which the theme of teenage rebellion was ideally suited. Stories of violent street gangs and lawless 'bad girls' offered a high octane mix of sex and violence; but they also offered a sharp bite of topicality at a time when America was seized by popular alarm about an apparent explosion of delinquency.

THE 'FIFTH HORSEMAN OF DOOM': THE 'JUVENILE CRIME WAVE' AND THE RISE OF 'YOUTH-SPLOITATION'

The rise of 'bad girl' fiction during the 1950s was indebted to wider developments in consumer markets and general shifts in American publishing. But the specific subject matter of 'bad girl' novels stemmed from another vital link in the books' cultural circuit—their social context and, specifically, the widespread perception that juvenile crime was spiralling out of control. As historian James Gilbert shows, Gallup surveys suggest a brief peak of public concern in 1945, followed by a more sustained period of alarm between 1953 and 1958 (Gilbert 1986, 63). The mood was captured in 1953 by Clymer Hendrickson, a New Jersey Senator, who contended that delinquent youth represented the 'fifth horseman of doom'. 'Juvenile delinquency', Hendrickson averred, was 'at its highest peak since World War II, and the crimes being committed by the young of our Nation are harder, fiercer, more shocking than ever before in our Nation's history' (*Washington Post*, 12 April, 1953). In response, that year saw the appointment of a Senate Subcommittee on Juvenile Delinquency to investigate the problem's cause. Headed by Estes Kefauver (Senator for Tennessee), the enquiry continued until the early 1960s, and its very existence helped confirm views that juvenile delinquency—or the 'J.D.' problem as it was often dubbed—was a major social issue.

Such perceptions, however, were vastly overblown. Notions of a quantum leap in delinquency seemed borne out by a relentless rise in crime statistics, but Gilbert shows how this 'juvenile crime wave' was largely a statistical phenomenon produced by new strategies of law enforcement and changes in the collation of crime data (Gilbert 1986, 66–70). As Gilbert argues, rather than being a response to a genuine eruption of adolescent vice, the post-war fears surrounding delinquency functioned as 'a symbolic focus for wider anxieties in a period of rapid and disorienting change'; the concerns about youth crime serving to articulate 'a vaguely formulated but gnawing sense of social disintegration' (Gilbert 1986, 77).[5]

Nevertheless, the newsworthiness of juvenile delinquency ensured it was a recurring theme in the popular media of the day. At the cinema, for instance, dysfunctional adolescence loomed large in a spate of 'J.D.' movies.[6] In 1955, for example, Warner's *Rebel Without A Cause* (dir. Nicholas Ray) catapulted James Dean to stardom as the prototypical teen rebel, while the same year saw MGM's *Blackboard Jungle* (dir. Richard Brooks) paint a sobering portrait of teenage violence in an inner-city high school. But not all J.D. films were homilies on the dangers of wayward youth. Whereas the pictures released by major Hollywood studios usually saw straitlaced adults moralizing to errant youngsters, the movies produced by independent studios were often more libertine. Dubbed 'exploitation' pictures in the film business, such films were largely geared to the youth market and shunned dominant notions of artistic merit and narrative finesse in favour of cheap, quickly made product that cashed-in on contemporary fads, luring audiences with the promise of spectacle and thrills. Hence many exploitation studios quickly seized on the theme of delinquency. American International Pictures (AIP, founded in 1954) led the way with a series of 'wild youth' films that included *Motorcycle Gang* (dir. Edward Cahn, 1957), *Dragstrip Riot* (dir. David Bradley, 1958) and *The Cool and the Crazy* (dir. William Witney, 1958). Superficially, these 'youth-sploitation' pictures purported to preach against the 'evils' of reckless adolescence but, beneath this veneer, the films gloried in their tableaux of the daring and the sensational; and much of their box-office pull lay in the way they offered young audiences the vicarious thrills of delinquent revolt.

Youth-sploitation sensibilities also surfaced in the book trade. 'Pulp' firms such as Ace, Pyramid and Popular Library predominated, but most paperback publishers (including Avon, Ballantine, Gold Medal and Signet) contributed to the hundreds of novels that, throughout the 1950s, paraded the misdeeds of American teens. With lurid covers and eye-catching titles, the J.D. paperbacks offered a breathtaking world of switchblades, zip-guns and gang rumbles. Author Hal Ellson was especially prolific. *Duke*, his tale of a black, fifteen-year-old gang leader in Harlem, was first published in hardback by Scribner's in 1949, but it became a bestseller in 1950 when Popular Library issued it in paperback, and by 1955 the book had clocked up sales of over 1.5 million. *Tomboy* came next in 1950, followed in 1952 by *The Golden Spike*, a novel that began a sustained relationship between Ellson and the publisher Ballantine, the company publishing many of the author's long run of J.D. novels, including *Summer Street* (1953a), *Rock* (1953b) and *Tell Them Nothing* (1956).

Other authors also stood out as *meisters* of J.D. fiction. Harlan Ellison, for instance, produced *Rumble* for the publisher Pyramid in 1958, and followed up its success with two short-story collections for Ace—*The Deadly Streets* (1958b) and *The Juvies* (1961). Wenzell Brown also carved out an impressive J.D. niche, producing *Run, Chico, Run* (1953b), *Teenage Terror* (1958), *Cry Kill* (1959a) and *Teen-age Mafia* (1959b) for Gold Medal, *Monkey on My Back* (1953a) and *The Big Rumble* (1955) for Popular Library, and *Gang Girl* (1954) for Avon. Edward De Roo was another genre recidivist, penning a succession of J.D. novels for Ace—*Go, Man, Go* (1959a), *The Young Wolves* (1959b), *Rumble at the Housing Project* (1960) and *The Little Caesars* (1961). There was also a multitude of J.D. one-hit-wonders. Jay de Bekker, for instance, proffered *Gutter Gang* (1954) for the publisher Beacon, Bud Clifton delivered *D for Delinquent* (1958) for Ace, Edward Ronn furnished *Gang Rumble* (1958) for Avon, William Cox supplied *Hell to Pay* (1958) for Signet and Morton Cooper dashed off *Delinquent!* (1958) for Avon. All were bold, brash and brimming with J.D. brutality.

The line-up of J.D. paperbacks also included some distinctive subgenres. Dope peddling was a regular ingredient in J.D. fiction, and in some novels 'reefers' and 'goofballs' edged out switchblades and gang rumbles as the chief preoccupation. Probably the best known 'druggie pulp' of the 1950s was beat icon William Burroughs' semi-autobiographical portrait of heroin addiction, *Junkie: Confessions of an Unredeemed Drug Addict*, published (initially under the pseudonym 'William Lee') by Ace in 1953. But this was just one among a slew of paperbacks that depicted ill-fated youngsters gripped by a desperate drug habit. Alongside Ellson's *The Golden Spike* and Brown's *Monkey On My Back*, there also appeared several first-person confessionals—for instance, Pyramid released Leroy Street's *I Was a Drug Addict* (1953) and Monarch published Valerie Jordan's *I am a Teen-Age Dope Addict* (1962)—while lurid exposés also emerged in the form of Joachim Joesten's *Dope, Inc.* (1953), written for Avon, and Sloane Britain's *The Needle* (1959), for Beacon. Ostensibly they sermonised against the perils of teenage drug addiction but, in the true tradition of 'exploitation' fare, the real appeal lay in their promise of a candid glimpse into a world of the forbidden. And 'bad girl' fiction, too, was another J.D. subgenre that capitalised on contemporary headlines and beguiled readers with a taste for the wild and the wanton.

'GIRLS GONE WRONG': DELINQUENCY, GENDER AND 'DOMESTIC CONTAINMENT'

While the 1950s 'juvenile crime wave' was mainly understood as a male problem, the issue of female delinquency also prompted alarm. Popularised in newspaper articles and magazine features, the image of the delinquent 'bad girl' also gained (supposedly) authoritative weight from professional pronouncements. Katherine Sullivan, for instance, drew on her experiences working on the Massachusetts Parole Board to author *Girls on Parole* (1956), a sobering account of 'why girls go wrong', while *Rebels in the Streets* (1964) saw journalist Kitty Hanson scour the files of the New York City Youth Board to deliver a portrait of femininity run amok:

> These are girls, of too much experience and too little knowledge, of violence and hatred, of impulse and recklessness. They know despair, but not pity. They often curse, but they seldom weep. These are girls who mug and steal, who maim and sometimes kill. (Hanson 1964, 3)

Concerns about female delinquency had already surfaced during war-time, when unease had a cohered around 'Victory-girls' or 'V-girls'— young women whose 'free and easy' liaisons with servicemen were interpreted by the media as evidence of a breakdown in national morality.[7]

But during the 1950s anxieties intensified amid the broader fears engendered by the apparent upsurge of juvenile crime. Indeed, as historian Rachel Devlin argues, the stories of 'girls gone wrong' seemed to underscore the seriousness of the delinquency 'problem', since the extent of the social disruption was 'made palpable by the fact that girls in particular had somehow slipped beyond the bounds of control, their "wildness" signifying the breakdown of the boundaries of gender as much as of civil behavior' (Deviln 1998, 89).

As Devlin suggests, the image of the female delinquent provoked particular unease because it resonated with wider tensions surrounding issues of gender and sexuality. Popular perceptions of 1950s America as a land of confidence and cohesion obscure the way US society was actually shot through with conflict and distrust. Historians such as Alan Nadel have drawn attention to the way Cold War America was characterised by a deep suspicion of dissension and stern pressures to conform; US foreign policies geared to the 'containment' of communist influence abroad finding their parallel at home in a cultural agenda infused by paradigms of 'containment', with literature, cinema and the spectrum of popular culture deploying narratives that 'functioned to foreclose dissent, pre-empt dialogue and preclude contradiction' (Nadel 1995, 14). Central to these strategies of 'containment' was a strict regime of gender and sexuality. As Elaine Tyler May (1988) shows, the 1950s saw intensified pressures for social and sexual stability, with ideologies of 'domestic containment' promoting marriage and homemaking as fundamental to the strength and vitality of the nation; a battery of media texts and academic discourse combining in an attempt to convince women that the role of housewife and mother was natural and fulfilling, and that to step beyond these normative roles was abnormal, even subversive. In this context, then, the so-called 'deviant femininity' of the girl delinquent seemed especially troublesome and provoked profound concern.

It was, however, exactly these fears that made the girl delinquent so attractive to the youth-sploitation industries. Her aura of deviance and trouble were, for example, grist to the mill for exploitation filmmakers, and throughout the 1950s a welter of cheap and quickly made pictures eagerly capitalised on the concerns. AIP, for instance, released a steady stream of 'bad girl' pictures, including *Hot Rod Girl* (1956, dir. Leslie Martinson), *Reform School Girl* (1957, dir. Edward Bernds) and *High School Hellcats* (1958, dir. Edward Bernds). But publishers also eagerly took advantage of the furore, hence the 1950s flurry of 'bad girl' paperbacks.

Across popular culture, images of the 'bad girl' were invariably characterised by a brazen sexuality. And, as Elizabeth McCarthy observes, the
'bad girls'' 'predatory, indiscriminate and rapacious sexual appetite' had a
marked edge of sedition given how far it was 'at odds with the concept of
female sexuality as geared towards marriage, homemaking and family'
(McCarthy 2011, 141). But 'bad girl' texts could also pander to pruri-
ence. The covers of 'bad girl' books, for instance, featured pouting lips,
bulging cleavage and tantalising tag-lines as a titillating lure; while sex
scenes that presented girls as boy-hungry hussies provided drooling readers with a rich seam of fantasy fodder. The output of firms on the fringes
of the publishing industry—for example, Beacon, Midwood and
Monarch—was especially salacious. With low production values (the
cheapest paper stock and shoddy bindings), their selling point was content
more explicit than mainstream rivals and they were sold under the counter
or in cigar shops rather than on newsstands. These firms' novels ran the
gamut of soft-core sleaze, but a staple were 'bad girl' tales such as Orrie
Hitt's *The Torrid Teens* (1960—'She came from a nice home [...] Yet at
seventeen she succumbed to vileness and twisted desire. Why?'), Leo
Rifkin and Tony Norman's *Gutter Girl* (1960—'The whole story of the
wild and wanton girls who run with the street packs and throng the cellar
clubs') and Julie Ellis's *Gang Girl.* (credited to 'Joan Ellis' 1960—'She
had her first sordid lessons in love on the dusty rooftops of rundown
tenements').

But other entries in the 'bad girl' genre were more reflective. In Hal
Ellson's J.D. novels, for example, the author's social conscience was never
far away. Ellson's 'day job' was working as a recreational therapist at
New York's Bellevue Hospital, where he became familiar with some of the
city's most troubled youngsters. The experience informed his novels, and
his tales of Manhattan's lawless delinquents often included elements of
liberal social critique. In his Preface to *Duke*, for example, Ellson argued
that the roots of delinquency lay not in intrinsic criminality but in deprivation and social exclusion. 'Where the gang exists as the "biggest" thing
there is', Ellson explained, 'it is only natural for a boy to join for he is
merely reacting logically to his own environment. He also finds acceptance
in a world that otherwise rejects him' (Ellson 1949, 4).[8] Ellson's liberalism
also emerged in *Tomboy*. The novel's fifteen-year-old protagonist—referred
to simply as 'Tomboy'—runs with an Irish street gang (The Harps), and
Ellson gives a hard-hitting account of her proclivity for violence as she
beats female gang initiates with a leather belt, burns a cigarette into the

breast of a traitor and pushes a rival gang's spy from a rooftop. But Ellson also presents Tomboy's delinquency as the outcome of her inner conflicts and dysfunctional home. Struggling with her sexual identity and seeking escape from her drunken father, Tomboy is presented as finding haven in the sense of belonging offered by the gang. Meanwhile, Ellson's liberal account of the 'environmental' causes of delinquency surfaces as Tomboy's gang reflect on a recent foray to the bright lights of Times Square:

> They forgot where they were and what they really belonged to, that dark, bleak world outside, a world of crowded tenements and dirty cheerless streets where drunks brawled in bars and lay in hallways, a world of bickering harassed women who carried the fear of poverty always with them, an area, which in spite of its desolation, knew the threatening pressure and growing pains of another on its border where a darker people lived and brawled yearning to break down the walls of its ghetto. (Ellson 1951, 94)

Similarly, the central character in Wenzell Brown's *Gang Girl* is more damaged than depraved. Like Tomboy, fifteen-year-old Rita is a feisty hellcat, and the novel follows her rise as a leader in a tough street gang. Dodging the cops, she smokes dope, deals drugs and pitches into fist fights. But, again like Tomboy, Rita is also the vulnerable victim of her circumstances. Living among the slum neighbourhoods of New York's Lower East Side, Rita's mother is an alcoholic ('fat and sloppy with the odor of gin constantly around her' [Brown 1954, 44]), while Rita is tortured by the loss of her father, a career criminal languishing on Death Row. Rita, then, is presented as a product of 'fear, bewilderment and a desperate need for love and security', always searching for 'somewhere to go, some place where she wouldn't be alone with the sickening dread that never seemed to leave her' (Brown 1954, 47).

'BAD GIRLS' CONTAINED?

Issues of textuality and representation are always an important component in a cultural circuit, and the characteristic features of 1950s 'bad girl' fiction were clearly informed by the concerns and controversies of the day. In particular, the depiction of characters like Tomboy and Rita as the traumatised products of dysfunctional family backgrounds reflected the way girls' delinquency was often understood at the time. It became common, after the Second World War, for psychoanalytic perspectives to be applied to the study of juvenile crime as a whole, but Devlin shows how such ideas 'proved to be particularly useful for describing and coming to terms with female delinquency' (Devlin 1998, 84). Psychoanalytic approaches were so popular in the analysis of female deviance, Devlin argues, because they 'managed simultaneously to express anxieties about the social meaning of female delinquency yet contain the meaning of that behaviour safely within the matrix of the family', so that 'female rebellion' could be interpreted as 'less an autonomous form of expression than a reaction to her familial circumstances' (Devlin 1998, 84–5). In these terms, then, the ideals of 'domestic containment' were effectively reinforced because delinquent girls could be viewed as psychologically disturbed, rather than as wilfully transgressive (or, more colloquially, as 'mad' rather than 'bad').

For some critics, 'bad girl' books like *Tomboy* and *Gang Girl*, were complicit in this 'containment' of challenging femininities. Ramona Caponegro, for example, argues that *Tomboy* reproduced the conservatism of psychoanalytic interpretations of female delinquency because

> as dangerous and as powerful as Tomboy appears on the streets, her actions can be read as mere extensions of her failed relationship with her father, not to mention her stepmother; consequently, according to the prevailing psychoanalytic theory of her era, her actions are robbed of self-determinacy, changing her from tough hood into the victim of a dysfunctional family— that is, a cause of juvenile delinquency that the public can understand. (Caponegro 2009, 320)

Indeed, suggestive of *Tomboy*'s implicit conservatism was the glowing endorsement it received from Frederic Wertham. The crusading psychiatrist sprang to fame with the publication of *Seduction of the Innocent* in 1954, a bestseller in which Wertham decried the mass media—and comics in particular—as a key cause of juvenile crime. The early 1950s saw Wertham deliver extensive testimony before Kefauver's Senate Subcommittee on Juvenile Delinquency, and his arguments were a key influence on the introduction of the notorious Comics Code in 1954, which effectively proscribed the 'horror' and 'crime' comics then popular with young readers.[9] But Wertham had nothing but praise for *Tomboy*. And, in his introduction to the book's paperback edition, Wertham championed the novel's 'psychological truth' and its presentation of delinquency as a problem whose roots lay in an adolescent's troubled upbringing (Wertham 1951, i–v).

Popular texts, however, are often replete with contradictions that can open them up to a variety of different readings. This was especially true of 1950s paperbacks, where representations of 'rogue' femininities had an ambivalence that left them open to a range of interpretations by different audiences. Many critics, for instance, point to the way lesbian-themed pulp novels of the 1950s were 'appropriated' by a gay readership.[10] Such books, Yvonne Keller argues, were 'intended for heterosexual voyeuristic male readers', but they had 'unintended productive, exactly nonrepressive, effects' (Keller 2005, 406). As Keller explains, at a time when lesbianism was virtually invisible in popular culture, for many gay readers the 'lesbian pulps' became an important vehicle for the formation of sexual identity since they 'put the word and idea of "lesbianism" into popular discourse, creating a category of people that had not—to most—existed before' (Keller 2005, 406–7).

Contradictions also characterised the 'bad girl' novels. They certainly had dimensions of conservatism. Written almost exclusively by men, their female characters were often constructed as sexual objects, while the configuration of girls' delinquency as a psychological disorder rather than an expression of social defiance worked towards a 'containment' of female agency. And yet 'bad girl' fiction *also* offered a walk on the wild side that went against the conservative grain. Throughout the 1950s the American media relentlessly promoted images of docile femininity, with women configured as 'happy housewives' rooted in a life of subservient and 'contained' domesticity. But the 'bad girl' books offered a beguiling alternative. They proffered a vision of outlaw girlhood that refused to toe the conformist line, and much of their appeal lay in the way they flipped an insolent middle finger to the straitlaced mainstream. Indeed, suggestive of the books' seditious aura were the efforts made by outraged moralists to ensure their suppression.

During the early 1950s, moral crusaders cast a puritanical chill over American publishing. First came localised, uncoordinated censorship drives by parental groups and religious bodies such as the National Organization for Decent Literature (NODL, formed by Catholic priests), together with state-sponsored lawsuits against specific books deemed 'obscene'.[11] Then, in 1952, the campaign was given focus by the appointment of a government inquiry—The House Select Committee on Current Pornographic Materials—tasked with investigating the publishing business and the influence of popular literature on young readers. Headed by Ezekiel C. Gathings (Democratic Representative for Arkansas), the committee gunned determinedly for the paperback market, announcing at the outset:

The so-called pocket-size books which originally started out as cheap reprints of standard works, have largely degenerated into media for the dissemination of artful appeals to sensuality, immorality, filth, perversion and degeneracy. The exaltation of passion above principle and the identification of lust with love are so prevalent that the casual reader of such 'literature' might easily conclude that all married persons are habitually adulterous and all teenagers completely devoid of any sex inhibitions. (United States House of Representatives 1952, 3)

From the start, the Gathings hearings were stacked against the paperbacks. Few witnesses were called from the publishing industry. Instead, a parade of religious leaders, police officials, teachers and judges testified to the pernicious influence of an array of popular titles. Hundreds of books were cited as reprehensible, but novels featuring wayward femininity seemed to attract particular ire, Gathings reserving special contempt for books like Treska Torres' 'lesbian pulp' *Women's Barracks* (1950), and 'bad girl' books such as N.R. DeMexico's *Marijuana Girl* (1951) and Hal Ellson's *Tomboy*. Published in 1952, the Committee's report pulled no punches, arguing for much tougher obscenity laws and stricter regulation of the publishing industry. The calls, however, had little impact. In contrast to the comic trade, the book industry carried political and cultural weight and, citing First Amendment freedoms, publishers successfully lobbied against strengthened controls. Gathings, meanwhile, became a figure of press ridicule as his report was left to gather dust.

The paperbacks, then, prevailed over puritanical attempts to clip their wings. And, during the 1950s and early 1960s, court victories further rolled back the legal checks on literature.[12] The changes in censorship were the final ingredient in the 'bad girl' books' circuit of culture. With the relaxation of legal constraints on novels' content and covers, publishers could milk J.D. themes for all their worth and, throughout the 1950s, the stream of 'bad girl' fiction was free to offer page-turning slices of 'youth-run-wild' melodrama.

THE END OF THE LINE FOR 'BAD GIRL' FICTION

The history of 'bad girl' fiction in 1950s America stands as a useful example of the way the concept of a 'cultural circuit' can be used to understand the development of media forms associated with youth cultures and subcultures. The rise of the 'bad girl' genre was clearly indebted to the broader historical context of mounting social concern around issues of both youth and gender. But other points in the cultural circuit were also important—in particular, the wider shifts in American publishing, the transformation of post-war markets and a textual ambivalence that opened up the 'bad girl' narratives to a variety of possible audience readings. And, with the relaxation of censorship controls, the genre steadily flourished.

'Bad girl' fiction—along with the wider J.D. genre, of which it was a part—hit its high-water mark around 1958, as publishers cashed-in on the crest of the juvenile crime furore. After this, however, the cultural circuit that had underpinned the rise of 'bad girl' books steadily unravelled. By the beginning of the 1960s tough street gangs were old news and, as the delinquency panic steadily dissipated, readers' appetites for 'bad girl' thrills also faded. Industry shifts were another nail in the genre's coffin. Increasing competition and a spate of business takeovers saw many smaller paperback firms either fall by the economic wayside or merge with larger publishing houses whose aesthetic inclinations were less outré.

Nevertheless, while 1950s delinquents became a thing of wistful nostalgia, the attitude and approach of the 'bad girl' books could sometimes resurface. Indeed, throughout the 1960s and 1970s media-fuelled fears of new subcultural bogeymen brought a spate of youth-sploitation paperbacks chronicling the menace of feral biker gangs, LSD-fuelled freak-outs and Charles Manson-*esque* hippie cults. And, within the line-up, there were a smattering of titles such as Dexter Knapp's *Girl Gangs* (1968) that harked back to the 'bad girl' glory days, with their tales of (as Knapp's front cover blurb put it) 'Gangs of girls banded together in their mutual thirst for sex and violence!' The 'bad girl' theme, then, may have waned, but it did not disappear entirely.[13]

Notes

1. The two histrionic quotations are taken from the back-cover promotional blurbs for, respectively, Quandt (1952) and Brown (1954).
2. See Osgerby (2017) for a discussion of the whole genre of 1950s 'delinquency' fiction.
3. For accounts of the rise of the American paperback industry, see Davis (1984), Schreuders (1981) and Walters (1985).
4. A more detailed analysis of the development of the American teenage market can be found in Osgerby (2008).

5. Gilbert does not use the term 'moral panic', but it can be aptly applied to American responses to delinquency during the 1950s. Popularised in Stanley Cohen's (1972) analysis of the 'battles' between mods and rockers at British seaside resorts during 1964, the concept of moral panic denotes episodes of overblown social alarm in which exaggerated and sensation-alised media reports fan the sparks of an initially trivial phenomenon, creating a self-perpetuating 'amplification spiral' that steadily heightens the phenomenon's social significance.

6. A full survey of 1950s 'J.D.' movies is provided in McGee and Roberston (1982).

7. See Heggarty (2008).

8. In this respect Ellson's attitudes echo perspectives elaborated by liberal sociologists and criminologists of the day. For example, Albert Cohen (1955) and Richard Cloward and Lloyd Ohlin (1960) argued that the poverty and privations of ghetto neighbourhoods excluded youngsters from mainstream routes to success and so, looking for an alternative source of status and security, they gravitated to street gangs. Given his position at Bellevue Hospital, it is likely that Ellson was familiar with such views.

9. For a history of America's horror comic panic during the 1950s see Hajdu (2008).

10. Analyses of 'lesbian' pulp fiction of the 1950s exist in Foote (2005), Rabinowitz (2014, 184–208), Walters (1989) and Zimet (1999).

11. An overview of the campaign is provided in Speer (2001).

12. See Davis (1984, 216–247) and Rabinowitz (2014, 244–280).

13. See Osgerby (2018, forthcoming) for a discussion of 'bad girl' fiction in Britain and the US during the late 1960s and 1970s.

REFERENCES

Britain, Sloane (1959) *The Needle*, New York: Beacon.
Brown, Wenzell (1953a) *Monkey on My Back*, New York: Popular Library.
Brown, Wenzell (1953b) *Run, Chico, Run*, Greenwich, CT: Gold Medal.
Brown, Wenzell (1954) *Gang Girl*, New York: Avon.
Brown, Wenzell (1955) *The Big Rumble*, New York: Popular Library.
Brown, Wenzell (1958) *Teenage Terror*, Greenwich, CT: Gold Medal.
Brown, Wenzell (1959a) *Cry Kill*, Greenwich, CT: Gold Medal.
Brown, Wenzell (1959b) *Teen-age Mafia*, Greenwich, CT: Gold Medal.
Brown, Wenzell (1961) *Girls on the Rampage*, Greenwich, CT: Gold Medal.
Caponegro, Ramona (2009) 'Where the "Bad" Girls Are (Contained): Representations of the 1950s Female Juvenile Delinquent in Children's Literature and *Ladies Home Journal*, *Children's Literature Association Quarterly*, Vol. 34, No. 4: 312–329.

Clifton, Bud (1958) *D for Delinquent*, New York: Ace.

Cloward, Richard and Ohlin, Lloyd (1960) *Delinquency and Opportunity: A Theory of Delinquent Gangs*, Glencoe: Free Press.

Cohen, Albert (1955) *Delinquent Boys: The Culture of the Gang*, Glencoe: Free Press.

Cohen, Stanley (1972) *Folk Devils and Moral Panics: The Creation of the Mods and Rockers*, London: MacGibbon and Kee.

Cooper, Morton (1958) *Delinquent!*, New York: Avon.

Cox, William (1958) *Hell to Pay*, New York: Signet.

Davis, Kenneth (1984) *Two-Bit Culture: The Paperbacking of America*, Boston: Houghton Mifflin.

de Bekker, Jay (1954) *Gutter Gang*, New York: Beacon.

DeMexico, N.R. (1951) *Marijuana Girl*, New York: Universal.

De Roo, Edward (1959a) *Go, Man, Go*, New York: Ace.

De Roo, Edward (1959b) *The Young Wolves*, New York: Ace.

De Roo, Edward (1960) *Rumble at the Housing Project*, New York: Ace.

De Roo, Edward (1961) *The Little Caesars*, New York: Ace.

Devlin, Rachel (1998) 'Female Juvenile Delinquency and the Problem of Sexual Authority in America, 1945–1965', in Sherrie Innes (ed.), *Delinquents and Debutantes: Twentieth-Century American Girls' Cultures*, New York: New York University Press: 83–108.

Du Gay, Paul, Hall, Stuart, Janes, Linda, Mackay, Hugh and Negus, Keith (1997) *Doing Cultural Studies: The Story of the Sony Walkman*, London: Sage.

Ellis, Joan (Julie Ellis) (1960) *Gang Girl*, New York: Midwood.

Ellison, Harlan (1958a) *Rumble*, New York: Pyramid.

Ellison, Harlan (1958b) *The Deadly Streets*, New York: Ace.

Ellison, Harlan (1961) *The Juvies*, New York: Ace.

Ellson, Hal (1949) *Duke*, New York: Scribner's.

Ellson, Hal (1951) (orig. pub 1950) *Tomboy*, New York: Bantam.

Ellson, Hal (1952) *The Golden Spike*, New York: Ballantine.

Ellson, Hal (1953a) *Summer Street*, New York: Ballantine.

Ellson, Hal (1953b) *Rock*, New York: Ballantine.

Ellson, Hal (1956) *Tell Them Nothing*, New York: Ballantine.

Foote, Stephanie (2005) 'Deviant Classics: Pulps and the Making of Lesbian Print Culture', *Signs: Journal of Women in Culture and Society*, Vol. 31, No. 1: 169–190.

Fortune (1953) 'The Boom in Paper Bound Books', September: 122–125.

Gilbert, James (1986) *A Cycle of Outrage: America's Reaction to the Juvenile Delinquent in the 1950s*, Oxford: Oxford University Press.

Goggin, Gerard. (2006) *Cell Phone Culture: Mobile Technology in Everyday Life*, London: Routledge.

Hajdu, David (2008) *The* Ten Cent Plague: *The Great Comic Book Scare and How it Changed America*, New York: Farrar, Straus & Giroux.

Hanson, Kitty (1964) *Rebels in the Streets: The Story of New York's Girl Gangs*, Englewood Cliffs, NJ: Prentice-Hall.

Heggarty, Marilyn (2008) *Victory Girls, Khaki-Wackies, and Patriotutes: The Regulation of Female Sexuality During World War II*, New York University Press.

Hilton, Joseph (1955) *Angels In The Gutter*, Greenwich, CT: Gold Medal.

Hitt, Orrie (1960) *The Torrid Teens*, New York: Beacon.

Jackson, Peter, Stevenson, Nick and Brooks, Kate (2001) *Making Sense of Men's Magazines*, Cambridge: Polity.

Joesten, Joachim (1953) *Dope, Inc.*, New York: Avon.

Johnson, Richard (1997) (orig. pub. 1986) 'What is Cultural Studies Anyway?', in John Storey (ed.), *What Is Cultural Studies?: A Reader*, London: Arnold: 75–114.

Jordan, Valerie (1962) *I am a Teen-Age Dope Addict*, Derby, CT: Monarch.

Julier, Guy (2000) *The Culture of Design*, London: Sage.

Keller, Yvonne (2005) '"Was It Right to Love Her Brother's Wife so Passionately?": Lesbian Pulp Novels and U.S. Lesbian Identity, 1950–1965', *American Quarterly*, Vol. 57, No. 2: 385–410.

Knapp, Dexter (1968) *Girl Gangs*, Clevelend, OH: Classics Library.

Lee, William (William Burroughs) (1953) *Junkie: Confessions of an Unredeemed Drug Addict*, New York: Ace.

Life (1959) 'A New $10-Billion Power: the US Teenage Consumer', 31 August: 78–85.

Margulies, Leo (ed.) (1958) *Bad Girls*, New York: Crest.

McCarthy, Elizabeth (2011) 'Fast Cars and Bullet Bras: The Image of the Female Juvenile Delinquent in 1950s America', in Darryl Jones, Elizabeth McCarthy and Bernice Murphy (eds), *It Came From the 1950s! Popular Culture, Popular Anxieties*, Basingstoke: Palgrave Macmillan: 135–157.

McGee, Mark and Roberston, R.J. (1982) *The J.D. Films: Juvenile Delinquency in the Movies*, Jefferson: McFarland.

Nadel, Alan (1995) *Containment Culture: American Narratives, Postmodernism, and the Atomic Age*, Durham: Duke University Press.

Osgerby, Bill (2008) 'Understanding the Jackpot Market: Media, Marketing and the Rise of the American Teenager', in Dan Romer and Patrick Jamieson (eds), *The Changing Portrayal of Youth in the Media and Why It Matters* Oxford: Oxford University Press: 27–58.

Osgerby, Bill (2017) 'The Pulp Delinquents', in Iain McIntyre and Andrew Nette (eds), *Girl Gangs, Biker Boys, and Real Cool Cats: Pulp Fiction and Youth Culture, 1950 To 1980*, Oakland: Pm Press: 21–37.

Osgerby, Bill (2018, forthcoming) 'Lithe, Lusty and Liberated: "Pulp Feminism"', in Iain McIntyre and Andrew Nette (eds), *Sticking It to the Man: Revolution and Counterculture in Pulp and Popular Fiction, 1956–1980*, Oakland: Pm Press.

Quandt, Albert (1952) *Zip-Gun Angels*, New York: Original Novels.

Rabinowitz, Paula (2014) *American Pulp: How Paperbacks Brought Modernism to Main Street*, Princeton, NJ: Princeton University Press.

Rifkin, Leo and Norman, Tony (1960) *Gutter Girl*, New York: Beacon.

Ronn, Edward (1958) *Gang Rumble*, New York: Avon.

Schick, Frank (1958) 'Paperback Publishing', *Library Trends: Trends in American Book Publishing*, Vol. 1, No. 1, July: 93–104.

Schreuders, Piet (trans. Josh Pachter) (1981) *Paperbacks, USA: A Graphic History, 1939–1959*, San Diego: Blue Dolphin.

Speer, Lisa (2001) 'Paperback Pornography: Mass Market Novels and Censorship in Post-War America', *Journal of American Culture*, Vol. 24, Nos. 3–4: 153–60.

Street, Leroy (1953) *I Was a Drug Addict*, New York: Pyramid.

Sullivan, Katherine (1956) *Girls on Parole*, Boston: Houghton Mifflin.

Time (1956) 'Bobby-Soxers' Gallup', 13 August: 72–3.

Torres, Treska (1950) *Women's Barracks*, Greenwich, CT: Gold Medal.

Tyler May, Elaine (1988) *Homeward Bound: American Families in the Cold War Era*, New York: Basic Books.

United States House of Representatives (1952) *Report of the Select Committee on Current Pornographic Materials, House of Representatives, Eighty-Second Congress Pursuant to H. Res. 596: A Resolution Creating a Select Committee to Conduct a Study and Investigation of Current Pornographic* Materials, Washington, DC: United States Government Printing Office.

Walters, Ray (1985) *Paperback Talk*, Chicago: Academy.

Walters, Suzanna Danuta (1989) '"As Her Hand Crept Slowly up Her Thigh": Ann Bannon and the Politics of Pulp', *Social Text*, No. 23: 83–101.

Washington Post (1953) 'Fifth Horseman', April 12.

Wertham, Frederic (1951) 'Introduction', in Hal Ellson, *Tomboy*, New York: Bantam: i–v.

Whittington, Harry (1959) *Halfway to Hell*, New York: Avon.

Zimet, Jaye (1999) *Strange Sisters: The Art of Lesbian Pulp Fiction, 1949–69*, London: Penguin.

Queering the Grammar School Boy: Class, Sexuality and Authenticity in the Works of Colin MacInnes and Ray Gosling

Lucy Robinson and Ben Jones

INTRODUCTION

In their writings on 'the Teenager' (often described as 'the Boy') between 1959 and 1961, Colin MacInnes and Ray Gosling translated teenage experiences and constructed memorable teenage subjects for both contemporary and later audiences. In this chapter, we will suggest that taken as a whole MacInnes's work constructs a complex understanding of 'the Boy's' political possibilities. By integrating an analysis of his novelistic work with his journalistic and activist writing, we will demonstrate the complexity of MacInnes's 'Boy' as an autonomous, queer political agent, embodied in the ultimate Boy: Ray Gosling. The two writers were close

We would like to thank Amelia Fletcher, Rob Pursey and Nick Bentley.

L. Robinson (✉)
University of Sussex, Brighton, UK

B. Jones
University of East Anglia, Norwich, UK

23
N. Bentley et al. (eds.), *Youth Subcultures in Fiction, Film and Other Media*, Palgrave Studies in the History of Subcultures and Popular Music, https://doi.org/10.1007/978-3-319-73189-6_2

friends, with MacInnes acting as a mentor to the younger Gosling, who in turn functioned as something of a confidant to the older man. We use the term 'queer' to mean both 'mode of analysis and deconstruction relating to identity politics and resistance to the norm, *and* as a mode of description relating to those who identify as lesbian, gay, bisexual and transgender' (Powell 2010, 283). For us, the significance of MacInnes's and Gosling's sexuality lies not in providing us with clues to their psychosexual motivation. Nor are we arguing that the Teenager was externally queered by gay Svengalis of the pop and fashion worlds. For our purposes, the Teenager is in itself a queered subject.

We will show how MacInnes's one time flat mate, Ray Gosling, described as the 'Professional Teenager' constructed and occupied a disruptive space between dependent child and productive adult. He showed how the Teenager was at once a cynical marketing ploy and a multiple shifting experience, queering the lines between the two. The Boy was a sexual as well as generational identity. It was at once impossible and obtainable. The Teenager was the inhabitant of a Dreamland always 'like a win on the pools, just around the corner' (Gosling 1960, 31). In both Gosling's and MacInnes's narratives of teenage life, the Teenager provided an identity that was 'progress' driven within a liberal narrative of the modern, and resonant of authenticity, resistance and transgression. The Boy Gosling therefore embodied the spectrum of queer-identified politics: multiple, and fragmented, whilst at the same time appealing to a set of collective, generational experiences. He was the template for the Teenager, providing inspiration for MacInnes's literary creation: an iconic character which sought to embody a generational identity. At the same time Gosling offered a process for unpicking the template. In the second half of the chapter we will explore how Gosling's Teenager was put together after his brief alienating experience of university life. Gosling 'the scholarship boy' found salvation in asserting the vibrant authenticity of working-class experience against the deadening norms of middle-class student life. We conclude the chapter by tracing Gosling's trajectory from the early sixties, analysing his activism on behalf of queer and working-class communities and his controversial confession to a mercy killing, shortly before his own death in 2013. We begin however by exploring how *Absolute Beginners* was interpreted and understood in the mid-1980s, as a prelude to a discussion of an alternative reading of the novel and MacInnes's queer politics.

COLIN MACINNES

In 1959, Colin MacInnes published the second of his London novels, *Absolute Beginners*. In it, the unnamed protagonist is constructed as the iconic teenager, slick, cool, creative, with his ex-lover Crepe Suzette as the object of his art, and his Achilles heel. The novel is episodically framed over one summer, against a backdrop of racial tension, and has become a standard option for reading lists on youth culture and masculinity in the 1950s. Often treated as social documentary rather than a work of fiction, it also stands as an infamous reminder of what 1980s retro could do to a novel when translated into film form. Julien Temple's 1986 musical adaptation starred Patsy Kensit as Crepe Suzette and featured David Bowie, Sade and Steven Berkoff. In the film the unnamed narrator, the Boy, is given MacInnes' name Colin, suggesting an identification with the author as protagonist, rather than as observer (Temple 1986). The film signalled the emergence of a particularly English soul jazz scene in the eighties, around The Wag Club and artists like Sade, Carmel, Working Week and Paul Weller's Style Council. Production had not run smoothly, and the film was not received well. Similarly the scene it articulated was written off by Simon Reynolds in 1988 as a 'Hipster London elite' (Reynolds 1988). Unlike Temple's punk films, *Absolute Beginners* has since become a marker of overblown, over-styled pop films. Over a decade after its release, Stephen Dalton described it as 'that nadir of vacuous Eighties style-whore cinema' (Dalton 1998).

By returning to MacInnes's original texts, rather than this later adaptation, both Paul Weller and Billy Bragg have used MacInnes's words to attempt to draw clear lines of inheritance back to an imagined 'authentic' teenage culture. In so doing they have called up 'the Boy' to stand alongside them in solidarity: a classed identity in a multicultural context with implications for a reimagined 'Englishness'. Weller described *Absolute Beginners* as 'the ultimate mod book' and wrote the preface to its new edition in the wake of the film's release. Bragg named two of his albums after MacInnes's books—*England, Half English* and *Mr Love and Justice*. In fact Bragg thought that it might have been Weller who gave him the copy of *England, Half English* that inspired him to connect with MacInnes. For Bragg, MacInnes's Englishness was a 'cultural notion' which encompassed ethnic diversity and celebrated multiculturalism and cultural hybridity (Staunton 2007).

PUTTING THE QUEER BACK—SUBJECT AND PROCESS

This diversity however had its own boundaries and borders. MacInnes's homosexuality and his acerbic personality provided his detractors with ample ammunition. His personal life has been used to wipe out his public political statements. When picked up by later writers and critics, the political potential of MacInnes's queer identity is either muted as in Bragg and Weller's recovery of 'The Boy' or erased entirely by the harshest critics of MacInnes's personal politics (see for example Howe, quoted in Vulliamy 2007).[1] Queer—whether conceived of as an approach or as an identity—gets lost in these more contemporary formulations. Despite the appropriation of MacInnes as the founding father of a classed and ethnically diverse Englishness, these identities, we argue, are inflected through a destabilising queerness. This is not a matter of reading MacInnes as either classed or as queered, but as we suggest class and queer identity can be read together, as inside/out, and as both subject and analysis.

MACINNES'S POLITICS

Although MacInnes was not always public about his homosexuality, he made political connections between the position of homosexuals and that of other marginalised groups. In his later life he became increasingly explicit about his queer politics. Prior to this he had spoken out against injustice and imperialism, particularly in relation to Northern Ireland and the situation of black Britons. Although himself a son of the imperial establishment, MacInnes was a friend to Michael X and defended the black community in Notting Hill from police harassment (Gould 1983, 193; Humphry and Tindall 1977, 51).[2] He was involved in and wrote about debates over immigration, the Elgin marbles,[3] Ireland (1962b), racism and discrimination,[4] censorship (1962a, 1971a), drug use (1965c), prostitution[5] and black liberation (1965b, 1967), and was part of the process that opened up public debate on these issues. A regular on the Radio 4 programme 'The Critics', he was also involved with 'the underground' and liberationist movements. He supported the defence of *Lady Chatterley's Lover* and *Oz*, also contributing to the latter publication (1962a, 1971b). Yet throughout it all, MacInnes was clearly the product of a privileged and literary background.[6] In short, MacInnes was a generational and cultural translator. Using his 'half in, half out' position he produced guides to hidden worlds; for example, his 'guide to jumbles' explains to the white community what MacInnes thinks various black communities think of them. His essays 'pop songs and teenagers' and 'Sharp Schmutter' were both guides to teenage life and style aimed at a much older readership. Although originally published in magazines, these essays were later included in his collection *England Half English* complete with annotated reflections and afterthoughts from 1961. In the process, of course, this work constructs the hidden worlds not just as unseen, but as other. He cannot step outside his own context however. His readers should, he wrote, appreciate 'pop discs' in the same way that they would 'the native masks and ivories' that he assumes they've collected.[7] Perhaps it is these seeming contradictions and crossovers, rather than his sexuality, that lead so many to describe MacInnes as 'perverse' (Calcutt and Shephard 1998, 180).

WORK ON MACINNES'S RESISTANCE

Beyond biography, academics have noted the layers of resistance in MacInnes' life and work and the ways in which he queered the fifties. As Nick Bentley (2003) has shown, MacInnes's 'radical experiment with narrative forms' reproduced the 'submerged worlds of London's 1950s' (2003). The episodic structure of MacInnes's writing, as attested by Bentley and Connor, indicated the fragmentary nature of subcultural lives. For Bentley, *Absolute Beginners* 'offers a diverse representation of identifying multiple subcultures within the term youth' (2003, n.p.). This diversity undermines the over-determinist coherence found in much of the early work on youth (for example, by Phil Cohen and Richard Hoggart) (Bentley 2010). Alan Sinfield's work on cultural materialism situates sexuality at the heart of post-war cultural change. Sinfield (1997, 178) uses both MacInnes and Gosling to demonstrate the blurring of British and American cultural codes. We want to build on these readings to trace a similarly disruptive element of his work across and between forms. Part journalism, part social commentary, part fiction, MacInnes's queered form and genre reproduced a queered subject. Matt Cook and Richard Hornsey have identified the 'bricolage' of fragmented narratives in the 1950s and early 1960s as ways of 'form[ing] provisional queer' positions 'against the heteronormative prescriptions of post-war British Culture' (Hornsey 2009; Cook 2011). Indeed, the queer bricolage of MacInnes's writing and life history was recognised by his peers. George Melly (1976), for example, saw MacInnes as an advocate of the 'portmanteau permissiveness of the sixties'. As Richard Hornsey has noted, MacInnes's fiction was 'far from explicitly queer' (2009, 2). Indeed it is this lack of explicitly queer *content* that has allowed us to situate MacInnes and his work as queer in a dual sense: both in terms of his subjectivity and his *mode* of analysis.

QUEER CONTENT

If MacInnes was implicitly queer in his fiction, his non-fiction writing explicitly addressed queer themes. MacInnes used his journalistic writing to extend the debates around homosexuality, and indeed personal politics more generally. In the 1950s MacInnes wrote articles condemning the homosexual subculture he saw around him. He described English Queerdom as 'one of the most unpleasant groups on the earth's crust' (MacInnes 1965a, 7). MacInnes rejected the reformism of the Wolfenden Report from its inception as a way of changing homosexual men's lives.[8] He challenged both the prurient interest in Oscar Wilde's trials and Wilde's status as 'the homosexual martyr' at a time when films such as *Oscar Wilde* (1959) and *The Trial of Oscar Wilde* (1960), were being used to ventriloquize the struggle from Wolfenden to what would become the Sexual Offences Act (1966, 159–60).[9] He was also critical of the reformist groups fronted by professional, heterosexual do-gooders (1965a). Much of his later journalism was written from a queer subject position. He wrote for *Gay Left*, *Gay News* and published his exploration of bisexuality, *Loving Them Both*, in 1973 (1965a, 1972b, 1973). These positions layered queer narratives in his work and queer identities in his biography.

QUEERED TEENAGER

This helps to understand how the queered Teenager has been constructed within the context of MacInnes's wider published work, particularly his journalism and his biographical context. As Bentley (2003) has argued, the lines between fact and fiction are disturbed in MacInnes's work, which makes it 'problematic for traditional literary criticism.' Sometimes his work is treated as documentary, particularly as MacInnes himself acknowledged in his writing about teenagers (MacInnes 1986, 148).[10] Stuart Hall, for example, found *Absolute Beginners* more 'authentic' in its understanding of both the social context and the collective strategies developed by teenagers than either memoirs or social surveys. Hall reviewed the novel alongside E. R. Braithwaite's memoir of his time teaching in an East End Secondary Modern, *To Sir, With Love*, and two social surveys for *Universities and Left Review* in 1959. Most notable, for Hall, was the way in which

MacInnes's Boy, 'comes straight at us' with his own moral compass. This, for Hall was what gave the book its status as 'social documentary' and took it beyond 'inspired journalism' (Hall 1959, 23). Yet to MacInnes the use of his work as social document could also undermine his craft, as he regarded his fiction as less documentary, and more poetic evocations of the human situation (MacInnes, 'Sharp Schmutter', 148).[11] This sense of MacInnes and his texts as inside/outside (both positionally and in terms of literary modes) is picked up by most commentators. In the queered sense, he was also both inside and outside in terms of his construction of his own sexual identity and of The Boy. The participant observer in fiction, life history and journalistic writing has helped construct a version of the period that privileges subjectivities whilst maintaining the possibility of detached and impartial social investigation, and the pull of authenticity, 'or of being there'. MacInnes did not, he wrote, 'document' an existing teenage culture and language; he made it up (149). He was both a participant observer *and* a creative writer. This has allowed the fifties as seen through MacInnes's works of cultural production to have their queer cake and eat it, to engage with queer as a mode of disruption of coherent identities, and as a way of articulating the same identities.

QUEERING THE BOY

Amongst the teenagers, MacInnes saw an international army for a new Children's Crusade.[12] It was, however, a distinctly masculine army. MacInnes and the Boy had their own limits when it came to girls. Where girls are acknowledged, they are, like Crepe Suzette, some 'sharp cat's bird or chick' (MacInnes, 'Sharp Schmutter', 153). The parents' generation may have accommodated women's rights, he wrote, but the youth culture was more tribal (instinctive perhaps) and therefore masculine. On the streets '[t]he boys walked ahead, their expressionless faces, surmounted by Tony Curtis hair-dos, bent in exclusive masculine communion' (MacInnes, 'Pop Songs and Teenagers', 55). Their scavenger style picked up from images of American and European dress and fed out to the streets via high street retailers like Marks and Spencer. The teenager was the product of their international and local economic base and their parade dress took advantage of the wonder of modern manufacturing; it was precise, lightweight and drip dry (MacInnes, 'Sharp Schmutter', 153).[13] MacInnes noted that rather than signalling an unmanly turn to the 'effete', this brought with it a welcome concern with hygiene and cleanliness (157).

The cleanliness market did, however, help to queer the Boy. It directed 'him' to window shopping, consumption, unisex hair salons and what MacInnes described as 'bisexual remedies for body odour' (157).

The Boy was not just transgressive of the boundaries between work and leisure, adulthood and adolescence, communities and classes, he was a profoundly sexualised, and sexually disruptive subject. If, as we have suggested, The Boy can be read as queer, furthermore, the Boy in *Absolute Beginners* queered the line between fact and fiction, representing for many a more 'authentic' teenager than those depicted in the contemporary journalism of MacInnes and others. In the next section we argue that this simultaneous pull of authenticity and disruption extends beyond the text, across the genres of MacInnes's writing and into the intertwined life histories of both MacInnes and Gosling. We analyse Gosling's self-composure as The Boy, in his own words, to demonstrate the queerness of the teenager, as both a subject and as a way of examining the world. Here we show that teenagers could be analysts of their own conditions in their own terms, and were not simply subject to MacInnes's constructions, despite the inherent messiness of Gosling and MacInnes's relationship. Gosling's class and youth were central to his appeal as both the embodiment of the working-class teenager, and as an 'authentic' guide to teenage culture. However, his educational experiences, metropolitan connections (including his relationship with MacInnes) and sexuality meant that he was, like MacInnes, simultaneously inside and outside the subcultures he was describing.

RAY GOSLING: FROM SCHOLARSHIP BOY TO DREAM BOY

As a teenager Gosling was both a Ted 'follower' ('part of the wave, but a believer') and, as he recalls, 'in a group of working class grammar schoolboys christened the "grubbies" or "arty-farties". We were interested in things of the mind. It was rather an elite set' (Gosling 2010, 49). Despite being from a working-class background, his identification as a *worker* began at 15 when he started a summer job as a signalman:

> I used to go back after working on the railway with an absolute contempt for everyone else in the school because they hadn't, or so I thought, the faintest idea of life [...] Mine was quite a big school—900 pupils—and I don't suppose there'd be more than a dozen boys who had any conception of what work was life for the mass of people. Your father can do it but you have to do it yourself to understand. (56)

At this stage of his life this feeling of being defiantly working class put Gosling in a rather different category from the 'uprooted and the anxious' scholarship boy depicted by Richard Hoggart in the *Uses of Literacy* (Hoggart 1958). Worker, Ted, "Grubbie" intellectual—Gosling moved across these roles with ease. It was only on leaving school to read English at Leicester University that Gosling began to feel distinctly out of place amongst his middle-class peers: 'Anything like the lively interest in life I'd found in the pubs, caffs and on the railway didn't exist. They'd no style [...] I liked the staff and made friends. I liked the library, but hated the students and there was nothing wrong with them' (61–2). Gosling made his escape—both to London, where he met MacInnes—and to the burgeoning music scene in Leicester where he began managing bands and set up the 'Chez Ray Rock' night at the Co-op hall (64).

By 1960 Gosling was 'The Boy'. He was however not simply a muse or protégé, he was the agent of his own construction. Like MacInnes, in blurring the lines between fact and fiction in his *own* writing Gosling acted as a spokesman for his generation. He used the label 'absolute beginner' to describe his generations' year-zero role in the history of youth (Gosling 1961, 5). For Gosling 'The Great Big Us' of absolute beginners had taken over from the Teddy Boy. At the conclusion to *Absolute Beginners*, MacInnes's Boy greets a group of Africans, newly arrived at the airport: 'They all looked so damned pleased to be in England, at the end of their long journey, that I was heartbroken at all the disappointments that were in store for them. And I ran up to them, through the water, and shouted out above the engines, "Welcome to London! Greetings from England! Meet your first teenager! We're all going up to Napoli to have a ball!"' (MacInnes 2011, 285).

Like MacInnes' hero, Gosling's role was to act as guide to the subcultural codes and spaces he inhabited, to present evidence and insights to the outside world (Bentley 2003). Gosling introduced the 'Dream Boy' and its multiplicities, performativities and queered rebellion in an article for *New Left Review* in 1960. Although introduced as a young signalman and youth club organiser, Gosling makes it clear that identities are far more complicated than job labels or bureaucratic roles: 'The Boy stands up in his sexual and phallic dress, a rebel against a sexless world of fear, and from his own he has made gods. In his dress, his walk, in his whole way of life he makes a private drama for the world that failed him to take note of' (Gosling 1960, 30). He goes on to note: '[The Boy] st[ood] in an age of frustration as a dreamlover', attracting both 'the society moll and the homosexual' (Robinson 2007, 57). Youthful masculinity and homosexual undercurrents were inseparable for Gosling. He spoke for those who were simultaneously '[d]reaming of being a Boy-God, [and] dreaming of being in love with a Boy-God' (Gosling 1961, 5). In his simultaneous position as agent and observer Gosling, and his self-made Boy-God, confounded categories. The Boy is not a mere object of study in the growing body of work on delinquency, nor is he the passive consumer of mass marketing—Gosling's Boy-God combines agent, analyst and organiser.

The article (described as a 'manifesto') was based on his experiences of helping to run a 'self-programming' youth club in Leicester. *The Daily Mirror* described it as the 'Toughest Youth Club in England', and it was run by young people, for young people. There was no table tennis table or '"administering angel" wanting to take [the young people] off the street'. It was potentially, 'the most daring and fruitful youth experiment of the century' according to the *Mirror* journalist who visited (Stonely 1961). Gosling wanted to use the lessons of this experiment to fill-in the considerable gaps in understanding evident in the 'Albermarle Report' on The Youth Service in England and Wales (1960). Whilst the report 'knew nothing about teenagers in 1960' Gosling's writing performed the Teenager from the inside out. Gosling wrote up the experience in *Lady Albermarle's Boys* the first Young Fabian Pamphlet in 1961. Like MacInnes's journalistic work, Gosling's report was designed to speak of his own experience, and to his own identified community, but also to act as a guide for the general public who had 'struck' him as being 'grossly ill formed' about the 'Service of Youth, [and] the habits and behaviour of the young generation' (Gosling 1961, 1). He provided a benchmark for the period in the construction of a number of categories: Boys, Dream Boys, Ordinary Boys, Lady Albermarle's Boys, Boy-Gods, as attested by Stan Cohen's use of Gosling's writing in *Folk Devils and Moral Panics*, which was reviewed by MacInnes (MacInnes 1972a).

We have long understood the need to talk about identities through the complex processes of their mutual production and intersections—not understanding masculinity without looking at femininity, understanding race as constructed simultaneously along lines of blackness and whiteness. However, our construction of teenage culture has largely focussed on the emergence of youth identity along its own lines of distinction between childhood, adolescence, youth and adulthood. When MacInnes constructed the Boy, and when Gosling composed himself as the Boy, we are able to see the ways in which ageing and youth are constructed together, at the time, and of course, over time through their autobiographical writings. MacInnes built the Boy in response to his own sense of ageing, and with hope for The Boy's imagined future. In 1961 he wrote 'I cannot deny I regret that youth is gone: not so much because I am no longer young, as because, when I was young, I didn't really know it: and thus missed many opportunities of using youth as now I wish I had.' He continues, 'one sad joy of being middle-aged is that most of us can love youth as we never could when we were part of it' (MacInnes 1962c). Unable to have experienced it himself, MacInnes framed, identified and disrupted the Teenager instead. Meanwhile Gosling was growing up. In so doing he became the commentator and composer, this time of MacInnes as much as of himself.

The Boy Grows Up

For Ray Gosling, Colin MacInnes was 'the man I looked up to, who was my mentor more than anyone else' (Gosling 2010, 79). He has been described by others as both a 'disciple' and 'protégé' of MacInnes' (Nehring 1993, 238; Fowler 2007, 75.), but we want to suggest that he was more than that, an embodiment of the Teenager, but also a site of disruption. MacInnes, the writer and The Man, was also reconstructed in relationship to Gosling, The Boy. Later in established adulthood Gosling gets relabelled as MacInnes' 'friend and memoirist', a reciprocal relationship. Having grown out of being MacInnes' Boy, after MacInnes's death in 1976, it becomes Gosling's turn to compose a self for MacInnes through his own biographical narratives. Each, therefore, composed the other. As well as a chapter dedicated to their relationship in *Personal Copy*, which is identical to the introduction dated 1978 that Gosling wrote to MacInnes's posthumous collection of essays *Out of the Way*, Gosling presented Radio 4's *Prophets, Charlatans and Little Gurus*, about MacInnes in October 1982 (Gosling 2010, 79; MacInnes 1979, 9–14). Gosling grew up to make up his mentor on his own terms as MacInnes had constructed his ageing process around the discursive centrality of The Boy.

Gosling's political activism from the mid-1960s and beyond encompassed both gay politics and advocacy on behalf of working-class communities. The bulk of the latter centred on the campaign against the wholesale redevelopment of the St Ann's district in Nottingham, to which Gosling dedicated the second half of *Personal Copy* to describing. A nineteenth-century neighbourhood of 10,000 houses with a population of over 30,000, the clearance of St Ann's, which took place over a period of about ten years from the mid-1960s, was one of the largest redevelopment programmes in Europe. It also proved to be one of the most controversial. 1966 saw the establishment of SATRA, the St Ann's Tenant's and Resident's Association—chaired by Gosling. SATRA strongly criticised the complete lack of public consultation regarding clearance and campaigned for selective renewal. In a report for Nottingham's Civic Society Gosling stated: 'We intend to show [...] that it is economically possible and humanly desirable to take the very bad out now, patch for the present the not so bad, improve the reasonable, preserve the good' (Gosling 1967, 2). Ultimately, despite the petitions, public meetings, challenges and small victories for democratic involvement and accountability, it was a battle which Gosling and his colleagues lost. As he reflected: 'Change came like a torrent, sweeping all before it: houses, streets, chapels, shops, pubs, the whole old life [...] A history was wiped away' (Gosling 2010, 221). Yet Gosling's nostalgia was inflected with a sense of standing both inside and outside the community he had chosen to represent:

> I wasn't born there, bred or raised. I'm not a native of what I call my district. I'm a latter day immigrant who freely chose to foist myself on "poor" people, like a Robin Hood, to fire slings and arrows at Aunt Sallies for the gratification of my own principles and for my own amusement as much as anybody's good. (251)

This privileged inside/outsider status was deployed to rather greater effect in his approach to the politics of gay rights.

Like MacInnes, Gosling engaged with queer politics as both a subject position and a mode of analysis. Throughout his activism Gosling's politics were queered and classed. He was critical of the elite reformism 'by stealth' of the earlier law reform campaigns and he became vice president of Campaign for Homosexual Equality in 1975.[14] Alongside his long-time comrade, Alan Horsfall, he ran the Gay Monitor website until his death. Like Horsfall, his focus lay beyond the relatively privileged metropolitan gay centres, to the provincial North and Midlands. In fact, no longer likely to be seen as a 'professional Teenager', he was instead represented (erroneously, given his East Midlands heritage) as a 'professional Northerner', whose documentaries recorded and to some extent romanticised working-class lives (Binnie 2000, 176).

Gosling's class, location and sexual identity made him an important critical commentator during the Bolton 7 case in 1998. The case saw the prosecution of seven men for consensual sexual acts in the 'privacy' of one of their homes in Bolton. All the men were known to each other, and the party had been videoed using a home camera. The video was used as the evidence in the trial in which all seven men were charged with a series of potentially imprisonable offences including buggery, and the rather catch-all charge of 'gross indecency'. All the defendants were convicted, three lost their jobs and the trial cost £500,000. The case made clear the boundaries between public and private left over from the 1967 Sexual Offences Act and further constructed two queer constituencies and ascribed each a value according to class. On the one hand the sophisticated, affluent Canal Street, on the other the 'unsophisticated', rough, working-class house parties (Binnie 2000, 166–78). The case also drew sharp lines according to age. The judge's sentencing pointed out the 'immature and unsophisticated' nature of the younger defendants. Their queerness denied them adulthood or agency; to the judge their same-sex activity was 'little more than [...] smutty-minded schoolboys tipsily experimenting with sex' (Binnie 2000, 176). Whilst the five younger men (between the ages of 18 and 25) were given community service, the two older men (aged 33 and 55) received (suspended) custodial sentences (Moran 1999, 39–55). Video footage had been at the heart of the case. Gosling responded in kind. He made a documentary about the case for Channel 4, *Sex, Lies and Video Tapes*. In the documentary he wielded his inside/outsider status to document working-class queer lives in northern England, in itself an usual thing.

Like MacInnes before him, Gosling continued to blur the lines between experience and memory, fact and fiction. The grown man Gosling was built up of the paper traces of his pasts. Gosling's *Sum Total* was a 'sort of autobiography', and his later *Personal Copy: A Memoir of the Sixties*, was a 'fairly true story'. Although presented and marketed as one of the ever-growing number of sixties memoirs, it was actually largely a collection of previously published journalism, topped and tailed to shift a chronology and compose a life narrative. In 2005 Gosling's ageing process became the subject of a documentary *Ray Gosling OAP* for BBC 4. A £5000 tax bill, left unpaid had spiralled into a massive debt. Gosling was bankrupt and about to lose his home. His impending move into sheltered accommodation meant he had to clear out the piles of paper notes and files that filled 'almost every square inch' of his home. He fought to remain in his own home and be allowed to keep and curate the mountains of 'documents' of his own past (Arnot 2005). As the Bolton 7 case had shown, sharp lines can be drawn across the more blurred lines of disruption. The slippery lines across fact and fiction, experience and documentary evidence came to a head for Gosling in 2010 at the age of 70. In a documentary he disclosed that he had 'smothered' to death a lover who was dying of AIDS. The documentary, for BBC East Midlands on the subject of death, was appropriately named *Inside Out*. He went on to repeat his confession on breakfast television. The story spoke of the contemporary debates on euthanasia, and of the tragedy of a generation of gay men lost or left grieving by AIDS. He told the filmmakers:

> I killed someone once. He was a young chap, he had been my lover and he had got Aids. In hospital, the doctor said, "There's nothing we can do." He was in terrible pain. I said to the doctor, "Leave me just a bit." I picked up the pillow and smothered him until he was dead. The doctor came back and I said, "He's gone." Nothing more was said. (Chalmers 2012)

It was a powerful story but it did not hold its own power for long. Gosling insisted that he would not identify the man, the hospital or town where the death occurred. But journalists offered cash incentives for anyone who would come forward to identify the dead man, or Gosling's previous lovers. The police investigated the 'mercy killing' as suspected murder and three days after the interview was broadcast Gosling was interviewed for over 30 hours before being bailed (Chaytor 2010a). During the interview Gosling conceded and named his lover: Tony Judson.

Newspaper reports of the events unravelled the story's emotional authenticity. As Gosling's life and writing had already shown there were 'laws in books and there is a law in your heart' (Chaytor 2010b). These were not the same thing. The fallout from the revelation also suggested that there are truths, or social documents, in books, and rather different truths in your heart. According to the *Mirror*, Gosling's younger lover had died in a British hospital in the late 1970s, 'in the early days of AIDS'. The first documented case of a gay man dying of AIDS, in New York, is generally recognised to have been in 1981. Gosling accepted that the story was fiction, not fact, and the usefulness of that fiction was lost. He was eventually charged not with murder but with wasting police time, and received a 90-day suspended sentence.

In one interview Gosling explained his confession as the product of slipped tenses, 'between the past and conditional' (Chalmers 2012).

Having written himself through boyhood and into the man he became, it was left to Gosling's obituary writers to make sense of the fictitious truth behind the story. Gosling had explained the layers of investment in his story, beyond its authenticity. He told his friend, Tony Roe, that '[a]t his friend's funeral [...] he was harangued for not ending the suffering sooner. So for the next 30 years he told himself and believed himself that he had. He had wanted to do the right thing and to have been seen to do the right thing' (Gosling 2013b). He had been moved to disclose the story as some sort of recompense for all the stories that he had collected over time; 'everyone else had revealed themselves to me', he said, 'and I felt I had to reveal myself to them' (Gosling 2013a).

NOTES

1. See the critical remarks of Darcus Howe in Vulliamy, 2007.
2. See MacInnes, "Letter to the Editor"; MacInnes 1967, 14; Gould 1983, 193; Humphry 1977, 51.
3. "Greeks and Vandals," in MacInnes 1966, 62–6.
4. "A Short Guide for Jumbles," in MacInnes 1966, 23–33.
5. MacInnes, "The Other Man," in MacInnes 1966, 141–7; MacInnes 1979, 338–9.
6. MacInnes was the son of Angela Thirkwell and was also Rudyard Kipling's cousin.
7. MacInnes, "Pop songs and Teenagers", in MacInnes 1966, 49.
8. MacInnes, "English Queerdom," 7.
9. "The Heart of a Legend: The Writings of Ada Leverson," in MacInnes 1966, 159–60.
10. Colin MacInnes, "Sharp Schmutter," in MacInnes 1966, 148.
11. "Sharp Schmutter," in MacInnes 1966, 148–57.
12. Colin MacInnes, "Pop songs and Teenagers", in MacInnes 1966, 50.
13. MacInnes, "Sharp Schmutter," 153.
14. See C.H.E., *Minutes of the Meeting of the Executive Committee Held on 16th November 1975*; C.H.E., *Minutes of the Meeting of the Executive Committee Held on 16th 17th July 1975*; and Grey 2011, 267.

REFERENCES

Arnot, Chris. 2005. "A Collection That Speaks Volumes," *The Guardian*, February 15, 2005.
Bentley, Nick. 2003. "Writing 1950s London: Narrative Strategies in Colin MacInnes's *City of Spades* and *Absolute Beginners*," *Literary London: Interdisciplinary Studies in the Representation of London* 1, 2, September (2003).

Bentley, Nick. 2010. "New Elizabethans: The Representation of Youth Subcultures in 1950s British Fiction," *Literature & History* 19, 1 (2010).

Binnie, Jon. 2000. "Cosmopolitanism and the sexed city," *City visions* (2000).

Calcutt, Andrew and Shephard, Richard. 1998. *Cult Fiction: A Readers' Guide.* London: Prion.

Chalmers, Robert. 2012. "Ray Gosling: Interview," *The Independent*, September 30, 2012.

Chaytor, Rod. 2010a. "Police quiz Gosling on mercy kill," *Daily Mirror*, February 18, 2010.

Chaytor, Rod. 2010b. "I killed my lover, but I'll tell cops nothing," *Daily Mirror*, February 17, 2010.

C.H.E., *Minutes of the Meeting of the Executive Committee Held on 16th November 1975.*

C.H.E., *Minutes of the Meeting of the Executive Committee Held on 16th 17th July 1975.*

Cook, Matt. 2011. "Homes Fit for Homos: Joe Orton and the Domesticated Queer," in eds. Brady Sean, and Arnold, John. *What is Masculinity? Historical Dynamics from Antiquity to the Contemporary World.* Basingstoke: Palgrave Macmillan.

Dalton, Stephen. 1998. "Glam Rock: Scary Monsters, Super Freaks #1", *Uncut*, November, 1998.

Fowler, David. 2007. "From jukebox boys to revolting students: Richard Hoggart and the study of British youth culture," *International Journal of Cultural Studies* 10, 1 (2007).

Gosling, Ray. 2013a. *Daily Telegraph*, November 21.

Gosling, Ray. 1960. "Dream Boy," *New Left Review*, 3, May/June 1960.

Gosling, Ray. 2010. *Personal Copy: A Memoir of the Sixties*, Second Edition. Nottingham: Five Leaves.

Gosling, Ray. 1961. *Lady Albermarles's Boys.* London: Fabian Society.

Gosling, Ray. 1967. *St Ann's.* Nottingham: Civic Society.

Gosling, Ray. 2013b. *The Glasgow Herald*, November 22.

Gould, Tony. 1983. *Inside Outsider: The Life and Times of Colin MacInnes.* London: Chatto & Windus.

Grey, Anthony. 2011. *Quest for Justice: Towards Homosexual Emancipation.* London: Random House.

Hall, Stuart. 1959. "Absolute Beginnings," *Universities & Left Review* 7, Autumn, (1959).

Hoggart, Richard. 1958. *The Uses of Literacy: aspects of working-class life with special reference to publications and entertainments.* Harmondsworth: Penguin.

Hornsey, Richard. 2009. "City of Any Dream: Colin MacInnes and the Expanded Urban Environment of Late 1950s London," (Paper presented at QUEER 50s, Birkbeck, University of London, 6–7 May 2009), 2, https://core.ac.uk/download/pdf/1348709.pdf

Humphry, Derek and Tindall, David. 1977. *False Messiah: The Story of Michael X*. London: Hart Davis.
MacInnes, Colin. 1959. *Absolute Beginners*. London: MacGibbon and Kee.
MacInnes, Colin. 1960. *Mr Love and Justice*. London: MacGibbon & Kee.
MacInnes, Colin. 1962a. "Experts on Trial: A Comment on Mr Sparrow," *Encounter*, March, 1962.
MacInnes, Colin. 1962b. "The Sad Joys of Middle Age," *The Listener*, 1962.
MacInnes, Colin. 1962c. "The Writings of Brendan Behan," *The London Magazine*, August, 1962, 53–61.
MacInnes, Colin. 1965a. "English Queerdom," *Partisan Review*, January–February, 1965.
MacInnes, Colin. 1965b. "Michael and the Cloak of Colour," *Encounter*, December, 1965, 8–15.
MacInnes, Colin. 1965c. "Out of the Way: Nicked," *New Society*, September 16, 1965, 27.
MacInnes, Colin. 1966. *England, Half English*. Harmondsworth: Penguin.
MacInnes, Colin. 1967. "Through a Glass, Darkly," *New Statesman*, August 18, 1967.
MacInnes, Colin. 1971a. "Out of the Way: Hustlers," *New Society*, August 19, 1971, 338–9.
MacInnes, Colin. 1971b. "Out of the Way: Trial of a Trial," *New Society*, August 5, 1971, 249–50.
MacInnes, Colin. 1972a. "From one generation to another," *The Guardian*, 1972.
MacInnes, Colin. 1972b. "Learning from Gays," *Gay News* 72, (1972), 11–12.
MacInnes, Colin. 1973. *Loving Them Both*. London: Martin, Brian & O'Keeffe.
MacInnes, Colin. 1979. *Out of the Way: Later Essays*. London: Martin Brian & O'Keefe.
MacInnes, Colin. 1986. *England, Half English* London: Chatto & Windus.
MacInnes, Colin. 2011. *Absolute Beginners*. London: Allison and Busby.
Melly, George. 1976. "Death of a rebel", *The Observer*, 1976.
Moran, Leslie J. 1999. "Law made flesh: homosexual acts," *Body & Society* 5, 1 (1999): 39–55.
Nehring, Neil. 1993. *Flowers in the Dustbin: Culture, Anarchy, and Postwar England*. Ann Arbor: University of Michigan Press.
Powell, Victoria. 2010. "QUEER 50s, Birkbeck, University of London, 6–7 May 2009," *History Workshop Journal*, 69, (2010): 283.
Reynolds, Simon. 1988. "Sinead O'Connor: Hammersmith Odeon, London", *Melody Maker*, January 2, 1988.
Robinson, Lucy. 2007. *Gay Men and the Left: How the Personal got Political*. Manchester: Manchester University Press.

Sinfield, Alan. 1997. *Literature, Politics and Culture in Postwar Britain*. London: Continuum.

Staunton, Terry. 2007. "Billy Bragg: Patriot Games", *Record Collector*, December, 2007.

Stonely, J. 1961. "The Toughest Youth Club in England," *Daily Mirror*, January 6, 1961.

Temple, Julien (Dir.) 1986. *Absolute Beginners*. London: Goldcrest and Virgin Films.

Vulliamy, Ed. 2007. "Absolute MacInnes," *The Observer*, April 15, 2007, accessed October 31, 2016, https://www.theguardian.com/uk/2007/apr/15/britishidentity.fiction

Punk Fiction; Punk in Fiction

Nick Bentley

Introduction: All the Young Punks

Punk is by its very nature irreverent. Punks are most often represented in motion, as an active force, challenging the cultures, mores and behaviours of mainstream society. They are not normally associated with the sedentary and thoughtful practice of reading. However, punk has been addressed in a number of novels and experiments with fiction over the years since it developed in the mid-1970s. This chapter will discuss the representation of punk and punks in literary fiction and has two main aims. Firstly, it discusses the way in which formal and literary techniques are used in fiction and writing about punk (or by members of the punk subculture) to reflect similar aesthetic practices in other artistic and cultural fields such as music and fashion. It examines narrative techniques in selected fiction as well as referencing a number of other literary manifestations of punk, including the new music journalism that appears in the 1970s (by writers such as Caroline Coon); the aesthetic characteristics seen in the rise of DIY punk

Some of the ideas in this chapter are a developed from another book chapter: Bentley (2018).

N. Bentley (✉)
Keele University, Newcastle-under-Lyme, UK

© The Author(s) 2018
N. Bentley et al. (eds.), *Youth Subcultures in Fiction, Film and Other Media*, Palgrave Studies in the History of Subcultures and Popular Music, https://doi.org/10.1007/978-3-319-73189-6_3

fanzines such as *Sniffin' Glue*; some of the stories collected in *Punk Fiction: An Anthology of Short Stories Inspired by Punk*, edited by Janine Bullman; and various other pieces of writing by participants in the subculture. In these stories and writing, in particular, the use of cut up narratives, typographical experiment, the shifting of register and perspective, and manipulation of language represent an attempt to offer a literary rendering of the anarchic expression of punk in music, fashion and attitude. However, it will also be shown that writing about punk at times draws on more established modes of literary realism in the attempt to convey authentic experiences. Secondly, it will examine the way in which punk has been used in fiction to indicate a transition or rupture in significant social, political and cultural discourses in Britain in the 1970s, especially with respect to the move from the consensus politics of the earlier part of the decade to a politics of confrontation marked by the appointment of Margaret Thatcher as leader of the Conservatives in 1975. The chapter analyses a number of novels including Gideon Sams's *The Punk* (2004 [1977]), Richard Allen's *Punk Rock* (1977), Hanif Kureishi's *The Buddha of Suburbia* (1990) and Jonathan Coe's *The Rotters' Club* (2001).

There are, of course, a number of definitions of punk and indeed a number of specific cultural and geographic locations that claim its origins: from New York's underground and post-glam culture to Brisbane's garage punk to London's King's Road; from The Roxy in Covent Garden and the 100 Club in Oxford Road, Soho to CBGB in Manhattan's East Village. There have, indeed, been several American novels that have engaged with, and been discussed with reference to, punk and post-punk such as Bret Easton Ellis's *Less Than Zero* (1985), Jonathan Franzen's *Freedom* (2010) and more recently, Garth Risk Hallberg's *City on Fire* (2015) (see Luter 2015; Bresnan 2015). This chapter, however, will concentrate on the British context. Punk appears, of course, in a whole range of novels from the 1970s to the present, and what follows can only be a snapshot of the coverage.

Dick Hebdige, following Paul Willis (2014), has identified a homology behind the apparent anarchic and diverse set of spectacular signifiers: 'The [punk] subculture was nothing if not consistent. There was a homological relation between the trashy cut-up clothes and spiky hair, the pogo and amphetamines, the spitting, the vomiting, the format for the fanzines, the insurrectionary poses and the "soulless," frantically driven music' (Hebdige 1988, 114). This has become one of the dominant critical readings of punk, based on Hebdige's semiotic approach to reading the cultural meanings generated by the subculture's spectacular elements. However, what becomes apparent when looking at the ways in which punk has been articulated in narrative fiction is the diversity of responses it has a gener- ated and the variety of styles and forms that in part reflects the anarchic nature of punk, but also often recourse to more established and conven- tional forms of literary realism. In this sense the homology model, which tends to reduce punk to a set of fixed attitudinal characteristics, is mislead- ing. Punk fiction, indeed, as we shall see, reveals a pluralistic set of diverg- ing representations, articulations and styles that reflect a diverse set of individual responses by novelists and writers.

Punk Fiction

One of the trickier elements of articulating punk in prose narrative is try- ing to capture the affective experience of being part of the punk subcul- ture. Several writers have tried to achieve this through direct description. Joolz Denby, for example, writes of attending a gig by The Ruts:

> It was like being in the eye of a hurricane, in a cauldron boiling with energy and a kind infectious epiphany. Outside the world could have vanished into Hell and nothingness, but in that shitty, murder-haunted, perfect box we were all warriors, shield-maidens, purified. None of us left unmarked by that experience and some of us were changed forever; some of us saw what we could aim for, what we could be, what we could break our hearts tryin for. What we still try for. (2009, 17)

The language in this section is interesting in that it uses clichés such as 'eye of the hurricane' and a 'cauldron boiling with energy' and mixes them with new formations such as the juxtaposition of 'shitty' and 'perfect' as adjectives to describe the venue. This is a prose striving for the tools to convey the experience adequately. The mixing of metaphors and registers is indeed indicative of the destructive energy that thrusts experiences together to form something new. What is also striking about this passage is the collective and ritualized feelings it produces. To express this, Denby reaches for very old formations: warriors and shield maidens; the term 'purified' appearing as wonderfully out of place in the description.

This is an attempt to describe a real physical location in a mode of social realism, but the prose extends beyond the documentary to convey the imagined feel of the experience itself. This combination of authenticity with an imagined and wrought style reveals something of the very nature of punk, which extends to the ways in which the participants consider themselves as occupying a space that is in some sense real and imaginary. Take for example, this description, excerpted from the band's website, of the history of the late-1970s punk band The Skeptix, by Ush, one of their original members:

> Let me take you back to them dim, distant and far off days of vinyl. In the beginning was THE PUSH, the best band to play in the singers garage, who did gig infrequently the length and breadth of STOKE! A rag-tag bunch of misfits who formed the band in 1978 *(ish)* but did pass away soon after. Upon the demise of said band, a voice spoke unto me, and said, 'OI, PRETTY BOY!! (*he had good taste in them days!*) D'YA WANNA BE IN MY BAND?' And lo, twas the voice of FISH! Local guitar hero! (*thats what he told me!*) Verily I said onto him, (*in a local dialect*) 'O'RATE! A WILL, AHH!!' So then The Skeptix were born. Pulled from the four corners of the town to conquer the evil and depraved world of 'pap pop' and other deranged forms of music that molested the ears of the youth and to bring light and meaning once more unto mankind!!!!!!!????? (Ush 2002, n.p.)

In this example of writing from within the subculture, the self-conscious myth-making is simultaneously undercut by the mocking side commentary, while the use of the mock-historic language, fluctuating registers, the typographical diversity and exuberant use of punctuation convey the energy and irreverence of punk.

The two examples quoted above can both lay claim to an authentic response to involvement in the subculture, but they convey two distinctly different approaches to the representation and articulation of punk in prose writing. The Denby extract attempts to offer a realistic and authentic description of the affective response of punk and tends towards a documentary testimony of what it felt like to be part of the punk movement. Its attitude to language, however, is relatively traditional in that it uses conventional prose writing as a linguistic claim to its authenticity. The Ush piece is more experimental in its rejection of conventional syntax and grammar, its movement between registers, and its deployment of parody. These two approaches also reflect some of the internal fractures within punk itself. The documentary aspect tends to focus on punk as an expression of broader social, cultural and political concerns of which it is read as an aesthetic and cultural expression. This approach can be seen, for example, in Julian Temple's film *The Filth and the Fury* (2001). Although it includes some appropriate stylistic elements such as the use of cut-up bricolage effects, the documentary style focuses on the emergence of the Sex Pistols and punk as a response to social and political contexts in 1970s Britain. In the film, interviews with the band are framed against *Richard III*'s 'winter of discontent' speech, referring to the famous description by political commentators at the time of the wave of strikes and social unrest in Britain in the winter of 1978–1979. The film also associates various issues of working-class disillusionment with the political system, and in particular the Labour Party as the political vehicle that had failed to represent their concerns sufficiently. Punk is thus read as an inevitable cultural manifestation of political discontent. In contrast, the aesthetic form represented by Ush is more irreverent towards conventional methods of articulation. It represents a carnivalesque disruption of the semiotics of power. There are of course aspects of this in Temple's film, but the Ush piece is more socially ambivalent in its irreverent playfulness. In filmic terms, Ush's approach is closer to Derek Jarman's evocation of punk in his 1978 film *Jubilee* with its avant garde and experimental evocation of punk rebelliousness.

It is perhaps in the combination of these approaches that a specific genre of 'punk fiction' can be identified, one that combines both an authentic account of the experience of punk with an anarchic response to the accepted and official forms of language and convention modes. This combination of form and content can be seen, for example, in Mark Perry's short story 'A Punk Life'

> what are we here for?/the same old questions/buzzing around in my head like some fucking stale Marquee gig/up there it all came back/standing— swaying/nervous up there but full of it/living on nervous punk energy/ blasted out on speed/hating the music/hating the crowd [...] punk was about being out of control/acting on impulse/setting things up/smashing them down/being better than the lot before but also being worse. (1996, 5)

In this passage, there is a clear sense of an authentic account of a real experience, however, the use of the disjointed and accumulated sentences represents a disruption of conventional modes of realism. Perry initially gained fame in the punk movement as the editor of the fanzine *Sniffin' Glue,* and this publication itself features elements of the anarchic and irreverent disrespect of conventional forms of writing with authentic and valued information about the punk scene.[1]

It can be shown that the influence of punk as a literary aesthetic extends beyond those texts that are directly connected with the subculture. For example, Jonathan Coe's *The Rotters' Club*, which although it includes aspects of punk in its narrative, embeds punk in a series of other concerns. In terms of literary form, *The Rotters' Club* borrows from punk's bricolage technique in its stylistic and typographical diversity. Coe's novel includes a series of narrators and points of view, and in driving forward its narrative the novel includes letters, diary entries, theatre reviews, political leaflets, sections from a character's journal, song lyrics and magazine articles. Elsewhere Coe has stressed the way in which 'the British novel has reinvigorated itself' by 'tapping into the energies of popular film, music and television', and this applies to his own work (Coe 2005, 6). Punk is one of the energies influencing Coe's writing, as can be seen in *The Rotters' Club* as well as in a number of his other works, including his most well-known novel, *What a Carve Up!* (1994).

Irvine Welsh's fiction could also be identified as drawing on the aesthetic of a punk sensibility. His ground-breaking first novel *Trainspotting* (1993), detailing the experiences of a group of heroin addicts in Edinburgh in the 1980s, also uses a bricolage technique of deploying diverse styles and points of view that mirrors punk's stylistic features in music fashion and pop imagery. Indeed, it could be argued that punk fiction as a genre can be identified not just in the sense of those novels that offer characters and narratives that are part of the subculture, but in a more subtle and profound influence on the stylistic direction of the British novel in the latter quarter of the twentieth century. British novelists such as Martin Amis, Julie Burchill, Angela Carter, Stewart Home, John King, China Mieville, Tony Parsons and Alex Wheatle, amongst others, can be identified as being influenced by a punk aesthetic, not to mention the more obviously direct links of literary genres such as cyberpunk and steampunk (see Elhefnawy 2015). Indeed, what is often identified as postmodern fiction includes work that borrows greatly from a punk aesthetic. In the next section of this chapter the formal aspects of punk fiction will be discussed with respect to a series of novels that have attempted to embed the subculture in broader narratives about the social, cultural and political contexts of Britain in the 1970s.

Punk in Fiction

Alongside stylistic aspects, punk has also been a rich source for novelists who are interested in commenting on the relationship between the subculture and the socioeconomic and political contexts from which it emerged. The contrast of approaches between the social realist and the experimental can also be found in the fiction that has tried to capture these contexts, ranging from works that came out at the time, such as Gideon Sams's *The Punk* (2004 [1977]) and Richard Allen's *Punk Rock* (1977), to novels that look back to the punk moment and use it in order to trace social and political changes, such as Hanif Kureishi's *The Buddha of Suburbia* (1990) and Jonathan Coe's *The Rotters' Club* (2001). Another distinction between Sams and Allen and Kureishi and Coe is that the former pair are working in a publishing context of pulp fiction/underground fiction, while the latter two have achieved critical as well as popular success.[2] Having said that, the removal of established distinctions between high and popular culture, of course, is a prominent feature of postmodernity, and punk had a central role to play in this blurring of boundaries. What seems to compare across all the novels is that punk is embedded in a broader view of the 1970s and used as a cultural manifestation of the profound set of political and social changes that were a feature of the decade. Even in Sams's novel, written by a 14-year-old member of the subculture (initially as part of a school English project), there is awareness that punk is a manifestation of deeper cultural changes afoot in society. As Adolph, the provocatively self-monickered hero of *The Punk* explains to an old man he encounters: 'Look mister, I am today's youth, and you're going to be hearing a lot more of us if you don't sit up and take notice. There's gonna be some changes in this country pretty soon, an' you better be prepared for it' (27). Although what these changes might be is left vague, it is clear that Sams's hero recognizes the place punk has in a broader set of sociocultural and generational changes.

This sense of change is often individual as well as social and several of the novels include moments (usually generated by attending a punk gig, party or event) where a main character experiences a profound change in identity. This can be seen in both *The Buddha of Suburbia* and *The Rotters' Club* where there is an attempt to convey the life-changing experience of attending a punk gig, notably for characters who are discontented with the direction youth culture was seen to be taking in the middle decades of the 1970s. Indeed, both novels deploy what are seen to be outmoded alternative subcultures as a contrast to the emergence of punk: in Kureishi's novel this is a combination of hippiedom and its post-hippy equivalent of art rock/space rock, and for Coe it is the British progressive rock of the late 1960s and early 70s.

Both *The Rotters' Club* and *The Buddha of Suburbia* contain scenes that attempt to describe the experience of attending a punk gig. In Coe's novel, one of the main characters, Doug Anderton, has ambitions to become a rock journalist and visits the NME offices in London on the basis of an informal invitation to 'drop in' after sending them an example of his writing. Although no one at NME is expecting him when he arrives, he is eventually asked to go to a gig to report on a Rock Against Racism gig in Forest Gate. Not knowing London he mistakenly goes to Forest Hill but, rather fortunately, ends up going to see The Clash playing at the Fulham Old Town Hall. The date is 29 October 1976 and this is a reference to an actual Clash gig marking Coe's attention to historical detail and revealing a level of authenticity in his representation of the lived experience of punk. The experience of attending the gig has a marked effect on Doug:

> He was transfixed by the sight and sound of Joe Strummer shouting, screaming, singing, howling into the microphone: the hair lank with sweat, the veins on his neck tautened and pulsing with blood. Doug surrendered to the noise and for an hour he pogoed like a madman in the dense, heaving heart of a crowd two hundred more or strong. (2001, 162)

This experience, combined with a one-night stand he later has with the 'preposterously named Ffion ffoulkes', an upper-class woman he had met earlier at the NME offices, represent a change in Doug's provincial outlook: 'Doug lost something important that night [...] It had to do with his sense of self, his belonging, his loyalty to the place and the family he came from' (164). In subcultural terms, Doug had, before this experience, been associated with his friend Philip Chase's love of prog rock, but his discovery of punk is couched in terms of a set of expanded cultural horizons that the introspection of prog had denied.

This transition from the so-called bloated, boring and outmodedness of the prog scene to the exuberance and rebelliousness of punk is, of course, a common trope in the cultural histories of the period. As Caroline Coon wrote in a *Melody Maker* review of a Sex Pistols gig in August 1976, 'The Pistols are the personification of the emerging British punk rock scene, a positive reaction to the complex equipment, technological sophistication and jaded alienation which formed a barrier between fans and stars' (1995, 491). This idea of punk representing a fresh and organic reaction to mid-70s rock extravagance is also registered in Sams's *The Punk*, for example, when the central character, the self-named Adolph, explains that he 'despised the rock stars and groups, such as The Who and Led Zeppelin.

They talked about fighting the system and capitalism but always ended up as rich as millionaires' (2004, 5).

That this transition from the hippy and prog to punk registered as a moment of both personal and societal change is perhaps most clearly expressed in Hanif Kureishi's *The Buddha of Suburbia*. The novel covers the span of the 1970s and when it begins, the main protagonist, Karim, is nineteen and affiliates with a late-hippie rock scene that is dominant in his school and appears to appeal to his mixed-race identity. However, Karim recognises that disillusionment is developing with the idealism suggested by the hippie generation. As he notes, 'the kid's crusade was curdling now, everyone had overdosed' (1990, 71). One of Karim's close friends is Charlie, the son of a white middle-class woman with whom Karim's father has an affair. It is Charlie who is presented as having his finger on the pulse in the various transitions in rock music culture the novel records as it moves through the 1970s. Initially Charlie forms a band based on the emerging space rock/art rock scene as epitomised in the figure of David Bowie, a scene that is presented as extending the hippie principles to a new focus on individual self-fashioning.

It is, however, Charlie's sudden attraction to punk that marks the main transition in the novel in terms of subcultural identity. Again this is presented as a visceral and emotive response to the experiencing of a live punk gig. On initially entering the venue with Karim, Charlie is sceptical of the band's anarchic approach: 'He's an idiot [...] I bet they can't play [...] Unprofessional' (130). But by the end of the gig it is the very abjection of the punk performance that Charlie lights upon as an indication of the power of this new subculture. 'The sixties have been given notice tonight. These kids we saw have assassinated all hope. They're the fucking future' (1990, 131). The event has a profound effect on Charlie, a character who is able to quickly jettison one subcultural identity and take up another: he changes his name to Charlie Hero and the name of his band to The Condemned (from the previously hippie-influenced 'Mustn't Grumble'). Charlie represents the power of punk to effect change in the individual as he opens himself to the anarchic power of the movement. Karim, however, is more sceptical and the representation of punk in the novel as a whole is ambivalent. The ability to latch on to the performative aspects of subcultural identity marks Charlie as engaged in an inauthentic response to punk subculture as a whole. As Karim points out, they cannot become punks because: 'We're not like them. We don't hate the way they do. We've got no reason to. We're not from the estates. We haven't been through what they have' (1990, 132) However, the question of authenticity and inauthenticity is always complicated in punk as much of it thrives on parodic performativity and self-reflexive mockery. As Dylan Clarke notes, punk offered a way of 'being subcultural while addressing the discursive problem of subcultures' (2003, 232). Clarke identifies punk as the 'last subculture' in the classical sense, but it can be equally argued that it ushers in the notion of the post-subcultural in its combined attention to demarcating a set of distinctive youth cultural behaviours and attitudes while at the same time promoting an attitude of self-loathing. When the abject becomes celebrated, the very notion of the subculture's success is itself always couched in ironic and postmodern terms. In this sense, Charlie's direct response to his first experience of punk exceeds evaluative judgments of the authentic/inauthentic, and in Kureishi's novel the arrival of punk's individualism is framed alongside the imminent appearance of Thatcherism on the political scene. In many ways, despite its claims of anarchism, punk and Thatcherism are parallel responses to the apparent failure of a centrist Labour Party that had claimed to represent working-class interests, but had resulted in widespread industrial unrest and political divisions within the Party by the late 1970s. As John Lydon states in *The Filth and the Fury*, with respect to the period that saw the emergence of the Sex Pistols, 'England was in a state of social upheaval. [...] Total social chaos [...] People were fed up with the old way, the old way was clearly not working' (Temple 2001, 00:02:15–00:02:46).

Punk as a response to sociopolitical conditions is also registered in Richard Allen's *Punk Rock*. In this novel, Danny Boy, the front man in a punk band who, like Charlie in Kureishi's text, has to a large extent self-fashioned his rebellious public persona, explains to the journalist narrator Kerr: 'We've reached the end of tolerance with bowler-hats telling us, in Queen's English, what to do and where to do it and when to do it. These kids are the nucleus of an army. A people's army. Not commies. Not any political, string-pulled puppets. But free kids wanting their music first, their country next' (Allen 1977, 79). Despite this claim of political non-partisanship, the particular articulation Allen places on punk emphasises a right-wing, racist element that is clearly different from Johnny Lydon's left-leaning anarchism. It should be noted, however, that Allen's claim to offer an authentic depiction of punk is dubious. Richard Allen is the pen-name of James Moffat, who had produced a series of lucrative subcultural pulp novels in the 1970s including *Skinhead* (1970) and *Suedehead* (1971). His 1977 *Punk Rock* was a continuation of this trend. Allen's style across all his works was to emphasise the violent aspects of subcultural practice and his novels tended to be lurid, soft porn entertainment that fed into moral panics about youth behaviours. *Punk Rock*, for example, includes an outdoor punk festival in which a skinhead is beaten up and trampled by the crowd while Kerr himself is punched and kicked. Allen's novel identifies the 'New Wave scene', as it describes it, as a commodified enterprise that combines insincere musicians, impresarios and music journalists whose main aim is to exploit a youth cultural movement. However, behind the commercial apparatus, Kerr begins to empathise with the authentic members of the subculture; after witnessing the violence at the festival he notes: 'I'm beginning to identify with the punk rockers [...] I can see the frustrations building inside them. Imagine ten quid for a ticket!' (1977, 52).

Violence also plays a prominent role in Gideon Sams's *The Punk*, which includes a scene in which a fight between punks breaks out at a gig resulting in one of the crowd fainting when his safety pin earring is ripped out. At another gig, featuring The Damned, The Clash and the Sex Pistols at the famous punk venue The Roxy, in Covent Garden, a fight breaks out between the punks when the headlining act are late in coming to the stage. The novel is loosely based on *Romeo and Juliet*, and the sectarian violence of Montagues and Capulets is transferred to violent encounters between punks and Teds with the inevitable tragic consequences for Adolph and his girlfriend Thelma who converts from Ted to punk. Violence is also an inherent part of the subculture in Stewart Home's *Tainted Love* (2005), a novel that is predominantly about the 1960s counterculture, but in its later stages includes description of a fight that breaks out at a Rock Against Racism gig between a politically engaged white punk band and its followers and a local skinhead group. As with Richard Allen, Home's narrative is more ambivalent towards punk than the more celebratory aspects of Sams's novel; in *Tainted Love* this particular punk scene has been infiltrated by Socialist Worker elements. The complexities of the subcultural conflicts are brought to the fore and are registered by Home in the fact that one of the members of the Reggae band headlining the Rock Against Racism gig defends the skinheads: 'Them Ladbroke Grove skinheads ain't racists [...] they're redskins and like old school reggae music' (2005, 222). Earlier, this ambiguous image of punk is registered by the narrator: 'when I returned to London in 1977 there were punks everywhere. Most of them seemed kind of cute to me but [...] they can turn savage (218).'

Alongside these descriptions of subcultural violence, the political complexities of punk are registered in the descriptions of fashion and appearance. In Sams's *The Punk,* Adolph wears a safety pin through his nose and an earring that comprised of 'a gold swastika surrounded by the star of David, painted in sky blue' (2004 [1977, 13]). Similarly, after Charlie converts to punk in Kureishi's *The Buddha of Suburbia*:

> He wore, inside out, a slashed T-shirt with a red swastika hand-painted on it. His black trousers were held together by safety-pins, paperclips and needles. Over this he had a black mackintosh; there were five belts strapped around his waist and a sort of grey linen nappy attached to the back of his trousers. (1990, 152)

As noted earlier, Hebdige has identified punk as a bricolage form with each object (and the combined juxtaposition of the objects) forming a homology of cultural signifiers that connotes chaos and rebellion. In the two extracts above, the fascist iconography is placed alongside the subversion of consumerism through the use of safety pins; this combines to present a performance, played out on the abjected body of the punk subject, of a total rejection of the dominant culture's ideas of taste. The sartorial statement is thus designed to shock not only the political centrist, but also evade conventional (1970s) demarcations of left- or right-wing politics. This is not to say that it evades hierarchies of taste, and indeed as Sarah Thornton has noted, following Pierre Bourdieu's concept of cultural capital (1984), the subcultural use of cultural knowledge and objects offers an alternative framework of *subcultural* capital (Thornton 1995). Indeed, for punk the more outrageous and offensive the dress and behaviour the higher the subcultural capital the subject accumulates. And in doing so, the aim is often to hollow out the political significance of objects such as swastikas.

The complexity of the political meaning of punk has been noted by a number of critics who themselves are divided over the effects of punk's desire to shock. Elizabeth Wilson, for example, has argued that 'Punk spoke the anger of youth in a crumbling economy administered by out-of-touch politicians, and, insofar as nihilism is political, it *was* political; it was anti-establishment, it was about outrage, shock, violence, pornography, anarchy and self-destruction' [emphasis in original] (2000, 135). Alternatively, punk can be seen to have attracted members from a broad political spectrum. As Roger Sabin points out, punk's 'political ambiguity left ample space for right-wing interpretation' (1999, 199) and as Dylan Clarke notes 'Some punks went so far as to valorize anything mainstream society disliked, including rape and death camps, some punks slid into fascism' (226).

These political ambiguities make punk a fertile subject for fiction, and both Kureishi's *The Buddha of Suburbia* and Coe's *The Rotters' Club*, in particular, deploy references to the subculture as a way of examining the political shifts in Britain in the 1970s. Both these novels, indeed, identify punk as coinciding with the shift from consensus politics of the immediate post-war to the culture wars of the Thatcherite period. For Kureishi, attention to pop-cultural contexts and histories has always been a way to examine broader social and political concerns; as Bart Moore-Gilbert suggests: 'For Kureishi pop epitomises the liberating energies of the "cultural revolution" which began in the 1960s' (2001, 115). We have already discussed Charlie, but the main character in *The Buddha of Suburbia* is Karim, who is described early in the novel as a 'new breed' of Englishman due to his mixed ethnic background and who is looking for 'trouble, any kind of movement, action and sexual interest' (1990, 3). Although he does not embrace punk in the same way as Charlie, his individualism and desire to succeed despite the racial prejudice he receives in 1970s Britain mirrors punk's desire to stand up for the marginalised and abjected of society. Karim is an engaging narrator; however, as the text moves forward into the later 1970s, his individualism is often self-serving and unthinking. Indeed, Karim and Charlie become emblematic of a new breed of selfish individualism, described by his friend Changez as representative of a new kind of identity: 'Here, in this capitalism of the feelings no one cares for another person' (1990, 215). The novel ends in 1979 with the election of Thatcher, and the implication is made clear that Karim and Charlie are themselves representative of a new culture that places individual ambition above the development of meaningful human relationships.

Coe's *The Rotters' Club* presents a similar deployment of punk as a cultural signifier of sociopolitical change. The novel details the relationships of a group of Birmingham school friends set against key political contexts of the 1970s: namely, Trade Union unrest, the Birmingham pub bombings, and the rise of racist political movements and attitudes. The school becomes the arena in which these concerns in the parent culture are played out, and subcultural affiliation thus becomes representative of broader political concerns. In this way, the novel follows one of the key ideas developed by the subcultural theorist Phil Cohen in its identification of the transference between youth subcultures and the parent cultures from which they emerge. As Cohen argues, 'mods, parkas, skinheads, crombies, are a succession of subcultures which all correspond to the same parent culture and which attempt to work out, through a system of transformations, the basic problematic or contradiction which is inserted in the subculture by the parent culture' (2004, 90).

In Coe's novel, punk represents an expression of rebellious individualism that is placed in contrast with the novel's other main subcultural reference—progressive rock. Richard Bradford, for example, notes that one of the main characters attracted to the subculture, Doug Anderton, is 'fascinated by punk, not because it is art but because it seems to him to distil a selfish disregard for collective or personal responsibility' (2007, 44). Doug is friends with Philip Chase and Benjamin Trotter, fans of prog rog bands like Hatfield and the North, who produced the album (1975) from which Coe takes the title of his novel. One key incident dramatises the arrival of punk on 1970s youth culture. The incident is recounted in one of the novel's shifts in temporal perspective that moves us to a written memory produced by Doug in 1999. Doug explains that Philip had been planning for a number of months to put together a prog rock band and had been writing material when the band met for its first rehearsal. The band is called Gandalf's Pikestaff and Philip's composition is a 32-minute prog rock masterpiece called 'Apotheosis of the Necromancer' which, in typical prog ambition, attempts to cover 'the entire history of the universe from the moment of creation up until roughly, as far as I could see, the resignation of Harold Wilson in 1976' (2001, 179). However, a chant—'the maws of doom', a phrase taken from a National Front leaflet introduced the previous day by one of the novel's other anarchic characters, is taken up by Stubbs, the band's singer. The drummer and guitarist in the band get bored with Philip's ambitious progressive rock and move into a 'ferocious back beat in 4/4', and Stubbs starts to scream 'The maws, The maws, the very maws of doom' repeatedly. This aggressive verbal interruption is indicative of the critic David Laing's argument that vocalists in punk bands tend to emphasise 'speech, recitative, chanting or wordless cries and mutterings' as a way of disrupting the 'musicality of singing' and thus avoiding the 'contamination of the lyric message by the aesthetic pleasures offered by melody, harmony, pitch and so on' (2015, 70). The anarchic overturning of Philip's ambitions at this point is thus emblematic of a particular rupture in rock history, and as Doug explains, 'Philip had chosen the wrong moment, historically, to make his personal bid for prog rock stardom' (2001, 179–80), and Philip himself later reflects that 'These were desperate times for someone like him, whose heroes—specialists, to a man, in fifteen-minute instrument [...]—had until recently commanded two-page features in the music press but could nowadays barely get themselves a recording contract' (2001, 250).

Behind the personal contexts and schoolyard antagonisms of this comic episode, however, is a deeper indication of underlying anxieties over political shifts in Britain. In subcultural terms, the rehearsal records some of the apolitical and escapist aspects of prog rock against the engaged (though often politically ambiguous) nature of punk. It is interpreted by Doug, as he reflects back on the period, as bound up with a shift in the political climate in Britain from the continuation of a broad consensus politics to the ideological stand-off between left and right as manifest in the emergence of Thatcherism. On the evening following the ill-fated rehearsal of Gandalf's Pikestaff, Doug recalls overhearing his father, a prominent trade unionist, enter into an edgy conversation with Benjamin's conservative father after the result of a by-election which the Tories had won a landslide victory. Doug later reflects: 'Meanwhile waiting in the wings was a new breed of Tory and these people meant business' (2001, 181). Philip's ambitions of producing a prog masterpiece are connected with 'the death of the socialist dream', as Doug comments:

This ludicrous attempt to squeeze the history of countless millennia into half an hour's worth of crappy riffs and chord changes seemed no more Quixotic than all the things my dad and his colleagues had been working towards for so long. A national health service, free to everyone who needed it. Redistribution of wealth through taxation. Equality of opportunity. Beautiful ideas dad, noble aspirations, just as there was the kernel of something beautiful in Philip's musical hodge-podge. But it was never going to happen. (182)

Doug associates progressive rock with a left-wing utopian sentiment that is no match in the 1970s and 1980s for the harsher ideologies of a Thatcherite politics of individualism, represented here by punk.

Coe's novel, then, is just one of a number of literary works in which punk is deployed as a cultural indication of broader social and political transitions in Britain and reveals the diversity of cultural associations with which it has been imbued. The subculture's anarchic rebelliousness is often used in fiction as emblematic of the shift in British culture from a politics of consensus to one of opposition. Taken as a whole, however, the fictional narratives discussed in this chapter reveal a complex set of political and ideological affiliations associated with punk that both registers the desire for a rude and often carnivalesque disruption of dominant ideologies and power relations, but one that evades traditional left-right markers. The anarchism of punk can thus be seen in a corresponding overturning of the prevailing modes and styles of the British novel as much as it can reflect profound changes in British society in the 1970s.

NOTES

1. For a history of the fanzine *Sniffin' Glue* see Perry 2000.
2. For a detailed survey of the importance of the context of publishing for punk fiction see Rivett 1999.

REFERENCES

Allen, Richard. 1977. *Punk Rock*. London: New English Library.
Allen, Richard. 1970. *Skinhead*. London: New English Library.
Allen, Richard. 1971. *Suedehead*. London: New English Library.
Bentley, Nick. 2018. 'From Prog to Punk: Cultural Politics and the Form of the Novel in Jonathan Coe's *The Rotters' Club*.' In *Jonathan Coe: Contemporary British Satire*, edited by Philip Tew. London and New York: Bloomsbury.
Bradford, Richard. 2007. *The Novel Now*. Malden, MA. and Oxford: Blackwell.
Bresnan, Mark. 2015. '"Consistently Original, Perennially Unheard Of": Punk, Margin, and Mainstream in Jonathan Franzen's *Freedom*.' In *Write in Tune: Contemporary Music in Fiction*, edited by Erich Hertz and Jeffrey Roessner, 31–42. London and New York: Bloomsbury.
Bourdieu, Pierre. 1984. *Distinction: A Social Critique of the Judgement of Taste*. Trans. Richard Nice. Cambridge, MA.: Harvard University Press.
Clarke, Dylan. 2003. 'The Death and Life of Punk, the Last Subculture.' In *The Post-Subcultures Reader*, edited by David Muggleton and Rupert Wienzierl, 223–38. Oxford: Berg.
Cohen, Phil. 2004 [1972]. 'Subcultural Conflict and Working-class Community [1972].' In *The Subcultures Reader*. 2nd edition, edited by Ken Gelder, 86–93. London and New York: Routledge.
Coe, Jonathan. 2005. *Like a Fiery Elephant: The Story of B.S. Johnson*. London: Picador.
Coe, Jonathan. 2001. *The Rotters' Club*. London: Penguin.
Coe, Jonathan. 1994. *What a Carve Up!* London: Viking.

Coon, Caroline, 1995 [1976] '1976: Rock Revolution.' In *The Faber Book of Pop*, edited by Hanif Kureishi and Jon Savage, 490–93. London and Boston: Faber and Faber.

Denby, Joolz. 2009. 'West One (Shine on Me).' In *Punk Fiction: An Anthology of Short Stories Inspired by Punk*, edited by Janine Bullman, 14–18. London: Portico Books.

Elhefnawy, Nader. 2015. *Cyberpunk, Steampunk and Wizardry: Science Fiction Since 1980*. Create Space.

Ellis, Bret Easton. 1985. *Less Than Zero*. New York: Simon and Schuster.

Franzen, Jonathan. 2010. *Freedom*. New York: Farrar, Straus and Giroux.

Hallberg, Garth Risk. 2015. *City on Fire*. London: Jonathan Cape.

Hebdige, Dick. 1988 [1979]. *Subculture: The Meaning of Style*. London and New York: Routledge,

Home, Stewart. 2005. *Tainted Love*. London: Virgin Books.

Jubilee. 1978. Dir. Derek Jarman. London: Whaley-Maley Productions.

Kureishi, Hanif. 1990. *The Buddha of Suburbia*. London and Boston: Faber and Faber.

Laing, David. 2015 [1985]. *One Chord Wonders Meaning in Punk Rock*. Oakland, CA: PM Press.

Luter, Matthew. 2015. 'More Than Zero: Post-Punk Ideology (and Its Rejection) in Bret East Ellis.' In *Write in Tune: Contemporary Music in Fiction*, edited by Erich Hertz and Jeffrey Roessner, 19–30. London and New York: Bloomsbury.

Moore-Gilbert, Bart. 2001. *Hanif Kureishi*. Manchester: Manchester University Press.

Perry, Mark. 1996. 'A Punk Life'. In *Gobbing, Pogoing, and Gratuitous Bad Language: An Anthology of Punk Short Stories*, edited by Robert Dellar, 5–8. London: Spare Change Books.

Perry, Mark. 2000. *Sniffin' Glue: The Essential Punk Accessory*. London: Sanctuary Publishing.

Rivett, Miriam. 1999. 'Misfit Lit: "Punk Writing", and Representations of Punk Through Writing and Publishing.' In *Punk Rock: So What?: The Cultural Legacy of Punk*, edited by Roger Sabin, 31–48. Abingdon and New York: Routledge.

The Rotters' Club [album]. 1975. Hatfied and the North. London: Virgin.

Sabin, Roger. 1999. '"I Won't Let that Dago By": Rethinking Punk and Racism.' In *Punk Rock: So What?: The Cultural Legacy of Punk*, edited by Roger Sabin, 199–218. Abingdon and New York: Routledge.

Sams, Gideon. 2004 [1977]. *The Punk*. London: Fortune Teller Press.

The Filth and the Fury. 2001. Dir. Julien Temple. London: Film Four.

Thornton, Sarah. 1995. *Clubcultures Music, Media and Subcultural Capital*. London: Polity Press.

Ush. 2002. 'The History of the Skeptix (well in my world, anyway!).' The Official Website of the Skeptix. Accessed October 31, 2017. www.theskeptix.com/.

Welsh, Irvine. 1993. *Trainspotting*. London: Secker & Warburg.

Willis, Paul. 2014 [1978]. *Profane Culture*. Princeton and Oxford: Princeton University Press.

Wilson, Elizabeth. 2000. *Bohemians: The Glamorous Outcasts*. New Brunswick NJ.: Rutgers University Press.

'Styles, 'Codes and Violence': Subcultural Identities in Contemporary Black Writing of Britain'

Dave Ellis

In an apparently unmotivated scene in Mike Phillips' *Blood Rights* (1990), the black private eye, Sam Dean, takes time out of his ongoing investigation to tutor his son on the visual details with which he can learn to map London streets and chart a safe course through the potential dangers therein. Dean is a voice of authority here not simply because he is a detective professionally attuned to, and experienced in, drawing significance from outwardly meaningless phenomena, but also because he is a veteran of London street life. He has grown up as a first-generation black Briton in the 1960s and '70s, and he is accustomed to, and has learned to anticipate, unprovoked acts of racial hostility from different social groups and from representatives of the white Establishment. The cognitive map he conveys to his son is based upon ethnic differences providing visual clues to the levels of threat they pose to a young black boy. The lesson is successful and his son learns that certain groups of people and certain situations

D. Ellis (✉)
Oxford Brookes University, Oxford, UK

N. Bentley et al. (eds.), *Youth Subcultures in Fiction, Film and Other Media*, Palgrave Studies in the History of Subcultures and Popular Music, https://doi.org/10.1007/978-3-319-73189-6_4

are dangerous and to be avoided: he has been given the means to read the streets. However, this intergenerational wisdom is somewhat destabilised as his son asks Dean why he always says hello to other black people on the street, whether he knows them or not. Dean replies, 'In the old days ... we'd speak because it would be kind of reassuring to be in contact with another black person' (Phillips 1990, 166). What has always struck me as interesting about this exchange is that Dean's son is offered tuition on what differentiates groups of people but must ask what binds them together. Perhaps Dean senior's sense of a communal identity based upon a shared history of migration is less evident to his son than it is to him: what does this suggest, I wonder, about the discursive construction of identity in black British literature that deals with characters two or more generations removed from the experience of migration?

In an analogous scene, Dennis Huggins, Alex Wheatle's central protagonist in *The Dirty South* (2008), performs his own cognitive mapping of South London: 'Tulse Hill estate where a trailer load of eastern European people and white trash families live [...] Myatts Fields estate where all the crack houses used to be ... Angel Town where every second brother seems to be packed with a gun. Stockwell, where the rude boys show off their guns in the local youth club and Vauxhall where the Portuguese shottas sell the best hash in London ...' (Wheatle 2008, 2). Dennis, like Dean's son, is a second-generation black Briton, albeit ten years his senior. It would be widely inaccurate to suggest Dennis has lost a colour consciousness or that he perceives white Britain to be any less harmful to his and his peers' life chances than Dean does. However, Dennis has learnt to map London differently to Dean, and the semiotic maps he employs owe less to colour codes than to postcodes: it is not so much whom you encounter, as where you encounter them that demarcates Dennis's London. This intensified parochialism drives the narrative of *The Dirty South* as it is Dennis's failure to observe the boundaries set out in his own mapping that leads to the tragic resolution of the novel.

In this chapter I will seek to explore the ways in which youth identity and affiliation are portrayed in works by two key figures in contemporary black British writing: Alex Wheatle and Courttia Newland. It takes a specific focus upon teenage culture and style as a means of picking out intergenerational differences not simply to suggest that youth culture defines itself in opposition to the generation that precedes it, since this is a well-established principle. Instead, it is to suggest that these books illustrate what I want to call the 'new parochialism' in which youth identity in working-class London draws upon an intensified sense of affiliation to a local area, estate or postcode. One consequence of this new parochialism is an alteration in the former codes of affiliation based upon a Caribbean heritage expressed through formal and family history and musical style which is supplemented (rather than replaced) by local histories, often held at the level of orality and myth. Central to the 'new' histories in each of the texts are myths of violence and reputation. In this respect, Sam Dean's colour coding of London becomes more complex, since the postcodes of the new parochialism blur the boundaries of 'race' and introduce new affiliations and disaffiliations that pertain more to new local histories than to the histories of migration.

The concept of a new parochialism is drawn from Homi Bhabha's intervention in 1999 when his 'Manifesto' stimulated a series of discussions and events leading to the *Reinventing Britain* Conference hosted by the British Council to debate British identities. In 'The Manifesto', Bhabha describes a contemporary reality in which 'the new cosmopolitanism has fundamentally changed our sense of the relationship between national tradition or territory, and the attribution of cultural values and social norms'. In the 'new cosmopolitanism', 'culture is less about expressing a pre-given identity (whether the source is national culture or "ethnic" culture) and more about the activity of negotiating, regulating and authorising competing, often conflicting demands for collective self-representation' (Bhabha 1999, 39). In these propositions Bhabha is seeking to progress beyond the multiculturalist debates of the 1980s wherein the notion of core and marginal cultures were challenged by decentring a dominant cultural tradition—in this instance, Englishness—in preference for a model of competing ethnicities within which no ethnicity could claim a prior value or innate or historical privilege. Instead Bhabha proposes a hybrid culture within which the essentialising tendencies of 'equal but different' are rendered 'increasingly sterile'. Central to Bhabha's vision of a new social landscape is the impact of a loosening of nationalist identities through the cultural borderlessness of transnationalism captured in the 'hybrid cosmopolitanism of contemporary metropolitan life' (Bhabha 1999, 39). One way in which this new, or hybrid, cosmopolitanism might be illustrated is through reference to 'Fresh for '88', a short story by Courttia Newland from his collection, *A Book of Blues* (2011).

In the story, a pair of London youths prepare for an MC contest being held in Wormwood Scrubs park. Here, 1988 is significant because it is 'the year young London went hip-hop crazy' (Newland 2011, 40). The enthusiasm for American style is evident in the street fashion of baseball caps, baggy jeans and unlaced Nike Air Max trainers and the eagerness of the narrator, Stone, to compare Harrow Road flats with Brooklyn brown-stones from *The Cosby Show* (Newland 2011, 39). However, this is not an unmediated adoption of American style: 1988 was also the year that British hip-hop established itself through the Demon Boyz and their *Recognition* album. Hip-hop, with its basis in sampling and borrowing, translating and transforming, ties closely to Bhabha's notion that there is 'no ideal norm of perfect translation or appropriation possible' when hybrid works contest origin or ownership. In this story, hip-hop is 'an all-encompassing culture' (Newland 2011, 40) not a narrow tradition, and, for Stone, the MC performance is not premised upon the reverential rep-lication of original performance but on the spontaneous interactivity of DJ, MC and audience: 'nothing supersedes that split-second moment of finding my flow and placing the words exactly on the beat …' (Newland 2011, 45).

Stone's bid to win the MC battle ends in failure as a fight breaks out in the audience during his act and disrupts his performance. Dispirited, he wonders whether his opinion of the power of London hip-hop was exag-gerated and would itself always remain parochial compared to the US acts. However, the transformative power of hip-hop to establish new configura-tions is reaffirmed in the denouement of the story: reflecting on what seems to be his perennial bad luck and persecution, Stone finally asks his friend, Reka, 'You think all dis shit happens to me—to *us*—because I'm white?' (Newland 2011, 60). Throughout the story Stone's character, voice, dress style and musical tastes have been indistinguishable from his (presumably) black associates, and Newland's intention is clearly to draw attention to the implied reader's assumptions about 'racial' markers. In addition, Reka's reply to Stone's query, 'Nah, blud', suggests that such markers are no longer relevant to a hip-hop generation who find a com-mon identity in musical subcultures that transcend national identities and cultural heritage: 'blud', here, is invested with additional meaning.

I do not want to overburden this short story with too much social sig-nificance, although some of what I have said here in terms of a shared street style that crosses ethnic boundaries can also be observed in Noel Clarke's screenplay for the film, *Kidulthood* (2006). The revelation of Stone's ethnicity, also, is not an uncommon narrative ploy, and parallels could be drawn with Gautam Malkani's *Londonstani* (2007), for example (it remains interesting, however, that a writer of Newland's experience and stature knows he can still exploit this authorial technique effectively). Similarly, UK hip-hop is not the first example of white youth adopting black cultural styles, although I would argue that this is a considerably more thoroughgoing adoption of black style than might be found amongst the white adherents of jazz, blues and reggae in earlier decades. However, I do want to return to Stone's question: if Reka responds negatively to racial difference being the source of their woes, one might ask why *does* all this happen to them?

Among Stone and Reka's associates are two older youths, P. Nutt and Sy, who bully Stone and, through the threat of physical violence, dominate the basement where the youths practice on borrowed record decks. Newland leaves it unclear whether Stone attracts particular attention from them due to his small stature rather than his ethnicity, not least because all the youths are equally intimidated by them. However, Nutt and Sy's repu-tation for violence is not wholly negative for Stone. Whilst window shop-ping away from their home neighbourhood, Stone is approached by a group of boys at a bus stop who try to rob him. The stand-off is only ended when one of the group recognises Reka and Stone as being associ-ated with Nutt and Sy. Now assumed to be under the protection of the duo, and with the unspoken expectation of reprisals should they go through with the robbery, the group withdraw: reputation and the assumption of local loyalties is enough to give them pause for thought. This correlation of locality, loyalty and violence is evident elsewhere in the story. Reka and Stone end relationships with girls mostly due, as Stone reflects, to the 'potential danger of visiting an area where he didn't live' (Newland 2011, 46). Similarly, Wormwood Scrubs Park is not just a site for competing music, it is also a ground for battling postcodes: 'Everyone from every manor in London came [to it], which made it a mad, bad and dangerous place to be' (Newland 2011, 46). Taken together, the 'shit' that happens to Stone emanates less from what he looks like, so much as where he comes from in the form of a heightened parochialism. Sy and Nutt must maintain their reputation for violence; that reputation must be recognised as an attribute of a highly localised area of London; and respect for it must be maintained irrespective of ethnicity.

This scenario is some distance from the positive potential of Bhabha's project to encapsulate a reinvented Britain within which a hybrid cosmopoli-tanism transforms the relationship between identity and a national tradition or territory. Instead, this new cosmopolitanism has been supplanted by a new parochialism in which the meanings of place are being reinvented by emerging urban histories that secure highly localised attributes of identity, communality and belonging. So, where Sam Dean was once able to point to the reassurance of a shared black history held together by oral links back to the Caribbean, arguably this oral history is not shared by his son, hence the confusion that sits behind his question. New social histories and identities are being forged that help to redefine the association of identity to place on much more restrictive historical and geographical bounds. To see if this can be illustrated elsewhere, it may be helpful to look at the longer chronological range afforded by Alex Wheatle's novels.

Brixton Rock (1999) is Wheatle's first novel and introduces the central character, Brenton Brown. Brenton has been placed into care at a young age and *Brixton Rock* recounts his reunion with his Jamaican mother and intense affair with his half-sister, Juliet. In the sequel set sixteen years later, *Brenton Brown* (2011), Brenton's unresolved feelings for Juliet, complicated by the growing demands of their child Breanna to know the truth of her parentage, eventually leads Brenton to migrate abroad. In both novels, Brenton's life in care is related through dreams and flashbacks and tells the tale of a black identity that must be learned through adopted styles and codes of behaviour and allegiance. In this respect, Brenton is severed from the pre-given identity of a national culture (as described by Bhabha) and so is his pick-and-mix invention of an identity, drawing upon diverse cultural sources that makes him a hybrid character, perhaps more so than the biology of his dual heritage.

Brenton is put into care because his mother, Cynthia, has an affair with a white man while her husband is in Jamaica. Pregnant when her husband returns, Cynthia is forced to give Brenton to his father who is unable to provide for him when his own family refuse to support a dual heritage relation. Brenton is brought up in Pinewood Hills, a care home in the countryside well to the south of London, and the novel itself is set in the hostel in Brixton Brenton is placed in when he turns eighteen. As might be apparent from this short summary, Brenton lacks a clear cultural heritage, having been brought up largely amongst white people, and his two principal sources of comfort are constructed ones: first a scarecrow called Mr Brown that he became fixated on as a child at Pinewood; and secondly, a poster of James Dean in which he continues to confide whilst at the hostel. The extent to which he must learn to be black is finally recounted by his hostel mate, Floyd, as an anecdote in *Brenton Brown*: 'His accent! There was some kind of BBC, Surrey fuckery going on with his accent ... I had to teach him to walk like a Brixtonian [...] He had no riddim, man. No bounce ... And then I tried to teach him how to crub with a girl' (Wheatle 2011, 240–1). It is while Brenton is still learning to be Brixtonian that he encounters his 'nemesis', Terry Flynn. Brenton initiates a longstanding feud with Flynn in *Brixton Rock* after he punches Flynn for calling him a 'liccle half-breed' at a blues party (Wheatle 2010, 19). Subsequently Brenton hospitalises Flynn by hitting him with a beer glass in a pool hall fight. From this point, Brenton is embroiled in a battle over reputations, since the ghetto press now has Brenton dubbed as 'the guy who crucially dealt with Terry Flynn' (Wheatle 2010, 21). This feud will lead eventually to both Flynn's death when he falls under a tube train during a fight with Brenton and to Brenton's enduring Brixton fame as the 'Steppin' Volcano': a nickname that companies him through most of Wheatle's novels. As Floyd puts it, 'Mashing up Terry Flynn has turned you into a celebrity' (Wheatle 2010, 249).

As the 'Steppin' Volcano', Brenton acquires a place in local mythology akin to Sy and Nutt in Newland's story and this reputation brings with it the expectation of behavioural patterns and other identity markers that Brenton learns alongside his education in being Brixtonian. For example, in the opening scenes to *Brixton Rock*, he deliberately adopts (and regrets) a 'bad bwai' pose' for the benefit of the police officers (2010, 3). In this respect, the cultural markers that Brenton also adopts, including the confusing combination of Jamaican reggae tapes and the James Dean poster that populate his hostel room, are themselves cut adrift from any authenticating point of origin: Brenton is not adopting a roots culture in terms of tracing back to his Caribbean roots. This becomes most evident in *Brenton Brown* when Brenton decides that his undimmed feelings for Juliet mean he must leave England altogether to achieve a fresh start. Whilst considering likely places to settle, Jamaica is quickly dismissed: 'I wanna go somewhere with decent weather. A place where I can hear reggae music. Forget Jamaica, I don't wanna spend my days there living behind some serious metal grille at the front of my yard and see a goat shitting on my gates and chickens walking around like they want to mug you ... Maybe the US?' (Wheatle 2011, 173). This is not the only point at which Brenton has dismissed a link back to the islands. Comparing the decoration of his mother's house with that of his friend Floyd's mother he notes, 'Mrs Francis's front room is similar to the way Mum had hers. The same black-and-white photos on their mantelpiece, Jamaican scroll souvenirs hanging from the walls [...] What a load of fuckery! [...] Did Jamaican women who came over here in the fifties and sixties all agree to have the same shit in their front rooms?' (Wheatle 2011, 134). Crucially, though, this is not as simple as saying that Brenton lacks the traditional family upbringing to provide old country ties to the Caribbean through memory and extended transnational family networks. For Brenton, this severance with the Caribbean is also true of his contemporaries for whom the notion of roots begins in Brixton. As he compares his sense of belonging to his friends, Floyd and Biscuit, Brenton states, 'My roots are not in south London. Not like it is with them. They belong here. This place has defined the way they walk, talk and carry themselves' (Wheatle 2011, 246).

The definition or construction of identity in this instance is as temporally and geographically specific for Brenton's friends as it is for Brenton himself. This ultimately begs the question of how Brixton has defined its black inhabitants, or perhaps more correctly, how they define it through their own cognitive mapping and history making. Linton Kwesi Johnson, a pioneer of black British culture from the 1970s, chronicled the same cultural terrain as Wheatle from the position of a first-generation migrant. His first volume of poetry, *Voices of the Living and the Dead* was hailed by Farrukh Dhondy as having 'contributed the first collective myth of English poetry for centuries'. Johnson's poetry, he continues, brings the 'experience of locality for his own audience—Brixton, Railton Road, Shepherds, the telegraph, Sofrano B, Neville King [...] what are these? Ask any young black in London' (Dhondy 1974, 133–4). In an interview Wheatle affirms his own belief in the continued significance he assigns to the importance of locality in the creation of identity through storytelling and the ownership of a parochial history: 'I feel the need to write those stories [of the black experience] because they're being neglected [...] we as a people have to write our own stories, otherwise, as what happened in the past, they'll be told for us. And, so, I feel this obligation sometimes to tell our stories' (Immonen 2007, 125). It is therefore interesting to see in Wheatle's novels the way in which this communal history of resistance gets diminished in the new parochialism of styles, codes and violence.

As noted above, the Brixton Riots in 1981 mark a crucial juncture in both the history of black Britain and the generational shifts represented in Wheatle's novels. Wheatle's views on the riots are made clear in an interview with Linton Kwesi Johnson where he states,

> people sometimes forget that these were the biggest upheavals on the mainland for 100 years, and that important moment in black history has not been properly recorded on film or drama or anything else, only in literature by

you [i.e., Johnson]. That is worrying. I'm thinking that this part of our history will just be wiped away and forgotten unless someone else makes up
their mind to address it. I think it needs to be addressed because our children need to know where they come from and of the struggles we have
waged thus far. (Wheatle 2009, 37)

Here again, the point of origin for the purposes of identity is assumed
to be British. In addition, the riots mark a significant place in recent black
history, not least because the Scarman enquiry that ensued brought an
official account of the daily experiences of black Britain into the political
and public domain. Specific reference is made in the Scarman Report to
the work of the Special Patrol Group and the operation of the 'sus' laws
that permitted almost random stop-and-search activities that were widely
perceived to be used to target black youths. *East of Acre Lane* is set against
the local events leading to these riots, and Wheatle acknowledges the
Scarman Report as a source for his novel alongside the anecdotal memo-
ries of his friends, joining together the official and unofficial accounts.
Wheatle's novel is significant because it dramatizes both an important historical event and a parallel parochial history. At the start of the novel
Brenton's place in the 'annals of Brixtonian folklore' as the 'Steppin
Volcano' is reaffirmed with Biscuit's nine-year-old brother, Royston,
already in awe of being in the presence of a 'real life Brixtonian bad man'
(Wheatle 2006, 24). By the end of the novel, this reputation would be
enhanced as Biscuit, Brenton and others kill local drug lord and pimp,
Nunchaks, in an endeavour to free Biscuit's sister, Denise, from prostitution. This reputation again falls into local legend and reappears in *The
Dirty South* where Dennis boasts about his father's (Biscuit's) fame as a
'shotta' involved in the death of a local 'Bricky crime lord' (Wheatle 2008,
3). It is in the intergenerational transition from Biscuit in *East of Acre
Lane* to his son, Dennis, in *The Dirty South* that one can observe the loss
of a Caribbean communal history in favour of the new myths of
parochialism.

East of Acre Lane features another recurrent character in Wheatle's fiction, the Rastafarian, Jah Nelson. Everton Pryce has described the link
between Rastafarianism and reggae music in a manner that accords with
Wheatle's sense of owning and linking together style, history and culture:
'Reggae music [...] played the role of linking the style and form of Afro-
Jamaican street-culture to the style and form of young Afro-Caribbean
blacks in Britain, and, with the rastafarian movement, gave these same

youths an orientation ...' (Pryce 1985, 37). Nelson attempts to bind Biscuit into this orientation so he so can 'try fe do somet'ing better, and nah get 'imself moulded by the environment where 'im live' (Wheatle 2006, 43). He does so by trying to provide Biscuit with a grounding in African history to help him see beyond the daily exigencies of being the breadwinner for his family (in the absence of his father) through dealing drugs and petty crime. Nelson is not wholly successful as Biscuit is swept along by the events that will lead to the fatal encounter with Nunchaks. However, at the close of the novel Biscuit sends Denise to Nelson to help her recover from the trauma of her abuse and witnessing Nunchak's death (Wheatle 2006, 306). Nelson's insistence that 'Education is de key' (Wheatle 2006, 308) will be picked up again in *The Dirty South* where it is dismissed by Dennis as being his father's 'mantra' (Wheatle 2008, 4). It is here that the cognitive map of London that Dennis described in my introduction can be placed into a longer history of youth subcultures into the (a)history of the new parochialism.

The Dirty South follows Dennis Huggins' entry into the world of drug-dealing in Brixton at the age of fourteen, until his eventual incarceration six years later. As noted above, Dennis's father, Biscuit, is the key character in *East of Acre Lane* who also appears in both *Brixton Rock* and *Brenton Brown* as a friend of the eponymous Brown during their youth in the earlier novel, and as adults in the latter one. Taken together, these loosely connected novels extend the range of Wheatle's novels from Brown's birth in 1963 to Brown's death and Dennis's release from prison in 2006. At the centre of this forty-year period sits the 1981 Brixton Riots around which the events of *East of Acre Lane* turn. Reading these novels as an account of the attitudes, codes and relationships of two successive generations of black Britons that come after Sam Dean (whose experience stretches back to the 1958 Notting Hill riots) allows us to think of Biscuit and Brenton as second generation and Dennis and his peers as third generation black Britons. In doing so, one can detect a social process within which the new affiliations, styles, codes and disaffiliations of the new parochialism get established.

Pivotal to understanding Dennis Huggins' character is recognising his highly parochial sense of place and the codes of behaviour that accompany such localised awareness. It is with a deliberate irony that Wheatle has Dennis dismiss his father's continued preoccupation with the 'numbers of young black employed in 19 fucking 80, long forgotten riots [...] and how Margaret Thatcher messed up the country' (Wheatle 2008, 4). Neither is

Dennis attracted by his African-Caribbean heritage. He has been taught black history by Jah Nelson when he was young, but he only uses this to impress Akeisha, his long-term love interest, and he only does so because another of his father's contemporaries, Yardman Irie, makes an appearance at a poetry jam in Brixton. Here, Dennis is utterly dismissive of the appeal to African roots by the host 'Queen Manashmanek from the golden and prosperous lands of Nubia' (Wheatle 2008, 110) and the consciousness-raising acts that precede Irie's performance. At the end of the evening, Dennis makes a clumsy attempted pass at Akeisha and she sees through his pretence: 'You've just spent the last half hour giving me a lesson in Jamaican history. And now this! I thought you was different from the rest, Dennis. But you're just like the other brothers in Angel Town and Bricky, just looking for a wok and you don't care how you get it ...' (Wheatle 2008, 119). This rejection of a cultural heritage and history is matched by Dennis's rejection of anything more recent. Even as he sits in his cell await-ing release, Dennis rejects new myths of belonging: 'burn the mayor's theory of multicultural society. It ain't real' (Wheatle 2008, 5).

What is real for Dennis is reputation. Without knowing the truth of events, he boasts about his father's past as a 'shotta', his association with the 'Steppin' Volcano' and their part in the murder of Nunchaks. In very much the same way as Stone, in Newland's short story, is attuned to the association of postcodes, codes and violence, Dennis tries to locate himself onto the cognitive map of London. Like Stone, he is aware of the dangers of the new parochialism, but unlike him, Dennis ignores his own advice and finds himself the object of an ambush in Peckham. Dennis is robbed, stripped and hospitalized but the core issue is less about money than a failure to observe the 'rules of the ghetto' (Wheatle 2008, 36). Having completed their assault, the leader of Dennis's assailants crows, 'Who's he think he is? A Brixton shotta coming down our ends and he wasn't even packed' (Wheatle 2008, 36). When his partner-in-crime, Noel, visits Dennis in hospital, he is unsympathetic: 'People been chatting [...] How you got honey-trapped by some bitch from Peckham ends. It's not good for our rep, bruv. Some brothers been laughing about it, saying that you and me are pussies. I ain't tolerating that' (Wheatle 2008, 43). Dennis and Noel plan a revenge attack wherein Brixtonian honour is satisfied and their parochial reputation restored as a more severe beating using iron bars and bricks is carried out on the original culprits.

In taking this action, Dennis and Noel are sustaining a parochial map of London in which the physical reality of violence and the discursive reality of reputation collide with the effect of strengthening their sense of collective identity: being a Brixtonian triumphs over any other form of possible allegiance. If such loyalties are highly parochial, they are also a-historical insofar as enmities are formed (as they are in Newland's story) from places of current residence rather than a longer history of migration. Consequently, Dennis's mapping of London is a radically synchronic arrangement that is dismembered from history. His tragedy is thus a failure to engage with history over both the short and the long term. For example, the cognitive map of Brixton Dennis provides in the introduction to the first chapter of the novel finally describes the 'Camberwell end of Coldharbour Lane where so-called Muslim gangs cruise and jack any shottas and run protection rackets' (Wheatle 2008, 2). It is precisely here and under these circumstances that he and Noel are ambushed once again, this time leading to Noel's death and Dennis's subsequent revenge killing of Courtney Thompson.

This potentially explains the complex interaction between reputation and reality in the new parochialism and particularly in its dynamic nature. If Brenton learns to adopt and adapt style to become a Bricky celebrity, the same is arguably true of Dennis who is suspected of pretence even by Noel: 'You're a pretend badman, Dennis. Everyone knows it. A motherfucking wannabe. You ain't too different from those white and Asian people who try to talk black. You're a motherfucking pimp! Pimping from street culture' (Wheatle 2008, 45). Similarly, Thompson is one of a group of young Blacks who have recently converted to Islam in the novel and who are bringing a new edge of violence to the area. For Dennis, these are merely 'so-called' Muslims and he suggests that their religious conversion is nothing more than the adoption of a new dissident street style that will not last (Wheatle 2008, 116). It is certainly true that Thompson fails to lead a recognisable life of Islamic convictions and that he is refused entry to a mosque by Muslim elders. In addition, Thompson and his gang demand that Noel 'converts' to being a Muslim as they beat him to death. But this is no religious crime and its motivation sits somewhere between parochial drug warfare and reputation since Dennis and Noel have 'disrespected' Thompson in front of his crew over a girl. In all three of Wheatle's novels, then, the death of a character serves not only to remove a violent threat, it also serves to place the surviving characters into a parochial history of London through which they and others can locate themselves. It is the new parochialism that Dennis uses to define his life—ironically since the legend of the killing of

Nunchak conceals the fact that the trigger was pulled by Biscuit's white neighbour, Frank. Thus Dennis's own mantra, 'only in Bricky', that also punctuates *The Dirty South* starts to feel as much of a historical as a social confinement.

Throughout *The Dirty South*, Dennis constructs a parochial London that continually reinvents codes of difference from which identity can emerge. For Bhabha, this emphasis upon the constructedness of identity characterises the multiculturalist thinking of the 1980s that missed the transformation of the public sphere occasioned by the new cosmopolitanism. However, this transformation is rejected by Dennis as itself being a myth, and his sense of localised identity based upon a parochial map of London is abandoned as he plans a new life in Leicester upon his release. This instability of character bears considerable resemblance to Stone in Newland's 'Fresh for '88', who adopts a language and a culture wholeheartedly but never feels fully as though it is his own. This is a theme that runs through Wheatle's novels, most notably in the character of Brenton Brown and thus confirms the role of the new parochialism in constructing identity through style in a process of affiliation and disaffiliation.

What this chapter has tried to show is a reversal of the positive trends gestured towards by Bhabha's proclamation of a transformed social space brought about by a new cosmopolitanism within a transnational, metropolitan Britain. Bhabha was working in response to the multiculturalist thinking of the 1980s in which multiple ethnic identities were envisioned as evidence of a plural society. For Bhabha, emphasising 'different but equal' policies operates within old paradigms of identities authenticated by myths of origin that were unsustainable in contemporary Britain. In these novels and short stories depicting black, teenage life in London within the same period, I think illustrations of new identities and loyalties being formed can be found. These loyalties are not based upon premigratory origin, as Bhabha suggests, but neither do they provide a transformed social space. Instead, a new parochialism based upon postcodes and local mythologies of reputation and social competition and rivalry occupy the space previously filled by social Rastafarianism in the 1970s. If social identities are being reconfigured in this new parochialism, they are not being weakened and the social signifiers of style and affiliation remain strong. So much so that, as Dennis watches his friend Noel being beaten to death in *The Dirty South* over a wholly predicted matter of reputation, one assumes these are not the 'teenage kicks' that The Undertones sang about.

REFERENCES

Bhabha, Homi K. 1999. 'The Manifesto,' in *Wasafiri* 14:29 (1999): 38–39.

Dhondy, Farrukh. 1974. 'Review of *Voices of the Living and the Dead*,' *Race Today* 6.3 (March 1974): 92.

Immonen, Johanna. 2007. 'Interview with Alex Wheatle, 11 March 2007, Clapham Library, London,' *Critical Engagements: A Journal of Criticism and Theory* 1.2 (2007): 117–138.

Kidulthood. 2006. Dir. Menhaj Huda. UK: Revolver Entertainment.

Malkani, Gautum. 2007. *Londonstani*, London: Harper Perennial.

Newland, Courttia. 2011. *A Book of Blues*, Newcastle-upon-Tyne: Flambard Press.

Phillips, Mike. 1990. *Blood Rights*. Harmondsworth: Penguin, 1990.

Pryce, Everton. 1985. 'The Notting Hill Carnival: Black Politics, Resistance and Leadership 1976–1978,' *Caribbean Quarterly* 32.2 (June 1985): 35–52.

Wheatle, Alex. 2009. 'A Conversation with Linton Kwesi Johnson,' *Wasafiri* 24.3 (2009): 35–41.

Wheatle, Alex. 2010. *Brixton Rock*. London: BlackAmber Books (first published, 1999).

Wheatle, Alex. 2006. *East of Acre Lane*. London: Harper Perennial (first published Fourth Estate, 2001).

Wheatle, Alex. 2008. *The Dirty South*. London: Serpent's Tail.

Wheatle, Alex. 2011. *Brenton Brown*. London: BlackAmber Books.

PART II

Subcultural Representations on Screen

Mod at the Movies: 'Face' and 'Ticket' Representations of a British Subculture

Stephen Glynn

The distinctly British nature of the Mod subculture is evident from the unending debate over the extent of its 'cross-class membership' (Muggleton 2000, 160), with its development and demographic, up to and beyond the acme of its media attention in the 1964 seaside riots against motorbike-riding Rockers, repeatedly documented and theorised (*inter alia* Melly 1972; Rawlings 2000; Weight 2013). In essence, beginning in the musical wilderness of late 1959, when groups of young men in and around London reacted to raucous Teddy Boys, pretentious beatniks and trad jazz fogies by fashioning themselves as well-dressed 'Modernists', by 1964 a nationwide but still selective 'gang Mod' escalation had developed its own codes, conventions and hierarchical structures. At the top were the 'Faces' (or 'Aces'), setting the pace and wearing the classiest combinations; in their wake came their epigones, the largely maligned 'Tickets' (or 'Numbers'), their out/look more working-class in flavour, their dance halls outings more often than not ending in a fight. The boys would arrive on the regulation Italian scooter, personalised with peacock fans of wing mirrors, headlights and

S. Glynn (✉)
De Montfort University, Leicester, UK

© The Author(s) 2018
N. Bentley et al. (eds.), *Youth Subcultures in Fiction, Film and Other Media*, Palgrave Studies in the History of Subcultures and Popular Music, https://doi.org/10.1007/978-3-319-73189-6_5

whip aerials, and wearing a US army surplus parka, practical for keeping warm while weaving through traffic and for protecting the expensive tight-fitting three-button mohair suit. The girls dressed androgynously, their hair cropped or bobbed, with trousers and shirts to match (and mostly borrowed from) the boys, flat shoes, bobby socks and minimal make up. Amphetamines kept the mind and body alert, maximising the weekend's fun potential, emphasising dancing before dating, being 'in' before 'putting out'.

Mod at the Movies is an equally select—and seemingly secretive—band. The BBC4 series *Oh You Pretty Things* (20 September 2014), exploring the cut and thrust between British fashion and music subcultures, cites as the starting point of this interplay a 'long forgotten' Mod movie: *Dateline Diamonds*, directed by Jeremy Summers, a 1966-released 'B' film that supported Leslie Phillips in the superannuated *Doctor in Clover*. *Dateline Diamonds* principally concerns diamond smuggling to Amsterdam via Kenny Everett's pirate radio ship—in reality Radio London—but it also features pop performers such as the Chantelles and Kiki Dee, and significantly captures the original line-up of Mod favourites the Small Faces, before Ian McLagan replaced Jimmy Langwith aka Winston. The group are hardly the film's 'star turn'—they play one song, filmed during a genuine Radio London night at the Rank Ballroom, Watford. It is an engaging, competently edited scene, but overall *Dateline Diamonds'* 'pop and cop' format was critically derided for falling between two stools: 'neither element is in anyway distinguished, and the intervals for music merely slow down the detection' noted the *Monthly Film Bulletin* (33, 385, February 1966, 22). Still, this had long been the standard procedure for pop performers: appear in a low-budget fiction film, boost box-office sales by bringing in a teenage audience, and boost record sales from the associated film publicity. This mutually beneficial commercial strategy had been undertaken by Britain's pop acts from its first indigenous stars Tommy Steele and Cliff Richard, through to the world-conquering Beatles and beyond (Glynn 2013). However, as a blatantly commercial venture, good timing was key, and the release of *Dateline Diamonds* was fatefully delayed, meaning that 'I've Got Mine', the Small Faces' follow-up single to 'Whatcha Gonna Do About It', came and went without the necessary publicity, and consequently failed to chart. Add in poor receipts and, in every aspect, *Dateline Diamonds* was also a commercial failure. Finally, Summers' film singularly fails to signify as 'the starting point' of Mod movies: indeed, there is much to contest with the pop-fashion Mod genealogy adumbrated in *Oh You*

Pretty Things. It was *Ready Steady Go!* (AR-TV, 1963–1966) with its presenter Cathy McGowan's clarion call that 'the weekend starts here' and mainstay group the Who that nationalised Mod fashion, while several prior and concurrent films, though largely maligned support features accompanying the principal programmed film, placed the subculture more centrally. Mods are sticklers for accuracy and this essay offers a corrective and comprehensive 'A to B' of Mod Movies.

Amsterdam was not the place to be seen: especially since teenagers and their spending power came to the fore in the mid-1950s, it was the libertarian reputation of Brighton that proved to be an irresistible attraction both to hormonal teenagers looking for lust and hard-nosed producers seeking a lucrative exploitation movie, and several cinematic outriders can now be located. Prophetic of Mod tropes to come, *Linda* (Don Sharp 1960) tells the story of gang member and scooter boy Phil (Alan Rothwell) taking his girlfriend Linda (Carol White) on a day-trip down to Brighton, hoping for something more than sightseeing and a stick of seaside rock: his advances are unceremoniously spurned. Though it was the support film to Tony Richardson's *Saturday Night and Sunday Morning*, and with Joe Meek producing its theme song, *Linda* was scantily reviewed: 'an unpretentious but amusing little film which combines action with humour and even some charm', noted the supportive *Cinema Exhibitors Association Report* (18 November 1960): so unpretentious it is currently listed as one of the BFI's 75 most-wanted 'lost' movies. Jim O'Connolly's *Smokescreen*, a Butcher's Film Services 'B' film from the apposite 1964, cannot be construed as a Mod movie—it even supported Elvis Presley's (enemy) biker musical *Roustabout* (John Rich) on the UK circuit—but it contains a memorable pre-credit sequence where a blazing Hillman Minx Convertible hurtles over the cliff at Beachy Head, we later learn, unoccupied: it is a film launch that, alongside its extensive location footage, rehearses *the* later definitive Mod foray down to Brighton. Optimistic on burgeoning musical 'scenes', Lance Comfort's *Be My Guest* (1965) sees David Hemmings' Dave Martin and his pop group prevent a devious promoter from stealing their hit song and subsequently set up the (Beach Boys-lite) 'Brighton Beat' movement. With a paucity of pantheon pop stars, the film's Mod credentials were enhanced by the casting, in an acting role, of Steve Marriott of the aforementioned Small Faces. 'A simple little tale, embellished with uncomplicated humour and music in the modern idiom. Good stuff for youngsters', patronised the trade press (*Kinematograph Weekly*, 25 March 1965). A support booking for Morecombe and Wise's spy spoof *The Intelligence Men* (Robert Asher), the film also featured a performance from Slash Wildly and the Cut Throats, in reality the Zephyrs, a London bluesy beat group then working with the Who producer Shel Talmy. The Zephyrs also feature in a scene, shot at the Scene, in *Primitive London* (Arnold Miller 1965), a minimal-budget Mondo-style documentary filmed by future *Adventures of* director Stanley Long. A portrait of the capital manoeuvring uncertainly between post-war austerity and 'Swinging' Sixties liberalism, it offers an eclectic set of Soho-based images ranging from a chiropodist session to chicken slaughtering and, whenever David Gell's transatlantic moralising voiceover begins to pall, cuts to a scene featuring a stripper. It mixes in brief interviews with 'freaky beatniks', Rockers at the Ace Café, London, and scenes with young Mods, overlaid with over-simple cod psychology on their 'peacock displays' necessitated by the post-war female majority and the concomitant 'trendsetter' male boutiques. At the other end of the cultural spectrum, another 1965 support film expressed, over 28 minutes, differences in scooter boys and ton-up boys through the medium of dance. *Mods and Rockers*, produced by pop Svengali Larry Parnes and directed by Kenneth Hume, employs the Western Theatre Ballet company, showcases Parnes' peroxide protégé Heinz, and uses a medley of Beatles' songs covered by the Cheynes (including 18-year-old Mick Fleetwood on drums). The original promotional synopsis extols the film's exposition thus: 'A symbolic ultra-modern coffee bar sets the scene for a girl in gold lamé jeans, bolero and bootees, to start moving to the pulsating rhythms beating out from a glittering juke box. A boy starts to dance with this red-headed dynamo of a girl, but is repelled when she accepts the advances of a second boy. The two men vie for her attentions.' 'Pulsating' and 'dynamo' strike as excessive: in truth, the warring Mods and Rockers offer up a series of stilted dance moves not far in advance of Sting's later efforts, though the trendy youth club-running vicar rings true to the spirit of the times. Further evidencing the pitfalls of misleading publicity, the film was folded into two Frank Gilpin shorts, *Swinging UK* and *UK Swings Again* and retitled *Go-Go Big Beat!* for a full-length US release: however, poster headlines implying a Beatles appearance led to Brian Epstein instigating litigation, and the removal of every Cheynes' cover number.

Mod then moves on, transforming itself either into a 'soft' hippy strain, as evidenced in the Howard Barker-scripted *Made* (John Mackenzie 1972) which brings Carol White, now as single mother Valerie Marshall, back to Brighton on a youth club outing: on the beach she meets and falls for insecure singer Mike Preston (Roy Harper), though he soon dumps her and writes a song about the experience. Or else Mod takes the harder route into the skinhead subculture, or its 'suedehead' variant, definitively portrayed in *Bronco Bullfrog* (Barney Platts-Mills 1970), a film which, with its shots of the Blackwall tunnel, terraced housing, kitchen and café interiors, undoubtedly influenced the booklet photographs in the Who's 1973 *Quadrophenia* album. A fast shimmy forward brings us to the late-1970s where, post-punk and largely due to Paul Weller and the Jam, Mod was once more part of the subcultural *zeitgeist*. *Steppin' Out* (Lyndall Hobbs 1979), a 25-minute support feature to Ridley Scott's first *Alien* movie, investigates London nightlife and, alongside punks and Blitz kids (precursors to the New Romantics), features 'Mod Night' at Legends with Mod revivalists Secret Affair and the Merton Parkas, and follows a coach party to a roller disco in Dunstable. Seemingly incompatible, that link of Mod and disco had also been central to John Badham's 1977 international success, *Saturday Night Fever*. A Mod movie in disco clothing, John Travolta and his Bay Ridge cohorts enduring their mundane jobs and living for their weekend high are, in fact, a cultural transposition of British 'Faces' and their 'Ticket' followers. Northern Irish rock writer Nik Cohn's 7 June 1976 New Journalism piece for *New York Magazine*, 'Tribal Rites of the New Saturday Night', had been immediately optioned by Robert Stigwood, the producer of *Tommy* (Ken Russell 1975), for his next epic venture—and overlaid with the inevitable upbeat Hollywood ending. While set in Brooklyn, recent arrival Cohn later admitted to compensating for his ignorance of American subcultures by borrowing characters and attitudes from what he knew best—the mid-1960s Mod scene in London's Shepherd's Bush: 'Tony and the Faces are actually Mods in everything—except the dances', he told *Melody Maker*, without fooling, on 1 April 1978. The obsession with appearance certainly strikes as a Mod influence, while Cohn even stole the Italian-American gang name, not straight from the Who's 1964 rebranding but from the fans their first manager, Peter Meaden, organised to swell their early gigs, the Hundred Faces.

If Travolta was a Mod manqué, the 'Face' of Mod movies soon arrived as the Who realised a feature film treatment of their musical Modyssey *Quadrophenia*, Pete Townshend's band-rebooting recreation of the 'short time' when they 'felt like Mods' (Townshend 2012, 245). In 1978 Townshend entrusted the £1 million cinematic version to a film debutant, 30-year-old television director, Franc Roddam, fresh from his award-winning docudrama *Dummy* (ATV, 9 November 1977). Roddam was given the brief that the double album's music should contribute to and support the narrative, but not, as they felt had regrettably occurred with *Tommy*, take over. It was a shrewd appointment, as Roddam, a Mod observer rather than obsessive, was central to the creation of a critical distance, taking the ideas Townshend had invested in the album and expanding them in line with his own social realist background. The film follows teenage Mod Jimmy Cooper (Phil Daniels) who lives at home, works as a junior clerk, and spends his evenings with friends in the Mod clubs of London. He is preoccupied both by scene regular Steph (Leslie Ash) and the upcoming weekend trip down to Brighton to fight the Rockers. He succeeds on both fronts but back home becomes increasingly disillusioned and leaves it all behind, returning to Brighton in the (vain) hope of reliving former glories. Roddam's addition of a backstory, a layer of London social context, was enriching, as was the writing in of additional characters since the young and largely unknown cast this necessitated introduced a fresh, punk-inflected sensibility to their portrayals of teenage dreams. These varied agencies all permitted *Quadrophenia* to accommodate competing modes of understanding, and the film's enduring appeal can be seen to reside largely in prising open a hermetic subculture to its social realist context: it is a cult film that dares to explore the dangers that reside in being part of a cult; it is a Mod film that exposes the potential mindlessness of Mod.

I have written extensively on *Quadrophenia* elsewhere, including a dedicated monograph (Glynn 2014) analysing the film's cult components such as its intertextual frames and its failings, notably myriad anachronisms and continuity errors. These components are doubly important for *Quadrophenia* since the 'private sectarian world' which Umberto Eco accords to cult movies (1986, 198) is true of Mod itself: as soon as the media and their misconceptions move in, the hard core move on. Indeed, Paulo Hewitt has questioned whether any 'real' Mods turned up at Brighton beach, arguing that the genuine Mod movement was finished by 1963, its cover blown by *Ready Steady Go!* (a media moment recognised in *Quadrophenia* when Jimmy devotedly watches the programme, to de rigueur parental disgust); thereafter, Hewitt asserts, it 'was taken up by idiots really, just beer boys and thugs—no self-respecting Mod would have been down at Brighton' (Catterall and Wells 2001, 161). It is a contentious claim, but for this particular subculture attention to detail undoubtedly mattered far more than attention-seeking: to 1960s Mod purists, not only was *Quadrophenia*'s portrayal hopelessly inaccurate, but it also encouraged gangs of raucous wannabes. Furthermore, 'original' Mod revivalists (such as myself) felt that they too were now losing their secrecy and exclusivity to a nationwide release. *Quadrophenia*, by its very popularity, was letting down its core audience, exemplifying the invariable conclusion: 'the simultaneous diffusion and defusion of the subcultural style' (Hebdige 1979, 93).

The portrayal of the Mod subculture, its identity construction through the ironic appropriation of mainstream signifiers, is treated elsewhere in this volume. Here I shall highlight the film's stylistic successes, its 'Ace' accomplishments in differing contextual cadres. The most spectacular—and most admired—'epic' scenes recreate the Brighton beach riots during the Whitsun Bank Holiday weekend of 17–18 May 1964. The source events can now be seen as a media-fuelled self-fulfilling prophecy, a mediation registered in *Quadrophenia* with the press photographer's snapping in front of Jimmy and Co. on the seafront providing the catalyst for their tribal chant of 'We are the Mods! We are the Mods!' Thereafter, with 2000 extras available to Roddam, down the slope and onto the beach to the west of the Palace Pier charged the Mods of 1978, while from the opposite direction came a set of (less authentic) leather boys, and caught in the middle police on horseback jostling and jumping over them. Cinematographer Brian Tufano, with his instincts as a documentary cameraman to the fore, placed himself amidst the flying stones and flying fists, filming mostly from a height of three to six feet and capturing the aggro 'on the hoof'. With its broad moves skilfully choreographed, the scene successfully pulls the audience in—it frequently draws applause at screenings—only then to push them away. On the film's release, Roddam stated that 'If there's any contemporary relevance in the film, it's in the way it tells young kids to be individuals and not to get carried away by group behaviour [...] Think for yourself, and don't follow group ideas' (*Screen International*, 191, 26 May 1979, 10). This call to self-reliance is considered a strong component of the film's enduring cult appeal: mirroring my 'placing' of the film in a Brighton lineage and providing a taxonomy for the 'tacky herbert' Jimmy, *Quadrophenia* is a film *about* the search for definition, the strong attraction—and insidious danger—of 'belonging'. Jimmy's teenage struggle for identity has, over time, become the film's predominant interpretation, but I would emphasise its equal exploration of the quest for *intensity*, for proving life on the pulses, be it through sex, drugs, rock'n'roll—or a good old punch up. When, after the seafront fracas, Jimmy screams 'On my life, I was there! I was there!' it is the intensity of performance that invites the spectator to recall their personal 'Brighton beach memoir'. For Danny Peary this is the universal, or at least American, entrée to the film: 'Who doesn't remember such a moment—the moment in your life when both the top dog in your crowd and your ideal lover saw you at your best, when you revealed your "true self"' (Peary 1984, 134). Jimmy's sense of belonging and self-worth is tied not so much to his identity with a movement but to the intensity of a moment.

Jimmy thereafter screws it up: *Quadrophenia* remains in people's affections finally because it is about *ineptness*, about human (rather than cinematic) failure. This 'quality' is embodied in the film's casting which Alan Fletcher, film consultant and author of the tie-in novelisation, thought 'inspired': 'Peer pressure drove the Mod machine and Daniels didn't look quite Mod, just missing it' (Catterall and Wells 2001, 149–50). The fulcrum of *Quadrophenia* is an analysis of someone trying to keep up with his subcultural peers and not succeeding. Jimmy fails in and is failed by the four key relationships in his life: his family, his job, the girl and the group—in short, a quadrophonic failing. For me, more than through its visceral realisation of the violent group dynamic, it is *Quadrophenia*'s focus on the uncertain individual that attains the apex of Mod movie achievement. Andy Medhurst has attributed to Dirk Bogarde's delivery of the 'confession' scene of *Victim* (Basil Dearden 1960) 'the rare power of genuine subversion in popular cinema' (1996, 128): Daniels' different performance mode during the return to Brighton can stand up close for affective comparison. Perfectly embodying the 'he-man drag' so 'greyly outrageous', announced by Roger Daltrey on the soundtrack, it is hard to locate a misjudged stress as, with eyes wide open but opaque, inflections both distant yet defiant, Jimmy (literally) attains a first-class ticket status. I have always found an awkward grace in this emotional stasis, sandwiched between two moments of vituperation, first when meeting his love Steph walking along the street and then espying his hero Ace Face (Sting) working at the hotel. Indeed, from the demise of his own scooter through to the cliff-face casting off of Ace Face's now vacuous Vespa, Daniels' Mod method unerringly conveys the internal conflict in its myriad evasions and betrayals, from agonised inarticulacy through to foul-mouthed releases of tension, from 'You slag! You cunt!' to the nadir of 'Bell-boy! Bell-boy!' This bleak breakdown is not a common cinematic conclusion, yet Jimmy's unresolved internal struggle undoubtedly contributes to *Quadrophenia*'s attraction for those in thrall to or recalling teenage turmoil. *Not* finding one's place, *not quite* being part of the pack, is a key aspect of the film's emotional honesty, and ultimately *Quadrophenia* endures because, as

Roddam later noted, 'it lets young people off the hook. They don't have to be great. You're allowed to fail' (*Cast & Crew: Quadrophenia*, BBC4, 22 March 2005). An *acceptance* of failure: this message, cutting through any cinematic or subcultural provenance, is arguably what makes *Quadrophenia*, in the final analysis, so *British* a subcultural investigation.

Mise-en-scène and music skilfully support this consummate collapse. Sitting in the seafront café, drugged up, depressed yet still striving to recapture happier days, the city and its iconic pier are visible in front of him on the window panes. The composition here adroitly illustrates Jimmy's diminished sense of reality and how the 'solid' Brighton, when the gang were united, has long departed. It is, in both visual and mental senses of the term, a reflection. Throughout *Quadrophenia* music's importance to the identity of young working-class people is explored, but, unlike tie-in fare such as *Dateline Diamonds* or *Be My Guest*, there are no 'star'-performed musical numbers. Fulfilling Townshend's brief, the Who's quasi-contemporary music, notably 'My Generation', features only in diegetic snatches at various parties, coffee bars, dancehalls and bedrooms, but still successfully offers an evocation of the period and an index of the depth of fan allegiance. The later rock-inflected album music also functions, especially in the film's last third, as a non-diegetic discourse, its 'melodramatic' employment 'siphoning off' Jimmy's increasingly fragile emotional states. For instance, when ejected from the Brighton dancehall, Jimmy spends the night on the beach, staring out at the pounding waves: with a long-shot dwarfing him against both pier and shoreline, visually the scene all but erases the insignificant human presence; instead the music, the instrumental section from 'Love Reign O'er Me' with lead guitar and synthesiser, foregrounds Jimmy's brooding psyche.

Such a combination of terrifying cosmic indifference and teenage experiential angst has made *Rebel Without A Cause* (Nicholas Ray 1955) the obvious, even obligatory point of comparison for *Quadrophenia*. But the tensions of social class were absent for Jim Stark and his bourgeois college colleagues, whilst in *Quadrophenia* 'the British working-class patois was so extreme it was almost the *point* of a lot of the dialogue' (Robert Sandall 2006). It also points to a more indigenous and informing genealogy as, alongside *Linda* et al.—and especially *Bronco Bullfrog* whose New Wave aesthetic, numerous plot turns, images such as the girlfriend riding pillion, and even snippets of dialogue ('bit flash, innee?') all echo Roddam's later treatment—Jimmy's return to Brighton, cinematically accomplished in its own right, has an extra enhancing resonance with the 1964 of Richard Lester's seminal *A Hard Day's Night*. Firstly, throwing his possessions out of the train corridor window wins

Jimmy the admiring glances of two schoolgirls, much as the Beatles' play-acting had drawn the attention of Patty Boyd and classmates. Then, as well as referencing a photo from the *Quadrophenia* album's artwork, Jimmy's attitude as he sits on the 5.15 between two bowler-hatted commuters silently encapsulates the class warfare previously articulated between the obstreperous plum-voiced commuter—'I fought the war for your sort'—and Ringo Starr, who sarcastically retorts: 'bet you're sorry you won!'

This key generational divide was repeated in the film's critical reception. The younger generation were thrilled: for Richard Barkley 'the film is a magnificent achievement in current British cinema, shatteringly honest in intent and stunningly photographed' (*Sunday Express*, 19 August 1979), while Nigel Andrews praised 'one of the most exultantly offbeat British films I can remember' with its Beachy Head finale 'as mad, memorable and modernistic as any sequence in recent British film history' (*Financial Times*, 17 August 1979). This positivity was not shared by Felix Barker, who fifteen years earlier had been swept up by the 'teenage enthusiasm', 'charm' and 'innocence' of the Beatles' first feature (*Evening News*, 9 July 1964): now, deeply disturbed by Roddam's brutal depiction of the Fab Four's supposed contemporaries, he wrote that 'Just about everything I dislike is to be found in *Quadrophenia*. The music is so loud and raucous that there should be a free issue of ear-plugs with every ticket. The film reeks with mindless violence' (*Evening News*, 16 August 1979). Similarly, *Films and Filming*'s end of year honours list (best film Terrence Malick's *Days of Heaven*) awarded *Quadrophenia* the accolade of 'most distasteful film of the year' (January 1980, 29). Nonetheless *Quadrophenia* was a commercial successful at the UK box office. It swiftly established itself as the definitive cinematic treatment of the Mod subculture, reigning supreme as its cult film reputation grew; its Mod revival re-release in 1997 earned favourable comparisons with the recent *Trainspotting* (Danny Boyle 1996) and critical encomia typified by Charlotte O'Sullivan for whom 'this is one of the best portraits we have of this frustrated little island. Too honest to be upbeat, too exciting to be bleak, even second time round it's unmissable' (*Time Out*, 29 January 1997).

At the time of writing, rumours of an unauthorised present-day-set sequel, to be directed by Ray Burdis with Daniels and Toyah Willcox on board, are prompting pre-emptive press outrage—'Like Jimmy's scooter, the original film's legacy risks being pushed off a clifftop' bemoaned James Hall (*Telegraph*, 10 June 2016). Still, however long it takes, subcultural leaders are inevitably challenged: the dynamic is discernible in *Quadrophenia* itself as young pretender Dave (Mark Wingett) locks horns with 'Face' elder Pete (Garry Cooper), shooting menacing looks and getting up too close for comfort before finally, down at Brighton, moving in on 'Pete's girl', Steph. *Quadrophenia* held unopposed dominion for 22 years before a south coast cinematic challenger emerged, via another Mod updating.[1]

Brighton Rock (4 February 2011) is the only British first feature, after *Quadrophenia*, to portray the Mod subculture. Here, though, from the outset lay a greater anxiety of influence. Graham Greene's 1938 source noir novel of fear and sin is considered, even by Greene, as the work that marked his emergence as a 'catholic writer' (Greene 1980, 74). Exploring the subculture of interwar racecourse gangs and their protection racketeering, its first film realisation, directed in 1947 by John Boulting and with 24-year-old Richard Attenborough giving a coruscating performance as the chilling teenage hoodlum Pinkie Brown, has become sufficiently revered to be voted number 15 in the BFI's 1999 poll for the 'Greatest British Film of the Century' and has drawn plentiful academic exegesis, including a dedicated monograph (Chibnall 2005). Several attempts to re-film the novel came and went—interested parties reputedly included Martin Scorsese, Terrence Malick and the Hughes Brothers—until Studio Canal, determined to maximise its back catalogue, eventually entrusted the £8 million reworking to feature film debutant, 36-year-old television director Rowan Joffe, fresh from his award-winning docudrama *The Shooting of Thomas Hurndall* (Channel 4, 13 October 2008). Writer-director Joffe, briefed not to do a straight remake of either the book or the Boulting version, but conscious that a contemporary version would reduce character credibility, decided to update the story to the seaside battles of Mods and Rockers in 1964, arguing that Britain 'still had some of the same kind of innocence it had in the 40s and 50s, but was by then forward-looking enough—with stuff like mods and the music of the time—to suggest that, in a film investor's mind, the current audience would see something modern about it' ('Mod Man Out', *Sight and Sound*, 20, 12, December 2010, 42). Significantly for the film's plot motivations, 1964 was also the last year where the death penalty was still in use for murder, while Joffe, who wrote a foreword to the 2011 tie-in rerelease of the novel, also saw a wider resonance in the warring subcultures as symbolic of Britain's new fear and hatred of the young who 'raise a challenging flick knife to the old pre-war order'. Largely shot in neighbouring Eastbourne since Brighton was now too gentrified to serve, and with a cast of A-list British acting talent, Joffe's reworking sees Pinkie vengefully murder Fred Hale (Sean Harris), the killer of his gang boss, and thus succeed to the position of leader. However, an incriminating snap by a seaside photographer leads Pinkie first to seduce timid waitress Rose Wilson (Andrea Riseborough) in order to secure and destroy the offending photo, and then to propose marriage so that Rose, like Pinkie a 'Roman', will be unable to give evidence in any prospective murder trial.

Brighton Rock invites a double comparison for its source and setting. Perhaps counter-intuitively, Joffe's plot changes work to tighten up on Greene's originals, adding a greater plausibility to events and pulling the various relationships into a closer orbit. Having Pinkie track down the photograph that shows his accomplice Spicer harassing Hale, rather than seek a circumstantial time-coded press card, adds a more acute urgency to his pursuit of Rose, while making Hale a rival gangster boss, rather than the prize-dispensing newspaperman 'Kolley Kibber', provides Pinkie with an accelerated rites-of-passage from 'runner' to mob leader. The avenging Ida Arnold (Helen Mirren) is not here a chance pub encounter but Hale's former lover and owner of the silver-service tea-room where Rose works, a transformation readable less as excessive coincidence than a credible depiction of Brighton's claustrophobic *demi-monde* where all actions have swift and localised repercussions. The plot's final third shifts clumsily, however, increasingly over-powered by Martin Phipps' intrusive score until all collapses at the denouement. Despite Joffe's protestations to the contrary, his film draws less on Greene's novel than the 1947 screenplay, rewritten by Greene after he rejected the version presented by Terence Rattigan: this cinematic influence is exposed in replicating the infamous finale where the screenplay softened the novel and spared Rose 'the worst horror of all' by having Pinkie's pier-booth recording ('You want me to say I love you—but I hate you!') stick on the record player and repeat 'I love you—I love you'. Joffe repeats Boulting's every move in a mawkishly melodramatic, indeed 'miraculous' conclusion, including the tilt up to a crucifix and the swelling angelic choir on the soundtrack. It is a cinematic (if not human) failing.

The deficiencies of this *Brighton Rock* become clearer, however, when Joffe stands up too close to Roddam. There is certainly a firmer attention to period detail, the squalid tenement blocks and Pinkie's stygian basement-lodgings authentically redolent of enduring post-war austerity, but while Mods, Rockers and the Brighton riots were central to Jimmy and *Quadrophenia*, subcultures are here contingent. This is narratively evident in a scene of (successfully realised) humour when Pinkie, having stolen a scooter as a getaway vehicle, finds himself inadvertently leading a Mod procession across the seafront. His pillion passenger, Spicer, is played by Phil Davis, whose previous casting as Jimmy's associate Chalky adds a minor Mod movie intertextuality, while Andy Serkis provides a mood-lightening cameo as gangland bigwig Colleoni, stirring his coffee with effete ennui as he pronounces on 'restless youth: the ravaged and disrupted territory between two eternities!'. The principal Mod casting, however, crucially lacks Daniels' intensity of performance, unwittingly missing not just the look—Sam Riley may offer a more brooding Pinkie than Attenborough, but at 30 years of age he cannot begin to pass for a 17-year-old psychopath—but also the sound, Andrew Lowry decrying 'a stage-school "fug" accent, breathy like the Italia Conti types trying to sound tough on *EastEnders*' (*Total Film*, February 2011). The characterisation of Rose rings equally false. Subcultural accounts of youth have long been accused of displaying an imbalance in gender divisions: by focusing on mainly working-class but overwhelmingly male subjects, 'women and the whole question of sexual division have been marginalized' (McRobbie 1980, 37). This is evidenced in the paucity of recognition of distinct female subcultures, but also in the failure fully to acknowledge female participation in a given subculture. This is not entirely true of *Quadrophenia*. When the boys all dash off from the Goldhawk Club to avenge a Rocker attack on one of their own, the girls are more than happy to stay behind and dance together to the Crystals' 'Da Doo Ron Ron': it is a brief scene but one foregrounding female Mod fashion and fun. Extrapolating from this, Steph and fellow Mod Monkey (Willcox) may not (yet) be strongly autonomous 'new' women, but the film portrays them very much in charge of their sexual activity. Steph in particular exercises agency over her desire: sexually liberated, she moves from man to man, uninterested in developing a stable relationship: Jimmy, by contrast, seems the pining romantic. *Brighton Rock* offers no such shifting sexual landscape: a woman as unworldly as Rose could, perhaps, have been found on the south coast in 1938, but the updating leaves her a socio-sexual anachronism—even her purchase of a mini dress to impress Pinkie is painfully subservient—while the couple's one-way romance remains stubbornly unconvincing, especially Rose's soul-damning devotion to a Pinkie so lacking in either menace or charisma.

And then there is the Brighton beach fight. Joffe's version serves as a plausible spectacle of disorder that Pinkie and his enemies can use as a cover for their own violence, notably the attack on 'milky' want-out Spicer. Principally, though, the riots provide at best a hinterland to the film's wider theme of the futility of violence, and at worst another hard-nosed commercial exploitation of Mod mores. And despite a promising prequel with pounding elemental waves, cinematographer John Mathieson's muted palette and Phipps' incongruous scoring exacerbate the fight scenes' stilted, dislocated character, sorely lacking the visceral, vital energy provided by *Quadrophenia* which entered the fray and pulled the audience in with it. Ultimately, though, the very presence of the warring Mod and Rocker subcultures problematises the film, blurring its narrative focus: if the racecourse gangs cede the spotlight to these later youth movements, it creates a confusing anti-climax that Pinkie et Co. remain discrete members of their own secondary collectives; indeed, down-playing the turf wars for a beach riot setting removes much of their intrinsic and internecine dramatic effect—here they play away, and lose.

Brighton Rock also failed to win large audience figures or critical plaudits. Simon Heffer fulminated without even seeing the film—the online trailer was enough for him to label it 'a farrago' and 'a masterpiece refashioned as a turkey' (*Telegraph*, 23 January 2011). Curmudgeonly perhaps, but all generations and journals felt a false move. Riley's performance was panned (often for not being Attenborough) while the repeat ending (in all senses) was pilloried: for Philip Kemp 'It's a major miscalculation' that 'finally sinks Joffe's movie' (*Sight and Sound*, 21, 2, February 2011, 51). The Modernisation, though, was most roundly condemned: for Tim Robey 'Sadly, the justifications for this, beyond indulging tacked-on *Quadrophenia* sequences of mods on mopeds, prove as shallow as puddles under the pier' (*Telegraph*, 3 February 2011), David Noh found the update 'needless' and 'emblematic of the entire enterprise's wrongheaded bloat' (*Film Journal International*, August 2011), while David Thomson thought the rioting 'a foolish moment, and it has nothing at all to do with the new film—but this film is too full of things that have too little point or impact' (*New Republic*, 30 August 2011).

Such a critique could never be applied to *Quadrophenia*, which, fighting off all 'Ticket' pretenders, remains the 'Face' of Mod movies, the definitive cinematic treatment of an enduring British subculture and its defining moral panic-inducing moment. To quote Jimmy: I mean, that's something, innit?

NOTES

1. The Mod revival and release of *Quadrophenia* occasioned gentler and sporadic Mod movements overseas, notably amongst art students in Southern California as evidenced by the US independent features *We Are the Mods* (E.E. Cassidy 2009) and *Young Birds Fly* (Leonardo Flores 2011), neither of which has (yet) exhibited beyond the festival circuit. For the sake of completeness, mention honourable or otherwise must be made of *Exhumed* (Brian Clement 2003) which transposes the Mods vs. Rockers battle to a post-apocalyptic world where Vampires ride Vespas and werewolves are leathered-up

bikers, and DreamWorks' *Madagascar 3: Europe's Most Wanted* (Eric Darnell, Tom McGrath and Conrad Vernon 2012) where the (villainous) animal control gang drive Mod-style scooters around the streets of Monaco.

REFERENCES

Andrews, Nigel. 1979. "*Quadrophenia* review," *Financial Times*, August 17.

Anon. 1960. "*Linda* review," *Cinema Exhibitors Association Report*, November 18.

Anon. 1965. "*Be My Guest* review," *Kinematograph Weekly*, March 25.

Anon. 1966. "*Dateline Diamonds* review," *Monthly Film Bulletin*, 33, 385, February.

Anon. 1979. "Frank Roddam interview," Screen International, 191, 26 May.

Anon. 1980. "*Quadrophenia* review," *Films and Filming*, 28, 4, January.

Barker, Felix. 1964. "*A Hard Day's Night* review," *Evening News*, July 9.

Barker, Felix. 1979. "*Quadrophenia* review," *Evening News*, August 16.

Barkley, Richard. 1979. "*Quadrophenia* review," *Sunday Express*, August 19.

Catterall, Ali. and Wells, Simon. 2001. *Your Face Here: British Cult Movies Since the Sixties*. London: Fourth Estate.

Chibnall, Steve. 2005. *Brighton Rock*. London: I.B. Tauris.

Eco, Umberto. 1986. 'Cult movies and intertextual collage', in *Travels in Hyperreality*. London: Picador.

Falk, Quentin. 2010. "Mod Man Out", Sight and Sound, 20, 12, December.

Glynn, Stephen. 2013. *The British Pop Music Film: The Beatles and Beyond*. London: Palgrave Macmillan.

Glynn, Stephen. 2014. *Quadrophenia*. London: Wallflower/Columbia University Press.

Greene, Graham. 1980. *Ways of Escape*. London: Bodley Head.

Hall, James. 2016. "This *Quadrophenia* sequel should be pushed off a cliff," *Telegraph*, June 10.

Hebdige, Dick. 1979. *Subculture: The Meaning of Style*. London: Methuen.

Heffer, Simon. 2011. "*Brighton Rock*: A masterpiece refashioned as a turkey," *Telegraph*, January 23.

Kemp, Philip. 2011. "*Brighton Rock* review," *Sight and Sound*, 22, 2, February.

Lowry, Andrew. 2011. "*Brighton Rock* review," *Total Film*, February.

McRobbie, Angela. 1980. "Settling accounts with subcultures: a feminist critique," *Screen Education*, 34.

Melly, George. 1972. *Revolt Into Style: Pop Arts in Britain*. Harmondsworth: Penguin.

Medhurst, Andy. 1996. 'Victim: Text as Context', in Andrew Higson (ed.) Dissolving Views: Key Writings on British Cinema. London: Continuum.

Muggleton, David. 2000. *Inside Subculture: The Postmodern Meaning of Style*. Oxford: Berg.

Noh, David. 2011. "*Brighton Rock* review," *Film Journal International*, August.

O'Sullivan, Charlotte. 1997. "*Quadrophenia* review," *Time Out*, January 29.

Peary, Danny. 1984. *Cult Movies 2*. London: Vermilion.

Rawlings, Terry. 2000. *Mod: A Very British Phenomenon*. London: Omnibus.
Robey, Tim. 2011. "*Brighton Rock* review," *Telegraph*, February 3.
Roddam, Franc. 2005. Cast & Crew: Quadrophenia. BBC4.
Sandall, Robert. 2006. 'A Way of Life: Making Quadrophenia', DVD Documentary, 2006.
Thomson, David. 2011. "*Brighton Rock* review," *New Republic*. August 30.
Townshend, Pete. 2012. *Pete Townshend: Who I Am*. London: HarperCollins.
Weight, Richard. 2013. *MOD: A Very British Style*. London: Bodley Head.

FILMOGRAPHY

A Hard Day's Night (Dir. Richard Lester, 1964).
Be My Guest (Dir. Lance Comfort, 1965).
Brighton Rock (Dir. John Boulting, 1947).
Brighton Rock (Dir. Rowan Joffe, 2011).
Bronco Bullfrog (Dir. Barney Platts-Mills, 1970).
Dateline Diamonds (Dir. Jeremy Summers, 1966).
Doctor in Clover (Dir. Ralph Thomas, 1966).
Dummy (Dir. Franc Roddam, 1977).
Exhumed (Dir. Brian Clement, 2003).
Linda (Dir. Don Sharp, 1960).
Madagascar 3: Europe's Most Wanted (Dir. Eric Darnell, Tom McGrath and Conrad Vernon, 2012).
Made (Dir. John Mackenzie, 1972).
Mods and Rockers (Dir. Kenneth Hume, 1965).
Oh You Pretty Things: The Story of British Music and Fashion (Dir: Matt Hill, 2014).
Primitive London (Dir. Arnold Miller, 1965).
Quadrophenia (Dir. Franc Roddam, 1979).
Rebel Without A Cause (Dir. Nicholas Ray, 1955).
Roustabout (Dir. John Rich, 1964).
Saturday Night and Sunday Morning (Dir. Tony Richardson, 1960).
Saturday Night Fever (Dir. John Badham, 1977).
Smokescreen (Dir. Jim O'Connolly).
Steppin' Out (Dir. Lyndall Hobbs, 1979).
Swinging UK (Dir. Frank Gilpin, 1964).
The Intelligence Men (Dir. Robert Asher, 1965).
The Shooting of Thomas Hurndall (Dir. Rowan Joffe 2008).
Tommy (Dir. Ken Russell, 1975).
Trainspotting (Dir. Danny Boyle, 1996).
UK Swings Again (Dir. Frank Gilpin, 1964).
Victim (Dir. Basil Dearden, 1960).
We Are the Mods (Dir. E.E. Cassidy, 2009).
Young Birds Fly (Dir. Leonardo Flores, 2011).

The Narrative Nightclub

Matthew Cheeseman and David Forrest

INTRODUCTION

This chapter brings together expertise in film and cultural studies to analyse representations of nightclub dancefloors in British films from the
1990s onwards: *Human Traffic* (Justin Kerrigan, 1999), *Sorted* (Alexander
Jovy, 2000), *Soul Boy* (Shimmy Marcus, 2010), *Everywhere and Nowhere*
(Menhaj Huda, 2011) and *Northern Soul* (Elaine Constantine, 2014). We
use these films to identify persistent visual iconographies and accompanying ideological underpinnings within the British dancefloor film. To
understand what these films do not do, we also look by way of contrast to
a film from France, *Eden* (Mia Hansen-Løve, 2014). Our approach links
academic writing on dance music and nightclub cultures with analysis of
filmic texts, and in doing so the chapter captures a sense of the wider
discourse surrounding nightclubs and especially the dancefloors that often
form their focus, on- and off-screen.

M. Cheeseman (✉)
University of Derby, Derby, UK

D. Forrest
University of Sheffield, Sheffield, UK

© The Author(s) 2018   91
N. Bentley et al. (eds.), *Youth Subcultures in Fiction, Film and
Other Media*, Palgrave Studies in the History of Subcultures and
Popular Music, https://doi.org/10.1007/978-3-319-73189-6_6

We propose that British film tends to use the dancefloor as a narrative device that occludes or disturbs notions of youth culture, turning it into a problem to be solved. For example, *Sorted* can be read as an attempt to purify club culture and strip it of deviancy whilst *Everywhere and Nowhere* is a search for a sublime state of identity work where the DJ as artist unifies a dissonant post-subcultural identity. In their positioning of the dancefloor as a problem to be solved, these films have much in common with the British social problem film in that they perpetuate conservative representations of youth cultures. In this post-war cycle (running between 1947 and 1963) youth culture was repeatedly equated with the notion of threat to an established social (and by extension) narrative order, with an underpinning 'concern with regulation' uniting the films (Hill 1986, 124). Race, sexuality, music and emerging subcultures were developed as themes that injected a veneer of radicalism, realism and relevance into an apparently staid and conservative film industry. The films of Basil Dearden, J. Lee Thompson and others have much to tell us about how British cinema continues to represent and indeed use youth and culture to enable narrowly focused narratives which support rather than destabilise dominant ideological positions. We turn here to John Hill's (1986, 125) seminal analysis of the social problem film:

> these films, for all their raising of problems, ended up confirming, rather than querying, a consensual view of the world. This was the result not only of what they did, or rather didn't, show, but of how such problems were then used to reconfirm a particular set of attitudes and assumptions. Images of teenage sex and violence, for example, not only functioned as indices of the 'problem' but also helped clarify the 'correct' standards of behaviour by which they were to be understood and judged.

This group of films, with their attendant dancefloors, all relate to early twentieth-century, pre-Chicago-school theories of deviancy, specifically ones that view deviant behaviour as resulting from deviant psychology. These films are often unsympathetic to the idea of subculture—uncomprehending that young people are engaged in a social group with its own norms and networks in opposition to mainstream society. While we are not suggesting that the representation of sex, violence or the consumption of drugs in the club culture films of the 1990s and 2000s is explicitly connected to a conservative moral order, it is, we propose, that deviant lifestyles and tendencies are similarly housed within narrative systems which emphasise order and restoration.

While this remains a common narrative device, further readings from the scholarship on youth culture and subculture are also apparent and relevant. We will briefly describe their scope here, beginning with the writers associated with the Birmingham CCCS (Centre for Contemporary Cultural Studies), who largely viewed subculture as emerging from working-class youth who focused on style to develop resistant and antagonistic cultures positioned against a mainstream culture. In the face of weakened class consciousness, such subcultures posited style as proxies for resistance against the system (see Cohen 1997; Hebdige 1979). One might expect such a dynamic to feature in club culture films. In our analysis, however, it typically manifests as a surface reading, in that the dancefloor is initially depicted as a communal, resistant space before being revealed as a deviant space. This trope turns the dancefloor into a narrative problem to be solved by the film's protagonist.

While we maintain that dancefloors are always presented as problems in British film, they are not always resistant or deviant to a wider society. They are sometimes problems in and of themselves: a stage on which the protagonist solves conflicting and opposing forces. We relate this to post-subcultural theory, which is understood as the mobilisation of Bourdieu's (1984) framing of distinction in relation to subculture in conditions of postmodernity. Subcultures are no longer seen as resistant but as a smorgasbord of styles and identities that can be fluidly borrowed from at will. Sarah Thornton (1995) writes in such a fashion about club culture, following Redhead (1993) in suggesting that subcultures are not necessarily resistant but elastic and porous. The individual's role in choosing, selecting and constructing their own style is thus emphasized (Muggleton 2000). This befits an age where consumer lifestyles have (allegedly) greater importance in establishing youth identity than subcultural affirmation (Miles 2000).

We recognise, then, that the debates in studies of subculture—between class and the individual, between ordinary life and spectacular style, worsened economic conditions and choice—are ongoing (Shildrick and MacDonald 2007) and note that there has been a recent (and persuasive) attempt at synthesis (Hodkinson 2016, 636) which argues for

> pursuing, drawing together and integrating two angles of study, one focused on how individuals negotiate with, draw from and position themselves in relation to different groups and the other centred on how particular groups work and the ways their operation provides structure and direction to the lives, orientations and identities of participants.

It is further noted, for our purposes, that many of the writers involved in this debate are British. Similarly, these debates are present in the British films we examine, although they may arrive at different solutions. As the nightclub plots of the protagonist frequently deal with familial obligation and social deprivation, issues of transition and social class (and its denial) are often present. As we shall also demonstrate, the individual mastering the dancefloor is often used to highlight post-subcultural issues of choice and stylistic performance. Sometimes, however, these do take into account negotiation between different groups, as per Hodkinson's call. We thus use the narrative space of the nightclub to poke at perennial questions concerning youth culture, seeking to depict and interrogate the position of British cinema's own exploration of youth culture.

While there has been much academic work on club culture, there has been relatively little written on the films depicting it. There is one monograph, by Stan Beeler (2007), *Dance, Drugs and Escape: The Club Scene in Literature, Film and Television Since the Late 1980s*. This depicts club culture as following a passage from subcultural to popular culture, which sees it 'become more apparent to the public eye' and in so doing 'develop[ing] an academic and literary superstructure' (11), that includes films. Some of these 'club fictions' are aimed at preserving the subcultural 'origins of the movement' whilst others present the club and the dancefloor as non-oppositional, part of 'the established cultural industry' (13). Beeler claims there are several elements essential to club fiction: dance music and venues, drugs and an attempt to 'escape to a better world' (in a combination of hedonism and futurism) (13). In terms of culture, club fictions function to 'describe the subculture to the mainstream' and 'to allow the members of the subculture to celebrate their participation in ways other than clubbing' (25). One might note that such a description positions these films as intermediaries, attempting to satisfy a range of viewers. There is thus a high degree of intertextuality between the dancefloor and the texts that inform, circulate and comment on it, all of which are part of a larger discourse about youth, style and identity (Morrison 2014). Our discussion of film is intended to explore this intertextual territory, sketching out its possible extent, in a manner approaching Nathaniel Weiner's (2015) comparable discussion of 1970s social realist films and their relation to subcultural thinking from Birmingham's CCCS. Weiner concludes that these films do 'reflect discourses at work among British radicals and filmmakers during the 1970s and 1980s ... who saw youth subcultures as a radical response to an experience of oppression shaped by age, class and race' (17).

In club culture films, the dancefloor has a communal and to some extent utopian iconography. Despite this, it is nearly always evoked as backdrop to facilitate the development of goal-oriented, classically configured narratives that emphasise personal agency and suppress the open-ended, non-restrictive possibilities of youth culture as a resistant collective. This move towards order is predicated on the privileging of the individual protagonist's narrative at the expense of a possible exploration of the dancefloor as enabling a more progressive sense of narrative dispersal. The dancefloor then, while appearing as a space for the flowering of communal identity, represents both a spatial and structural entity to be mastered or overcome in pursuit of conservative structures of goal completion. We would like to suggest that this is a convention for British film. That is not to say that film does not entertain notions of youth culture, but rather that the use of the dancefloor as a narrative device occludes or disturbs these notions, turning, in each film, the notion of subculture (post- or otherwise) into a problem to be solved. So, the area we explore in our case studies is the peculiar tension between the dancefloor as a space that consistently individuates various films, despite those films holding variegated attitudes and beliefs towards subculture.

Our analysis suggests that the cinematic dancefloor remains an inherently conservative space due to its construction within rigid and inexpressive narrative and ideological parameters. Other critics have, however, adopted more complimentary perspectives. Like us, Simon Morrison, acknowledges the well-trodden 'discursive traits' of what he terms the Electronic Dance Music Culture (EDMC) film, with its 'parabolic storyline arc' that 'maps the genesis, zenith and the nadir of the narrative: the anticipation [...] the actuality [...] the aftermath that orientates us through the story of the film' (2011, 54). For Morrison, despite its formulaic nature, this structure does appropriately reflect the 'journey of a night-out: going out [...] coming up [...] coming down. Indeed, it is the story of club culture itself' (54). Morrison is right that the dancefloor film has the capacity to evoke the visceral ambience of the club space, and that such experiences, do indeed, resemble something of a narrative journey with distinct phases and points of conclusion. There is not necessarily a mutual exclusivity between linear storytelling and the evocation of the narrative nightclub.

Andrea Rinke is similarly positive in her approach to such texts, specifically Justin Kerrigan's 1999 film *Human Traffic*. She praises the apparent absence of a moralising structure, the film's refusal to discipline its protagonists' transgression and its 'carnivalesque celebration of youthful deviance' (2015, 38). Rinke's argument also centres on the disruptive self-aware narration as further evidence for the strength of the film's 'polemic against the condemnatory master discourse about recreational drugs' (40). Certainly, Kerrigan's approach to his subjects—a group of twenty-somethings who the film follows over a weekend of clubbing—is sympathetic, and Rinke is right that the 'film does not problematize the taking of dance drugs by young clubbers' (43). In this sense, *Human Traffic* is not a 'social problem film' and as Rinke would argue, its dispersal of narrative focus across its ensemble, resists reductive, instrumental conclusions. However, as ever we must look to the ending to better understand the film's ideological enterprise. An alternative reading of *Human Traffic* might suggest that despite its non-judgemental evocation of a utopian dancefloor community, these elements are ultimately superficial authenticators of the deeply conservative and goal-oriented emphasis on the protagonist's Jip's (John Simm) battle to overcome his impotence and consummate his relationship with the object of his desire, Lulu (Lorraine Pilkington). The film finishes with a crane shot as the two kiss and embrace. Although the deployment of such a cliché could well be seen as part of the film's ironic, self-aware register, the apparent need for *Human Traffic* to be anchored by the journey towards heterosexual romantic union reveals once more the limited project of the dancefloor film.

The relationship between genre and subcultural theme is central to our understanding of the ways in which the cinema might seek to represent the individual and the dancefloor. As mentioned, Nathaniel Weiner's work on British cinema's relationship with subcultural representation is particularly useful here. Weiner's argument, that films such as *Pressure* (Horace Ové, 1975), *Bloody Kids* (Stephen Frears, 1980), *Babylon* (Franco Rosso, 1980) and *Made in Britain* (Alan Clarke, 1983) reflect the approaches, concerns and sensitivities of the research undertaken by the CCCS, identifies a more resistant and progressive subcultural impulse within British film history. In his discussion of *Babylon*, a film about soundsystem culture in South London, Weiner indicates how the film 'celebrates the independence and vitality of the London reggae scene, echoing the CCCS' interest in the politics of style and its analysis of reggae as "cultural resistance"' (2015, 11). His case studies all have in common looser, more non-prescriptive narrative structures than the nightclub films we discuss. For example, *Babylon* concludes with 'Blue' (Brinsley Forde) defiantly MCing at a party as the police break down the doors, and the viewer's need for closure is overwhelmed by the vitality of the performance; and Ové's *Pressure* oscillates between a vivid documentary realist style and a more poetic and expressionistic examination of the dream state of its troubled protagonist as he confronts institutional racism and moves towards a position of political radicalism at the film's conclusion. The films are capable of such nuance because they are unencumbered by the narrative doctrine of social problem that would define the dancefloor film of the 1990s and 2000s.

In Alexander Jov's *Sorted*, made in 2000, Matthew Rhys plays Carl, a provincial lawyer who comes down to London to investigate his brother's death. Carl's brother, it is soon revealed, was an active member of a community of clubbers. The film tracks Carl's flirtation with the subcultural pleasures of the dance and drug scene; it subjectifies (and to some extent celebrates) his first experience of the drug ecstasy; it celebrates the kinship of the dancefloor and the intensity of the group friendships it accommodates; and it attempts to posit the alternative lifestyle of the clubber against normative narratives of everyday life. The film is thus very sympathetic to a classic view of club culture, as a contingent, consistent group united by strong group bonds and a regular consumption of club styles and music. It follows the classic initiation of a neophyte, descending into a clubworld that is depicted as subterranean, existing in a transcultural London underworld, where, nevertheless, the dancefloor provides glimpses of redemption. A group of clubbers offer friendship and support to the neophyte, literally styling him in the clothes and footwear of the underground.

These elements are, however, marginalised in favour of the central emphasis on Carl's journey: that of the naïve but virtuous northerner, dispatched to the exotic and dangerous capital in his search for truth, revenge and the restoration of moral order. His subcultural exploration is necessary to reveal the antagonist, the evil figure to his good, the spatial overlord of the dancefloor, Tim Curry's devilish Damian, a fantastical drug dealer. Carl orchestrates a clubbers' uprising against the drug lord who owns and oversees the very nightclubs they dance in. Thus evil is purged from the dancefloor by the outsider. The film concludes with Carl overseeing Damian's death, avenging his brother and happily consolidating his relationship with Sunny (Sienna Guillory), his brother's ex-girlfriend, and tellingly the only one of his brother's associates who exists outside of the narrow confines of the dancefloor narrative—the clubbers are seen in the end titles, as afterthoughts.

The protagonist kills the drug lord poisoning the subculture, thus achieving not only narrative cohesion and completion in terms of avenging his brother, but also purging the drug dealer from the nightclub: a strange plot for a film that also extols the mind-bending, group-enhancing joys of ecstasy. Thus *Sorted* represents an updated social problem film in a way that is typical for the club culture films: (1) drugs, hedonism and utopian possibilities do not exist without the criminal; (2) the dancefloor itself is indeed a criminal space; (3) pleasure cannot exist without the presence of evil; (4) the club or the party is a narrative obstacle that must be overcome by the virtuous outsider; (5) the dancefloor becomes an authenticating device to veil an inherently simplistic binary. In subcultural terms *Sorted* is concerned with deviancy, in a fashion reminiscent of the post-war social problem films, but with a different goal: an attempt to purify club culture itself. It is thus sympathetic to the idea of subculture (and sympathetic to the idea of subculture as resistance) but cannot help but also frame subculture as a problem to be solved, largely due to the way the dancefloor is positioned as an obstacle.

Menhaj Huda's *Everywhere and Nowhere*, made in 2011, is a more acute representation of the dancefloor to perpetuate and promote individual agency. Here, rather than overcome the dancefloor, the protagonist, wannabe DJ Ash (James Floyd), must master and control it in order to succeed in completing his linear coming-of-age narrative. He is torn between his love for DJing (and apparently production, although like many dancefloor films no distinction is made between the two), and his conservative first-generation Pakistani father's desire to see him take on the family business. Of course, the DJing wins out, but this narrative completion does not endorse subcultural creative endeavour. Indeed, the odd (and inauthentic) fusion of drum'n'bass and mass-market electro house played by the senior DJ, Ronnie (Simon Webbe), emphasises that the passage to the DJ booth is not about music as much it as about status—musical authenticity and its inherent para-textual potential cannot be allowed to distract from the protagonist's quest.

Ash's own productions are put forward as evidence of his uniqueness as a creative force. They are fusions of Bollywood musical soundtracks, dubstep, and amen breaks commonly associated with drum'n'bass, yet the music merely serves as a narrative device to assert—in a heavy-handed manner—Ash's conflicted cultural identity, the film's apparently utopian conclusion confirms this: Ash's triumphant appearance in a DJ booth sees him return to the populist sanitised drum'n'bass of earlier scenes. Ash's central position within the narrative and his pursuit of the star status of DJ is supported by a persistent emphasis on his difference in contrast to other, less developed agents within the film. His character is predicated on a pervasive resistance towards communal possibilities. He is too intelligent and too sexually attractive to find affinity with his cousin, who is enchanted by radical Islam (seemingly because he cannot get a girlfriend); he is too serious to enjoy the pleasures of drug consumption and the pursuit of sex that his other friends enjoy, and he is too moral to prescribe to the flawed and hypocritical version of Islam represented by his father, who preaches family values while maintaining a sexual relationship with a family friend. These factors symbolically converge through the dancefloor that Ash must master—a figurative distillation of the narrative obstacles that he must overcome, spatially represented in the journey towards the booth to become an artist.

Despite the similarity in individuating narrative, the film's treatment of club culture is completely different from *Sorted*. Much of this is due to the eleven years that separate the films. By 2011, when *Everywhere and Nowhere* was made, club culture is presented as synonymous with being young. There is no underground journey here: whatever your ethnicity, sexuality, religion, you must engage with the dancefloor. It is ubiquitous and ordinary, the floor that youth friendship is necessarily enacted on. Such ubiquity certainly reflects the structural and social changes that saw club culture municipally reframed as the night-time economy, which regulated and legitimated the idea of rave with that of the creative municipality (Chatterton and Hollands 2003). Indeed, many of these changes were already underway by the time *Sorted* was made in 2000, yet that film certainly depicts a club culture that was distinct and underground, capable of being learnt and not already ambient, non-negotiable by youth.

Following Stan Beeler's typology of club fiction, *Sorted*, thus, takes the dual role of both explaining club culture to outsiders but celebrating it to insiders. The distinction is lost by *Everywhere and Nowhere*, where there are only distinctions in style, no initiations or discovery. The outsiders are Ash's immigrant parents and radical Islam. This is clearly expressed in the dialogue:

> 'Everyone is living a big fuck off lie'
> 'That's what we do, that's what we have to do.'

In one way this could be interpreted as presenting a view of youth as a generation, with only non-whites identifying with any concept of subcul-

ture, which in this case is fundamental Islam, positioned as an intensifica-
tion of his father's patriarchal, restrictive attitudes. The dancefloor is the
true reality that must be mastered, that cannot be ignored. When Ash's
father is revealed to be corrupt, the world of family, ethnicity and wealth
can be shunned, and Ash can finally be open about the fundamental ubiquity of the dancefloor. He has conquered an overbearing father and can
journey to the DJ booth as its master.

Ash has journeyed from being a club culture participant with multiple
and conflicting identities, to a master, in charge of a coherent identity at
the centre of youth culture. He has been true to his self and true to the DJ
booth, which represents his perfect individuality amongst a crowd of individuals, fluid only in the styles of music they consume. Thus, the dancefloor posits a purification that solves a problem: post-subculturalism
stripped of interfering family, ethnic and religious obligations (turning
away from the position Hodkinson argues for and towards the classic post-
subcultural analysis of Muggleton 2000). Ash is free to immerse himself in
the post-production art of the DJ, mixing styles without consequence,
and has thus achieved mastery of a generation of individuals united by the
consumption of club culture.

In recent years the generic concerns of 'club fiction' have been enacted
in British films interested in other dance subcultures, namely Northern
Soul. 2010s *Soul Boy*, directed by Shimmy Marcus, feels strikingly familiar.
A young, naïve protagonist enters the dancefloor space and his life is transformed by an immersion into the 'scene'; drugs and crime threaten to
derail the euphoria, but the resolution of a 'love triangle' and, in the case
of *Soul Boy*, success for the protagonist in a climactic 'dance off' offer
redemption and closure. The film's eye for period detail, with its authentic
soundtrack and recreation of the iconic Wigan Casino, is mere decoration
for the delivery of a tried and tested structural formula.

Elaine Constantine's *Northern Soul* released some four years after *Soul
Boy*, however, promised something more. Constantine was and still is an
avid attendee at Northern Soul all-nighters; as a photographer she had
documented the scene in its heyday; and she drew on her own experiences
to ensure authentic locations: 'I knew to do it justice I had to shoot up
north' (Scullard 2014). A radical social media and online strategy also
helped build the sense of 'authenticity' around the film. The long process
of *Northern Soul's* production (it took years to raise finance) had the effect
of generating publicity and the film's Facebook page swelled to 50,000

followers before it was even released. The page was used to recruit extras for the dance scenes and to solicit photo submissions and stories for Constantine's accompanying book *Northern Soul: An Illustrated History* (with Gareth Sweeney). The page was also critical in enabling distribution as fans lobbied their local cinemas to show the film via initiatives such as 'Ourscreen' which 'empowers film fans and local communities to create and attend screenings at their local cinema', and screenings were hosted in club settings alongside DJ sets and exhibitions across the country (Anonymous 2016). The participatory nature of *Northern Soul*'s audience development, and its mining of collective (sub)cultural capital, appeared to enable a penetration of the diegetic boundary between the passive audience and the imagined narrative dancefloor. We remember watching the film at The Showroom cinema in Sheffield on the day it was released. The theatre was packed full of Northern Soul fans. They sang at the screen, a few even danced. This was certainly, in Beeler's terms, a film made (and marketed) to celebrate the scene to insiders.

This sense of euphoria, however, was curtailed by the collective realisation of the film's fundamental limitations. Constantine's background in photography is evident in the claustrophobic compositions, the interplays between light and dark and the granular evocation of the 1970s. The film is thus more stylistically impressive than *Soul Boy*, yet its style cannot excuse its rigid storytelling. In a fictional Northern town, John (Elliot James Langridge), a frustrated, socially awkward school-leaver, meets a kindred spirit, Matt (Josh Whitehouse), and discovers Northern Soul. The two become DJs and plan to accumulate enough money to travel to America to buy records. Drugs and crime pollute the dream, when Sean (Jack Gordon), a shadowy (Southern) outsider, botches a drug deal and the euphoria of the dancefloor gives way to a hellish comedown. John and Matt fall out, and then, at the film's conclusion, rekindle their friendship, but not before Matt has affirmed his heterosexuality by having sex with the angelic Angela (Antonia Thomas), offering him a path of redemption outside of the dancefloor with its homoerotic undertones. There are momentary spaces in the film for what Constantine calls the:

> pleading, yearning, largely adult, black American voices [...] initially very alien to our ears [that] seemed to speak to us so directly [...] with a degree of intimacy that we rarely got from our own friends and family. (Anonymous 2015)

While these communal impulses were bound up in the fostering of engaged participative audiences, the film still falls back on tried and tested narrative strategies which seem, in their subordination towards individual resolution, to directly contradict Constantine's evocation of a utopian subcultural moment. The dancefloor here acts as a magnet around which the plot assembles in a predictably orderly fashion, forming straight lines and refusing to disperse and evoke the transformative potential of the subculture.

If the narrative nightclub's conservatism is defined by the relationship of causality to narrative space, we must look to representations of dance-floors that reject the instrumental nature of such structures. From the period we focus on (post-1990s), we have turned to a French film as an example. Mia Hansen-Løve's *Eden* (2014) is co-written by and based on the experiences of Hansen-Løve's brother, Sven. The film follows 20 years in the life of Paul (Félix de Givry), a Garage DJ in Paris, from the beginnings of his love affair with dance music, to his rise to prominence, before the second half of the film deals with the melancholy of his descent into debt and drug addiction. Although the trajectory might seem familiar for the dancefloor film, its expansion across a dispersed, twenty-year timeline, with its loose episodic structure closing and opening points of narrative interest at seemingly arbitrary junctures, imbues the film with an opaque ambience that offers no easy solutions.

Eden was originally billed as a film about the so-called French touch scene that produced Daft Punk. Although Thomas Bangalter and Guy-Manuel de Homem-Christo are characters in the film, their roles are minor, their lack of prominence making conspicuous *Eden*'s more universal, quotidian concerns. The duo is, however, central to a critical moment within the film. At a house party early on in the film they play, for the first time, their classic, breakthrough track 'Da Funk'. For Hansen-Løve the scene anticipates their elevation to stardom:

> In the profile shot, Bangalter and Homem-Christo still belong to the group [...] Then, from the far shot, we see them face on but suddenly they are somewhere else. We have lost them. They are here, but you don't hear what they say any more because they are stars. I love how we captured that moment. (MacInnes 2015)

As the track progresses and its seminality becomes evident, Hansen-Løve cuts to a two-shot of another hopeful production duo, Paul and his partner

Stan (Hugo Conzelmann). Our expectations of the nightclub film suggest that this should be a critical point: perhaps they will respond negatively, because they know they will never be able to match 'Da Funk's' quality, or this moment will signal the setting of a narrative goal, inspiring them on their own path towards stardom. Instead, Paul merely comments to Stan: 'They finished their track.' Hansen- Løve cuts back to the animated dance-floor, Daft Punk just visible behind their decks, and Paul continues: 'It fucking rocks.'

Like Constantine, Hansen-Løve struggled to finance her dancefloor film, with potential backers put off precisely by the film's rejection of the principles of the narrative nightclub: '[a]ll the comments I've had about the script were that nothing was happening and that there wasn't enough conflict' (Ehrlich 2015). In another interview she again seems to invoke the rigid generic expectations of the dancefloor film:

> Some people think when you have characters that are doing something illegal or wrong, they should be punished in a way. They were punished but in a different way than people expected, a much quieter way. (Mertens 2015)

For *Eden*, then, the staples and structuring devices of the dance music genre are secondary to a more ambiguous and poetic examination of music and dancing as a way of dramatizing everyday life, as Sven Hansen-Løve's notes:

> [Paul] has one big thing in his life, he is driven by music like [most people] are for a woman or a guy, he falls in love deeply and passionately [with that], and it's difficult to find room for both. (Montgomery 2015)

The multiple romantic relationships that Paul has across the film are of course interwoven within its aforementioned elliptical narrative structure, as Jonathan Romney argues in his review: 'when you focus on one character's intense, sealed-in experience, it makes sense that other people's lives happen offstage, in an abrupt, fragmentary fashion' (Romney 2015). Thus the pursuit of romance, the beginning and ending of affairs, otherwise so central to the narrative nightclub, are secondary to the film's central organising structure: Paul's experience of and immersion in the subcultural space.

As such, the nightclub scenes are critical to *Eden*'s poetic energy. Hansen-Løve shot on digital rather than film, which, as she recalls 'means we didn't have to have extra lights in the nightclub scenes. We were using the lights of the nightclub' (Vishnevetsky 2015). As such, the camera's subtle presence is reflected in its position often amongst the crowd and alongside the playing of the music diegetically, generating another layer of sensory realism. The crowd often sing along with the soulful lyrics of the tracks that Paul and Stan play, adding an experiential, interactive quality to the representation of the club. Again, Hansen-Løve is keen to emphasise her wilful rejection of the iconographic clichés of the narrative nightclub:

> I wanted to make it so much more real life and much less like cinema. I didn't want to embrace that vulgarity that is so common now, [that] MTV language, I wanted to get rid of that and find my own. (Montgomery 2015)

The film's realism, both subjective in its focus on Paul's nostalgic, dream-like reflections, and objective in its visceral, almost participatory evocation of the feeling of dancing to and playing of house and garage music means that the conventional narrative cues of the dancefloor are absent. *Eden* is instead organised along more associative and rhythmic patterns, in line with its themes. When Stan and Paul are interviewed on a radio show, Paul introduces a track as being 'exactly what we like, between euphoria and melancholy' in a moment which seems to condense the film's underlying tone. Indeed for Lindsay Jensen this tension represents 'the theme of Paul's life over the years explored by the film. Between is a constant state.' *Eden* ends with a solitary Paul on his bed reading a poem, 'The Rhythm' by Robert Creeley:

> It is all a rhythm,
> from the shutting
> door, to the window
> opening,

The poem's cyclical quality, both in form and content, reminds us that Paul's melancholy is a condition of his euphoria and vice versa. *Eden* succeeds where *Northern Soul* does not, in embedding the nightclub in a narrative structure that can tackle and encompass its shifting position across and along a person's life. In doing so it explores the scope of youth and style and takes a long view of subculture, society and commitment. It comes closest to representing the synthesis between subcultural and post-subcultural which Hodkinson discusses.

Eden is, in our survey, an exception. As a French film with an ostensible focus on a historically specific French dance music subculture, *Eden* is unmoored from the trappings of the British cinema's colonisation of the nightclub as a cinematic space. Much of its success comes from Hansen-Løve's nuanced approach, unburdened as it is from the expectation of narrative order and focussed instead on evoking a *feeling* of the experience of dancing and listening to music. *Eden* shows that the narrative nightclub need not be constrained by a linear treatment of the dancefloor, yet it is hard to find a space within British cinema for a similarly imaginative treatment of the subculture(s). Indeed, one has to look to the world of contemporary art, and Mark Leckie's *Fiorucci Made Me Hardcore* (1999) for a visual text which seeks to realise rather than curtail the possibilities of the British dancefloor. In the British films that we have discussed here, the trace of the social problem genre lingers: that is a way of dealing with youth and subculture which demands order, and which denies the possibilities and potentials of transgression, both within and beyond the narrative. British films concerned with the dancefloor, despite showing the potential of communality, tend to force an individuating narrative, whereby the space becomes an obstacle to be overcome and mastered, in the course of which it is frequently turned into a tool by the protagonist. This is a narrative function that also relates to these films' instrumental approach to subculture, where the dancefloor uncomplicates, makes linear, purges and purifies.

REFERENCES

Anon. 2016. "About Ourscreen" available online: https://www.ourscreen.com/about-ourscreen/ [Last accessed: 13/12/16].

Anon. 2015. "Keep the faith: Elaine Constantine on filming the Northern Soul story," available online: http://www.bbc.co.uk/programmes/articles/2jrXD9q1bpKVP19TwdcCBFt/keep-the-faith-elaine-constantine-on-filming-the-northern-soul-story [Last accessed: 13/12/16].

Beeler, Stan. 2007. *Dance, Drugs and Escape: The Club Scene in Literature, Film and Television Since the Late 1980s.* Jefferson: McFarland.

Bourdieu, Pierre. 1984. *Distinction*. London: Routledge.

Chatterton, Paul and Hollands, Robert. 2003. *Urban Nightscapes: Youth Cultures, Pleasure Spaces and Corporate Power*. London: Routledge.

Cohen, Phil. 1997. *Rethinking the Youth Question: Education, Labour and Cultural Studies*. Basingstoke: Palgrave.

Ehrlich, David. 2015. "Interview: Mia Hansen-Løve Talks 'Eden,' Daft Punk, French Disco & Her Next Film 'The Future'," Available online: http://www.indiewire.com/2015/06/interview-mia-hansen-love-talks-eden-daft-punk-french-disco-her-next-film-the-future-262813/ [Last accessed: 13/12/16].

Hebdige, Dick. 1979. *Subculture: The Meaning of Style*. London: Routledge.

Hill, John. 1986. *Sex, Class and Realism*. London: BFI.

Hodkinson, Paul. 2016. 'Youth cultures and the rest of life: subcultures, post-subcultures and beyond' in *Journal of Youth Studies* 19 (5), pp. 629–645.

MacInnes, Paul. 2015. "*Eden*: 'There was no film that took club culture seriously," Available online: https://www.theguardian.com/film/2015/jul/21/mia-hansen-love-eden [Last accessed: 13/12/16].

Mertens, Max. 2015. "Interview: Eden Director Mia Hansen-Løve." Available online: http://daily.redbullmusicacademy.com/2015/06/mia-hansen-love-interview [Last accessed: 13/12/16].

Miles, Stephen. 2000. *Youth Lifestyles in a Changing World*. Maidenhead: Open University Press.

Montgomery, Hugh. 2015. "Why the Daft Punk-featuring EDEN is the dance music film fans have been waiting for." Available online: http://www.independent.co.uk/arts-entertainment/films/features/why-the-daft-punk-featuring-eden-is-the-dance-music-film-fans-have-been-waiting-for-10396530.html [Last accessed: 13/12/16].

Morrison, Simon A. 2014. "'Surely people who go clubbing don't read": Dispatches from the dancefloor and clubland in print' in *IASPM Journal* 4(2). Available online: http://www.iaspmjournal.net/index.php/IASPM_Journal/article/view/735 [Last accessed: 3/12/16].

Muggleton, David. 2000. *Inside subculture: The postmodern meaning of style*. Oxford: Berg.

Redhead, Steve. (ed.) 1993. *Rave Off!: Politics and Deviance in Contemporary Youth Culture*. Farnham: Ashgate.

Rinke, Andrea. 2015. "'The weekend has landed!' Carnivalesque youth rebellion in the Ecstasy film *Human Traffic* (Justin Kerrigan 1999 UK)" in *Studies in European Cinema*, 12:1, pp. 35–45.

Romney, Jonathan. 2015. "Film of the Week: *Eden*." Available online: http://www.filmcomment.com/blog/mia-hansen-love-eden-review/ [Last accessed: 13/12/16].

Scullard, Vickie. 2014. "Director Elaine Constantine brings Northern Soul to Bury." Available online: http://www.theboltonnews.co.uk/leisure/the_big_interview/11530979.Director_Elaine_Constantine_brings_Northern_Soul_to_Bury/ [Last accessed: 13/12/16].

Shildrick, Tracy A. and MacDonald, Robert. 2007. "Street Corner Society: Leisure Careers, Youth (Sub)Culture and Social Exclusion" in *Leisure Studies* 26 (3), p. 399–355.

Thornton, Sarah. 1995. *Club Cultures: Music, Media and Subcultural Capital.* London: Polity Press.

Vishnevetsky, Ignatiy. 2015. "Mia Hansen-Løve on trying to make the *Heaven's Gate* of house music." Available online: http://www.avclub.com/article/mia-hansen-love-trying-make-heavens-gate-house-mus-220876 [Last accessed: 13/12/16].

Weiner, Nathaniel. 2015. "Resistance through realism: Youth subculture films in 1970s (and 1980s) Britain" in *European Journal of Cultural Studies.* Available online: http://ecs.sagepub.com/content/early/2015/11/06/1367549415 603376 [Last accessed: 3/12/16].

You're All Partied Out, Dude!: The Mainstreaming of Heavy Metal Subcultural Tropes, from *Bill & Ted* to *Wayne's World*

Andy R. Brown

In this chapter I explore the apparent contradiction that a youth subculture at the centre of a mass-mediated, high-profile moral panic was also the inspiration for a string of successful Hollywood movies, which placed the male-teen-buddy 'metalhead' experience at the centre of the narrative, in the form of characters like Bill and Ted (Alex Winter and Keanu Reeves), and Wayne and Garth (Mike Myers and Dana Carvey). While previous studies (Hunter 1996; Best and Kellner 1998) have been concerned to locate such films and characters within a recognisable landscape of youth-oriented consumer capitalism, they have been unsuccessful in identifying the centrality of heavy metal culture tropes, including argot, electric-guitar virtuosity and music and album references, to the ways in which such characters negotiate their relationships to such an environment. While such

A. R. Brown (✉)
Bath Spa University, Bath, UK

© The Author(s) 2018
N. Bentley et al. (eds.), *Youth Subcultures in Fiction, Film and Other Media*, Palgrave Studies in the History of Subcultures and Popular Music, https://doi.org/10.1007/978-3-319-73189-6_7

films are clearly comedies and depend upon a postmodernist pastiche of conventions common to the late 1980s teen film, this satirical style is also one that is constantly in 'dialogue' with heavy metal culture. Without this aspect, such films would lack authenticity and their characters would not be credible, let alone liked by a cross section of teenagers and adults, many of whom are nonetheless not heavy metal fans. The question I want to pursue is how such films translate heavy metal subcultural tropes into credible mass cultural forms, examining what is inevitably lost in such a process as well as what is gained, suggesting overall that satire and humour are central to such strategies and to their success.

HEAVY METAL AND MORAL PANIC

> We have certain rules. Removal of heavy metal albums or tapes, not allowing the child to dress in any style of heavy metal, which would mean taking these kinds of things away from him. Not allowing him to wear the heavy metal t-shirts that depict the band members or pictures of monsters, skeletons, graves or whatever.

Darlyne Pettinicchio, co-founder and Director of *The Back In Control Training Center*, Orange County, CA.[1]

In the period from 1984 to 1991, the genre of heavy metal and the youth culture identified with it were subject to a sustained campaign of elite condemnation and mass-mediated 'moral panic', to an extent unprecedented even within the troubled history of the reception of popular music in North America (Chastagner 1999; Weinstein 2000, 265–70; Walser 2014, 137–51). The initiators of this campaign were an organisation that called itself the *Parent's Music Resource Centre* (PMRC), largely 'composed of Washington D.C. wives and mothers' (Martin and Segrave 1993, 292), such as Susan Baker and Tipper Gore. The PMRC charged that rock music had become sexually explicit, morally depraved and pornographic. They produced a list of offending songs ('the Filthy Fifteen'), the majority of which were by heavy metal bands, and called for a ratings system that would control access to such music by minors. The campaign, which typically focused on quoting 'explicit' lyrics and 'objectionable' album covers from the PMRC's 'bad list' (Martin and Segrave 1993, 293–4), received widespread coverage in national media, such as *Newsweek*, the *Washington Post*, *The Donahue Show*, *CBS Morning News*, and *Today*.

Following a presentation on the 'evils of rock music' by the PMRC to the Justice Department's Commission on Pornography, the Senate Committee initiated proceedings into 'porn rock' and record labelling, held in September 1985. There, a number of 'expert' witnesses claimed a causal connection between 'epidemic' rates of male suicides and heavy metal songs, citing Ozzy Osbourne's *Suicide Solution*, Blue Oyster Cult's *Don't Fear the Reaper* and AC/DC's *Shoot to Thrill*. In October 1985, Osbourne was sued by a nineteen-year-old youth's parents, who claimed that the young man was listening to the artist's record the night he took his own life. In the summer of 1990, the band Judas Priest were taken to court by the parents of two boys who acted out a suicide pact, allegedly at the behest of 'subliminal (or backward) messages' placed on the album, *Stained Class* (1978). Such claims reflected widespread fears among religious organisations, such as Parents Against Subliminal Seduction (PASS), over the impact of Satanism and satanic symbols on impressionable youth (for example, Raschke 1990, 171). The outcome of the campaign was a 'voluntary agreement' between the Recording Industry Association of America (RIAA) and the PMRC that the industry would label potentially 'offensive' records with a 'Parental Advisory: Explicit Lyrics' warning. This practice came into effect in 1986 and is now the industry standard, occurring most frequently on heavy metal and hip-hop/rap releases (Christenson 1992).

Despite the unprecedented and excessive nature of this elite-orchestrated and media-sustained 'demonisation' of heavy metal youth and their music of choice, during this same period fictional or filmic representations of the 'metalhead' teenage archetype actually *increased*, finding their way into a number of popular films. These include the conflicted character(s) who were able to go *Back To The Future* (1985) or, to complete a post-modernist history assignment, as in *Bill and Ted's Excellent Adventure* (1989) and *Bill and Ted's Bogus Journey* (1992), *Airheads* (1994) and the low-budget *Clerks* (1994), *Mallrats* (1995), *Jay and Silent Bob Strike Back* (2001) and *Fubar* (2004). Also, during this period (1989–1995) the growing popularity of the 'kidult' characters Wayne and Garth, of *Saturday Night Live's* comedy-skit Wayne's World, led to the release of the very successful *Wayne's World* (1992) and the sequel, *Wayne's World II* (1993). The period 1993–1997 also saw the development, by the animator Mike Judge, of MTV's *Beavis and Butt-head* show, which although initially controversial, gained widespread success. How are we to explain this?

IDIOT DANCING: SUBCULTURAL THEORY AND HEAVY METAL YOUTH CULTURAL STYLE

It is tempting to place this account of heavy metal youth culture within the classic CCCS model of resistance and incorporation, in particular the moral panic and industry commodification phase described by Hebdige (1979, 92–9). Here we witness both the societal 'folk devil' subject to symbolic and institutional censure *and* the industry-commercial phase where a once-threatening teen subculture is rendered safe and manageable, in this case, within recognisable 'youth' comedic conventions. However, it is important to note that the majority of subcultural theorists failed to recognise the existence of a heavy metal subculture at all or, if they did, rejected any claim it might have to be a youth culture of 'resistance' (Cashmore 1984); ironically, in the case of Hebdige, because its style was viewed as 'idiotic' (Brown 2003, 211). The object of this idiocy is heavy metal's 'dance-style', which he fails to identify as 'head-banging'.

For Cashmore, reports of this 'head-banging' (*The Times*, 5th April 1982), provided the 'only genuine moment of panic about heavy metal' when a youth died from brain damage caused by 'continually jerking his head at a concert' in 1982 (1984, 37). Despite this coverage, 'heavy metal generally failed to arouse the kind of hysteria or panic associated with most youth subcultures' (Cashmore 1984, 37). Rather it 'gave the appearance of being threatening without actually being threatening'. Heavy metal fans, according to Cashmore 'didn't want to change society... They just wanted a little corner of it where they could introvert to their own sphere, escaping to a fantasy world in which they played imaginary guitars and shook their heads into states of concussion' (1984, 37). And yet, as we have seen, within a year of this judgment heavy metal was at the centre of the largest and most sustained panic of any post-war subculture.

In retrospect, it seems plausible to argue that the campaign by state and local institutional apparatuses of repression, focused on the music of heavy metal and its fans, announces a neoliberal New Right attack on a perceived area of youth resistance to Regan (and Thatcherite) policies within youth and civil society in this key period (Brown 2013, 24–5). Despite the claims made that heavy metal music was a darkly sinister fringe music that encouraged its fans to 'oppose the traditional values of those in authority and encourage rebellious and aggressive attitudes and behavior towards parents, educators, law enforcement and religious leaders', and to promote 'behaviors that are violent, immoral, illegal [such as] drug and alcohol abuse' (Pettinichio 1986), heavy metal music during the PMRC campaign was far from a fringe music. As Walser notes, in this period heavy metal was transformed from a subculture-identified music into the 'dominant genre of American music' (2014, 11), with *Rolling Stone* magazine pronouncing it the new 'mainstream of rock and roll' (2014, 3). But, as a marketing survey conducted during this same period found, while 'ten million people in the United States "like or strongly like" heavy metal'—a further 19 million strongly disliked it (cited in Walser 2014). Perhaps one of the reasons for this negative perception is that, unlike many other youth subcultures, the relationship between the music of heavy metal and its fandom has been central to its coherence as a youth formation, meaning that when it experienced a period of commercial success it still retained a subversive edge, despite its popularity.

Central to this subversive edge was a performative expression of hyper-masculinity, one that attempted to cohere a narrative of 'heroic' masculine virtuosity and control but which was subject to challenges within its own logic from glam, romance and androgynous styles, that signalled in their different ways, an instability to any masculinist narrative of certainty. For Walser (2014), the appeal of heavy metal in this period, was in how metal 'musicians and fans [...] developed tactics [and strategies] for modeling male power and control within the context of patriarchal culture' via 'enactions of masculinity', including 'varieties of misogyny as well as "exscription" of the feminine [...] supported by male, sometimes homo-erotic, bonding' (p. 110). Walser's (2014) exploration of these modes identifies: the misogyny of the 'male victim' ensnared by the dangerous sexuality of the 'femme fatale' in such songs as *In the Still of the Night* by Whitesnake; the *Nothing But A Good Time* androgyny and to-be-looked-at-sexual-display of glam-metal bands like Poison; and the 'romantic sincerity' projected by hard-rock/metal bands, like Bon Jovi, who began to soften their sound with ballads 'where the only mystical element was bourgeois love' (p. 120).

Previous work, such as Plantinga (2014) on the mockumentary *This is Spinal Tap* (1984), read this hyper-masculine display as an *over-conformity* to hegemonic masculinity, and identified the comedic aspects of such films as centring on the pathos of the central characters inability to recognise the impossibility, and indeed *absurdity*, of achieving the 'phallic mastery' required of the heavy metal performer. However, I argue that not only is a 'self-referential' humour central to the subcultural identity of heavy metal culture (Konecny 2014) and thereby a key factor in the affectivity of its filmic appeal to wider audiences, the over-investment of fans and musicians in the absurd and overblown narratives of mythological monsters, horror, the satanic, war and apocalyptic nemesis reflects a wider project of resistance that, drawing on a neglected aspect of Connell's (2005) hegemonic masculinity thesis, I want to describe as 'protest masculinity'.

The term 'protest masculinity' is variously employed to explain the aberrant behaviour towards the social compact that supports hegemonic masculinity, exhibited by males in habitual situations of unemployment or insecure work, males lacking a father figure in deprived households and those resisting the authority of other men in work situations or apprenticeships. Poynting defines it as 'compensatory claims to imagined powerfulness on the part of marginalised young men experiencing social injury at their lack of real power, expressed through a hypermasculine style' (2007, 511), while Gregory Wayne Walker argues: 'Protest masculinity is a gendered identity oriented to a protest of the relations of production and the ideal type of hegemonic masculinity' (2006, 5). Connell explores how various 'marginalised' masculinities, such as white Australian bikers, embrace a compensatory 'outlaw' masculinity and thereby make 'a claim to power where there are no real resources for power' (2005, 111). Connell's point is that these marginal men receive little benefit from the patriarchal dividend, while their attempts to resist the gender order bring them back into conflict with authority. Their choices are therefore limited: accept marginality and subordination, adopt a mode of conflict or seek to reject hegemonic masculinity.

From a macro socio-cultural, and indeed psychoanalytic perspective, heavy metal's 'protest masculinity' is rooted in a deeply sublimated resistance to regional and global *deindustrialisation* and the consequent cultural marginalisation of working class identities, particularly those identified with skilled manual work, which is not only 'magically' recovered (as the CCCS subcultural theorists would have it), but subject to multiple reinvestments over the years. Heavy metal's protest masculinity has become a complex cultural phenomenon that invites multiple readings, from the humorous to the profound, the subcultural to the 'universal'.

Oedipus Most Complex: Time-Travelling with Marty McFly and Bill & Ted

In the realm of popular culture this 'magical recovery' is most often dramatised as a teen-male Oedipus complex, where the central characters are consciously aware that they must challenge the male authority of their tyrannical and/or inept 'fathers' while trying to resist the (real or imagined) attentions of their mothers: 'She's your step mum, dude!', Ted repeatedly reminds Bill. This Oedipus complex is played out, often literally, through the role that heavy metal guitar culture plays in the lives of these teens. It is the key to shaping the future, as in *Bill and Ted,* or to reshaping the past so that it can become the future, as in *Back to the Future.* Of course, what is also recovered is a 'good' kind of patriarchal 'father' figure. For example, the central character of the breakthrough teen franchise *Back to the Future* (1985) is a conflicted male-teen who lives in suburbia, in a lower-middle-class family, and who is described by his school principal as a 'slacker' 'just like your father'. Marty McFly (Michael J. Fox) skateboards around his hometown and plays guitar in his band, the Pinheads. In the opening sequence of the film Marty plugs his guitar into Doc Brown's 1950s sci-fi console, turns the volume and distortion dials up to 'maximum' and then blows the main speaker cone and his own body across the room, with one touch of his magic pick. Looking back over his aviator shades at the broken speaker at the centre of the giant amp, Marty is heard to softly exclaim: 'Rock n roll!'. But he fails the school prom audition because the head of the assessment panel (played by Huey Lewis)[2] halts the band's performance, commenting: 'I'm afraid you're just too darn loud'.

In a key sequence towards the climax of the film, Marty—having played lead-guitar on the ballad that allows his Mom and Dad to kiss for the first time and thereby ensure his future existence—is then invited by the band leader and fictitious cousin of Chuck Berry (Marlon) to play another number. Reluctant at first, Marty then launches into Berry's *Johnny B. Goode* (1958), thereby introducing the all-black R&B band (who were booked to play an all-white fifties college prom night) to the 'new' genre of rock 'n' roll. But after the bridge, Marty unleashes a guitar solo 'from the future', which leads to the premature end of the song (as the band can no longer keep up) in a haze of feedback and wailing lead guitar: "I guess you guys aren't ready for that yet. But your kids are gonna love it," he says to the stunned audience. During the performance of this solo, Marty makes reference to many of the styles that define the guitar-centric culture of heavy metal (and its uneasy relationship to black music), including Berry's string bends, the speed-surfing guitar runs of Dick Dale, Jimi Hendrix's stage-craft and virtuosity, the aggressive power-chords of The Who and the neo-classical "tapping" of Eddie van Halen.[3] Much of this guitar repertoire can be found in the instrumental solo piece, 'Eruption', performed by one of the most celebrated metal guitarists, Eddie van Halen, which combines pentatonic blues 'licks', Chuck Berry-esque string bends and 'quotations' from well-known classical-violin primers, combined with 'fast picking and hammering', precise string-harmonics and 'dive bombs'.[4]

It is surely not a coincidence that in the opening sequence of *Bill & Ted's Excellent Adventure* (1989) the boy's dilemma is that their failure to make a promotional video for their band, the *Wyld Stallyns*, is because they can't play well enough; yet the purpose of the video is to enlist the help of 'guitar god', Eddie Van Halen to help them to achieve this aim. Not only does Ted 'steal' his father's keys, but Bill, in order to rescue his friend, phones the house pretending to be 'Officer Van Halen', saying the lost keys have been handed in to the local police station. At various points in the film, we are told by the 'good' father-figure, Rufus (George Carlin) (who has travelled back from the future to assist them), that the boy's guitar playing will 'get better', since without their 'future' music the new world order cannot come into being. Like *Back to the Future*, the key to achieving their mission is a time-travel machine.[5] However, first they must pass their history exam, or Ted will be packed off to the military as punishment for being a high school 'slacker'.

What follows are their adventures back in time to transport a number of 'historical' figures, including Billy the Kid, Napoleon, Genghis Kahn, Plato, Joan of Arc, Beethoven, Freud, Abraham Lincoln and some 'medieval babes' from the court of King John, to the Californian suburb of San Dimas, where they are introduced to the delights of the local shopping mall before appearing as guest speakers in their 'rock concert' themed, end-of-term presentation. During this postmodernist journey, the film takes every opportunity to reference heavy metal tropes, sometimes quite literally. For example, when hiding in knight's armour, attempting to rescue the medieval teen 'babes' who have been promised in marriage, the boys find it difficult to walk:

Ted: 'Bill'
Bill: 'What?'

Ted: 'These are heavy'
Bill: 'Yea, heavy metal!'

When attempting to woo the young women, Ted quotes lyrics from the power-ballad 'Every Rose Has Its Thorn' by Poison. When their rescue plan is exposed, the King's henchmen order that they be placed in an 'Iron Maiden', to which they boys reply: 'Excellent!' (accompanied by air-guitar). When introducing the philosopher Socrates to the San Dimas high school graduates, Ted declares: 'He was the teacher of Plato, who was in turn the teacher of Aristotle and like Ozzy Osbourne, was repeatedly accused of corruption of the young'.[6]

For I.Q. Hunter (1996), Bill and Ted are part of a 'mini-genre' of American cinema: the Dumb White Guy Movie. Owing something to anarchic gross-out comedies like *Porky's* (1981) and *National Lampoon's Animal House* (1978), 'films such as *Wayne's World, Forrest Gump, Dumb and Dumber, Airheads* and the TV show *Beavis and Butthead* glorify the Dumb White Guy as an all-American cultural hero' (p. 111). But rather than viewing them as 'lurid symptoms of anomie and cultural degeneration' or as 'boorish manifestations of a white male backlash', for Hunter, they represent the 'simultaneous triumph of consumer capitalism and American popular culture', as predicted by Fukuyama in his 'end of history' thesis (1996, 111). Despite this somewhat sweeping claim, for Hunter the 'key joke' of the film is that the 'salvational music' of the *Wyld Stallyns*, that will put 'an end to war and poverty', align the planets and lead to 'communication with aliens' from the future, 'is white heavy metal, the most despised and unhip (and monocultural) of genres' (p. 123). What Hunter fails to note however is the overriding 'dialogic' conversation that the film has with heavy metal youth culture, transforming an outsider subculture into a satirical but ultimately likeable set of characterisations, that are then able to comment on contemporary youth experience more generally. Relevant here is that the scriptwriters originally envisaged Bill S. Preston, Esquire and Ted Theodore Logan as '14-year-old skinny guys, with low-rider bellbottoms and heavy metal T-shirts' (Quoted in Freeman 2014). In fact, it appears that an early scene was scripted of Bill and Ted walking past a group of popular kids who 'hated them'. However, once Alex Winter and Keanu Reeves were recruited into the project, this scenario was dropped (Freeman 2014).

Bangers, Thrashers and Burnouts:
The Mainstreaming of Heavy Metal Character Tropes

In many key respects, heavy metal is paradigmatic of post-subcultural
youth styles that followed in the wake of punk, such as goth, grunge,
industrial/dance, rap and hip-hop, styles that have a more complex relationship to the commodity form than simply *appropriation* (Brown 2007).
What this means is that the integrity and identity of the subculture and the
kind of youth identities that it allows is a function of its passionate but
conflicted relationship to the *authenticity* of its commodity forms, to the
extent that they are seen to truly 'represent' metal's subterranean values.
At the same time, like the working-class subcultures of teds, mods and
skins celebrated by the CCCS school, heavy metal culture is grounded in
a classed cultural experience, one that defines the biographies of its origi-
nator bands (Black Sabbath, Judas Priest, Budgie, Deep Purple, Uriah
Heep), as well as providing the mythological canvas upon which the genre
is able to transform the overwhelming loudness of its industrial origin
environment into a metrically 'heavy' expressive musical form. But it is
one that has the requisite sonic weight to carry other-worldly narratives
and flights of musical fantasy that darkly embrace human corruption, the
devil, evil and hell on earth. It is not surprising then that histories of the
remarkable longevity of the genre demonstrate that heavy metal culture is
articulated in the space between industry and 'underground', between the
authentic and 'sell out', where the authentic forms of heavy metal music
are often paradoxically the most theatrical, overblown and ridiculous,
either in their borrowings from classical music and literature, pursuit of
overwhelming musical loudness and dramatic 'OTT' ('over the top') performances (Brown 2015).

   In this respect, it is important to recognise that the 'comedic' conventions and representations of heavy metal on film cannot simply be interpreted as an industry/hegemonic attempt to render the genre 'ridiculous',
but rather, they are reflective of these long-standing tensions and contradictions. While the genre of the teen film is certainly a relevant framework
for understanding the production cycle that I examine here, and the history of exploitation and distortion that often accompanies such productions (Shary 2005), by the mid-eighties the Hollywood producers of this
popular genre were increasingly aware of the need to address particular
youth identities in ways that were seen to be credible, often because the
success or failure of such films depended on a perception of 'authenticity'

among the increasingly cynical and segmented youth consumer audiences such productions were marketed at. So, despite the fact that many of the films are comedic, such comedy is informed by a satirical intelligence, which both laughs at but also celebrates its object of mirth.

The significance then of the emergence of a number of documentaries, feature films and *mockumentaries*, from the mid-1980s to the early 1990s, is in how such productions make reference to and articulate the character of the teen (or kidult) 'metalhead' and the ways in which they are defined by a heavy metal culture that inform their collective 'values' and shared 'norms' of behaviour. Thus, whether they are aspiring bands (actual or fictional) or male-buddies, such as Bill and Ted, Wayne and Garth or Jay and Silent Bob, they consistently display and embrace a set of values that 'mark' them out as a generational cohort, as bangers, thrashers, slackers or burnouts. This is so for argot ('this sucks', 'party on', 'excellent'), gestures, (air-guitar, headbanging, the horns), shared musical references (AC/DC, Metallica, Black Sabbath, Megadeth, Scorpions, Van Halen), mode of dress (long hair, denims, patches, t-shirts, trainers), socioeconomic circumstance (lower middle-class, skilled or semi-skilled working class), urban locations (suburbia), and social and 'political' demeanour (school-slacker, college-dropout, dead-end-job employee). Central to this also are modes of consumption, particularly styles and their typical 'youth' locations (the shopping mall, the fast-food takeaway, the chain store, college campus), but also the search for identity and authenticity where it seems to be most absent, in the midst of youth consumer capitalism.

"WE'RE NOT WORTHY": THE SATIRICAL RELATIONSHIP OF WAYNE'S WORLD TO HEAVY METAL CULTURE

'Let me bring you up to speed. My name is Wayne Campbell. I live in Aurora, Illinois, which is a suburb of Chicago—excellent. I've had plenty of joe-jobs; nothing I'd call a career. Let me put it this way: I have an extensive collection of nametags and hairnets. Ok, so I still live with my parents, which I admit is bogus and sad. However, I do have a cable access show, and I still know how to party. But what I'd really like is to do Wayne's World for a living. It might happen. Yeah, and monkeys might fly out of my butt' (*Wayne's World*, 1992).

Drawing on the character of Wayne, the fast-talking, wise-cracking, heavy metal kidult, who with his 'excellent' friend, Garth, hosts his own 'open access' cable television show from his mum's basement, this hugely successful mainstream film, and it sequel, offers an insight into heavy metal fandom and its subcultural tropes, which is both celebratory of the guitar-gods and bands that define the genre, while poking fun at big business and 'lame' male figures of authority who fail to respect its integrity or seek to exploit it. So strikingly original was this characterisation of North American, male-teen suburban culture in the mid-1980s that it has found its way into rock iconography and *You Tube* fandom, particularly the syn-chronised head-banging that accompanies *that riff* from Queen's 'Bohemian Rhapsody', when Wayne, Garth and partied-out friends, 'head-bang' in unison, from the seats of their car, in the famous opening sequence of the movie.

Mike Myers, who created the comedy skit for *Saturday Night Live* and co-wrote and starred in the film, observes: 'Wayne's world is the subur-ban, adolescent, North American, heavy metal experience as I knew it in the mid-70s, growing up in Scarborough, Ontario, which is a suburb of Toronto, Canada'.[7] Rob Lowe, who plays the 'sleazy TV exec' (Benjamin Kane), who wants to transform Wayne and Garth's public-access cable show into a commercially sponsored TV show in order to steal Wayne's musician girlfriend, has observed:

> *Wayne's World* takes place in Aurora, Illinois, and I grew up in Dayton, Ohio. So, it's basically the same place. I grew up in downstairs, naugahyde-panelled basements with bean bag chairs and really bad shag carpeting with a TV that had four legs, and that gold mesh over the speaker [...] so I related to *Wayne's World*. Wayne's World was real to me'.[8]

Although the plot involves the teen-film conventions of boy-meets-girl, loses her to the suave but cynical baddie, falls out with his best friend, but then in the last reel the buddies unite in a mission to save the heroine and expose the duplicity of the baddies, the film spoofs these conventions along the way, and especially in the finale, where different postmodernist endings are enacted, including references to *Scooby Doo* and other TV shows. However, from the opening scenes, the film spends time establishing the characters, Wayne and Garth and their friends, as 'kidults' who are defined by their teen allegiance to heavy metal music culture and their patterns of symbolic consumption amongst the fast-food takeaways, shopping malls and drive-ins of middle-America suburbia. The satirical intent of the film and the source of its inclusionary humour are established from the outset as

Wayne speaks direct-to-the-camera, introducing himself and then his bespectacled 'best friend' Garth, who pulls up outside his house in the 'Mirthmobile' (a 1976 AMC Pacer, with flame body work). Once in the front seat, the eponymous hero slots a cassette tape into the dashboard player and announces to his metal dudes: 'I think we'll go with a little *Bohemian Rhapsody*, gentlemen'. 'Good, call' replies Garth. This classic hard rock soundtrack then accompanies the characters as they drive into the heart of teen suburban uptown, singing along to Wayne's lead, as the camera frames the neon logos and signs of shops, bars and take-out venues.

This soundtrack is interrupted twice: first when Wayne and Garth stop to rescue a fellow metalhead (wearing a Deep Purple t-shirt): 'Phil, what are you doing here. You're all partied out, man—again'. Once Wayne has given Garth a 'no puke guarantee', their friend is taken on board where the Queen song momentarily revives him. After the headbanging sequence, the Pacer pauses so that Wayne can gaze into the window of the local guitar store, where a white 1964 Stratocaster is on display. Garth, speaks direct to camera: 'He does this every Friday night'. And then to his friend: 'Stop torturing yourself, man. You'll never afford it. Live in the now.' But Wayne, lost in a mystical reverie (accompanied by ethereal music), turns to camera and says: 'It will be mine. Oh yes. It will be mine'. Later, after a visit to their favourite donut 'munch-bar' (where the waitress says: 'Don't you guys ever get tired of ordering the same thing' and they all reply: 'No'), we move on to the Gasworks (where Meatloaf is a bouncer). 'An excellent heavy metal bar and always a babe-fest', declares Wayne. It is here that Wayne falls instantly in love with Cassandra, the lead singer and bassist of the band: 'She's a babe. Schwing. Yady-yady-yah. Hugh'. And the plot set-up of the film is complete, as Wayne speaks to camera: 'She will be mine. O yes, she will be mine.

The 'protest masculinity' that informs the humor of the film, centrally involves deflating the pretensions of male authority figures, employing 'toilet jokes' and 'juvenile' sexual innuendo. For example, when the arcade owner and sponsor, Noah Vanderhoff (Brian Doyle-Murray), tries to take over a Wayne's World slot, Wayne holds up a card to camera, that points in his direction, declaring: 'This man sucks goats. I have proof', before hitting him with his favorite put-down:

Wayne: 'All I have to say about that is: ass-sphincter-says-what.'
Noah: 'What?'
Wayne: 'Exactly!'

Like Bill and Ted, Wayne and Garth share a modified 'surfer' or 'valley' speak idiolect, which includes the ubiquitous: 'Excellent. Party on', 'No way. Yes, way', 'Bogus' and the double-negative qualifier, 'Not'; as well as a 'babe' lexicon: Robo-babe, Babe-licious, Fox, Babe-raham Lincoln, and so on. However, the phrase 'we're not worthy' is key to the alternative value structure of their heavy metal fandom. This phrase, accompanied by much bowing and scraping, is reserved for 'name' hard rock and heavy metal musicians. It is also notable that whenever Wayne interviews such musicians he always throws in a 'serious' question that the musicians are (surprisingly) able to answer in great detail. As for example,

Wayne:	'So, do you come to Milwaukee often?'
Alice Cooper:	'Well, I'm a regular visitor here, but Milwaukee has certainly had its share of visitors. The French missionaries and explorers were coming here as early as the late 1600s to trade with the Native Americans.'
Pete (band member):	'In fact, isn't "Milwaukee" an Indian name?'
Alice Cooper:	'Yes, Pete, it is. Actually, it's pronounced "mill-e-wah-que" which is Algonquin for "the good land."'
Wayne:	'I was not aware of that. Say, does this guy know how to party or what?'

The satirical intelligence then that informs *Wayne's World* offers the audience an insight into a youth subculture that has a set of values that are rooted in notions of authenticity, drawn from the music and style-culture of heavy metal fandom. While we are able to laugh at how Wayne and Garth reflect the sexual fantasies and insecurities of male-teens who are not quite adults, as in the subplots of Garth's late puberty and Wayne's 'psycho' ex-girlfriend, it is ultimately their naïve commitment to their subcultural world that gives them the strength to contest the pomposity and power of male authority figures who seek to exploit it and them. While it could be argued that the subculture it portrays is one that is easily accessible to youth (and adult) audiences who 'recognise' the bands, and the style and argot the film exaggerates for comic effect what the film ultimately celebrates is the *authenticity* of the youth cultural experience itself.

CONCLUSION

As Best and Kellner (1998) note 'the popularity of heavy metal for over two decades [...] requires sociological scrutiny in an era of quick turnover of musical fads' (p. 98). However, except for a passing reference to Donna Gaine's book, *Teenage Wasteland* (1991), they fail to offer such a scrutiny. As I have argued here, the demonisation of heavy metal youth culture in the 1984–1991 period in North America not only coincides with the period of its most sustained chart success, it is also a period in which the image of the male metalhead conveyed in moral panic media is paradoxically transformed into a series of teen-buddy characters, most notably Bill and Ted, and Wayne and Garth, that are central to the success of a string of Hollywood teen-comedy films and their sequels. While classic models of subcultural theory argue that periods of youth moral panic are accompanied by a process of mainstreaming that effectively make 'safe' the threat such youth cultures are seen to pose to dominant culture, in the case of heavy metal it could be argued that it is the mainstreaming of heavy metal music in this period that provokes the panic in the first place. Whatever is the case, it is surely the popularity of heavy metal music culture among a large section of North American youth that is the motive for scriptwriters and film producers in this period to develop these teen-comedy projects. The fact that such films are comedies, where the object of mirth is the central characters and their relationship to heavy metal culture, might suggest that the role of satire here is to 'make safe' a troubling youth culture by simplifying and distorting it using established comedic conventions. But, as we have seen, although the films do simplify the musical references of heavy metal culture, a form of 'protest masculinity' is central to the plot and narratives of such films, allowing the central male-metalhead 'loser' characters to triumph against hegemonic forms of male authority that are depicted as pompous, oppressive and corrupt. However, the answer as to why such films were popular with a cross section of teen and adult audiences is unquestionably the way(s) in which heavy metal music and culture provides Bill and Ted, and Wayne and Garth, with a unique vocabulary, shared sense of humour, core values and group identity that informs their world view and consumer lifestyle, so that in a teen world of fads and fashions they communicate a taste-culture that has a strong sense of continuity and authenticity.

NOTES

1. Interview from the documentary film *The Decline of Western Civilization, Part II: The Metal Years* (1988).
2. Of Huey Lewis and the News, whose 1985 hit 'The Power of Love', features in the film. Ironically, the number the band are performing is a 'heavy metal version' of this song.
3. Michael J. Fox confirms (2002 DVD Feature) that the choreography for this sequence was conceived as a homage to these 'guitar heroes'.
4. The band Van Halen are also named on a cassette tape of 'future music' that Marty plays to George McFly (Crispin Glover), while pretending to be an alien visitor to earth, to command him to take his future mother, Lorraine (Lea Thompson) to the Prom in order to break the oedipal-complex he finds himself trapped within.
5. The time machine originally scripted was a 1969 Chevrolet van, not a Phone Booth. But the director (Stephen Hereck) felt this was too *Scooby Do* and also *Back to the Future* had just come out, featuring the DeLorean car.
6. In the sequel, *Bogus Journey* (1991), the 'dead' Bill & Ted have a great deal of fun with their guide Death (the Grim Reaper, a pastiche of the Bergman character): 'Ted, don't fear the reaper.' Death: 'I heard that.'
7. Interview included with 2001 DVD of the film.
8. Interview (as above).

REFERENCES

Best, Steven and Kellner, Douglas. 1998. "Beavis and Butt-head: No future for postmodern youth." In *Youth Culture: Identity in a Postmodern World*, ed. Jonathon. S. Epstein. Malden, Mass, Oxford: Blackwell, pp. 74–99.

Brown, Andy R. 2015. "Everything louder than everyone else: the origins and persistence of heavy metal music and its global cultural impact." In *The SAGE Handbook of Popular Music*, eds. Andy Bennett and Steve Wacksman. London: Sage, pp. 261–277.

Brown, Andy R. 2013. "Suicide Solutions? Or, how the emo class of 2008 were able to contest their media demonization, whereas the headbangers, burnouts or children of ZoSo generation were not." In *Heavy Metal: Controversies and Countercultures*, eds. Titus Hjelm, Keith Kahn-Harris and Mark Levine. Sheffield: Equinox, pp. 17–35.

Brown, Andy R. 2007. "Rethinking the subcultural commodity: The case of heavy metal t-shirt cultures." In *Youth Cultures: Scenes, Subcultures and Tribes*, eds. Paul Hodkinson and Wolfgang Deicke. London: Routledge, pp. 63–78.

Brown, Andy R. 2003. "Heavy Metal and Subcultural Theory: A Paradigmatic Case of Neglect?" In *The Post-Subcultures Reader*, eds. David Muggleton and Rupert Weinzierl. London: Berg, pp. 209–222.

Cashmore, Ellis. 1984. *No Future*. London: Heinemann.

Chastagner, Claude. 1999. "The Parents' Music Resource Centre: From Information to Censorship" *Popular Music*, 18(2): 179–92.

Christenson Lewis, Peter. (1992) "The Effects of Parent Advisory Labels on Adolescent Music Preferences," *Journal of Communication*, 42(1): 106–113.

Connell, Raewyn. 2005. *Masculinities*, 2nd edition. Cambridge: Polity.

Freeman, Hadley. 2014. "Bill & Ted's 25th birthday: party on, dudes!," April 17: https://www.theguardian.com/film/2014/apr/17/bill-and-ted-25th-birthday-party-on (accessed 2 Oct 2016).

Gaines, Donna 1991. *Teenage Wasteland: Suburbia's Dead End Kids*. Chicago: University of Chicago Press.

Hebdige, Dick. 1979. *Subculture: The Meaning of Style*. London: Routledge.

Hunter, Ian Q. 1996. "Capitalism Most Triumphant: Bill & Ted's Excellent History Lesson." In *Pulping Fictions: Consuming Culture across the Literature/Media Divide*, eds, Deborah. Cartmell, Ian. Q. Hunter & Imelda. Whelehan. London: Pluto Press, pp. 111–124.

Konecny, Brandon. 2014. "Heavy Metal Monsters!: Rudctio ad Ridiculum and the 1980s Heavy Metal Horror Cycle," *Film Matters* (Spring) pp. 13–18.

Martin, Linda & Segrave, Kerry. 1993. *Anti-Rock: The Opposition to Rock 'n' Roll*. Cambridge: Da Capo Press.

Pettinichio, Darlyne. 1986. *The Back in Control Centre Presents the Punk Rock and Heavy Metal Handbook*. Fullerton, CA: Back in Control.

Plantinga, Carl. 2014. "Gender, Power, and a Cucumber: Satirizing Masculinity in This Is Spinal Tap." In *Documenting the Documentary: Close Readings of Documentary Film and Video* eds. Barry Keith Grant and Jeannette Sloniowski. Detroit: Wayne State University Press, pp. 339–355.

Poynting, Scott. 2007. "Protest Masculinities." In *Encyclopedia on Men and Masculinities*, eds. Michael Flood, Judith. K. Gardiner, Bob Pease & Keith Pringle. London: Routledge, pp. 511–12.

Raschke, Carl A. 1990. *Painted black: from drug killings to heavy metal: the alarming true story of how Satanism is terrorizing our communities*. San Francisco: Harper and Row.

Shary, Timothy. 2005. *Teen Movies: American Youth on Screen*. London: Wallflower.

The Times Diary. 1982. 'A Head Start on a New Beat Generation', 5th April, 1982.

Walker, Gregory W. 2006. "Disciplining Protest Masculinity," *Men and Masculinities*, 9:1, pp. 5–22.

Walser, Robert. 2014. *Running with the Devil: Power, Gender and Madness in Heavy Metal Music*. Hanover: University Press of New England.

Weinstein, Deena. 2000. *Heavy Metal: The Music and its Culture*. Cambridge: Da Capo Press.

Don't Look Back in Anger: Manchester, *Supersonic* and *Made of Stone*

Beth Johnson

The last five years has seen the release of two 'rockumentary films'—*The Stone Roses: Made of Stone* (Dir. Shane Meadows, 2013) and *Oasis: Supersonic* (Dir. Mat Whitecross, 2016)—which will be the central focus of this chapter. Both documentaries function to bring their respective Mancunian British bands (who originally found popularity in the 1980s and 1990s) back into contemporary cultural focus via their positioning of the pre-digital 80s and 90s as authentic subcultural music eras. Whilst this framing provides a significant degree of similarity, there are clear differences between the texts. While *Made of Stone* ultimately traces the revival and tour of The Stone Roses since their 2011 reformation, *Supersonic* uses the present and, I will argue, draws on a recent trend for nostalgia as a springboard to look back at the past.

The release dates of these rockumentaries coincide more broadly with a recent indie 'revival' trend in the cultural public sphere evidenced through reformations of bands such as James, Republica, Pulp, Cast and Blur. Critical responses from the national, web and music press toward revival and retro culture, coupled with what Paul Long and Jez Collins (2018) have referred to as the 'mythologizing of certain cities and bands as musically exceptional' have been largely unfavourable and even antagonistic. Drawing on the

B. Johnson (✉)
University of Leeds, Leeds, UK

© The Author(s) 2018   127
N. Bentley et al. (eds.), *Youth Subcultures in Fiction, Film and
Other Media*, Palgrave Studies in the History of Subcultures and
Popular Music, https://doi.org/10.1007/978-3-319-73189-6_8

legacy of FAC51 (Manchester's original 'Factory Records') and in response
to the building's 2010 reinvention as a three-floor nightclub, FAC251, run
by Peter Hook and club operators Tokyo Industries, an anonymous website
branded 'FUC51: Manchester Deniers' carried the following introduction:

> Manchester will have you believe it is a forward-thinking city. A Northern
> Republic standing up against the tide of Londoncentric nonsense. However,
> what Manchester fails to realise is that it cannot ever move forward because
> it is so determined to rest on recent history. While slating Liverpool for
> being a Beatle-museum, Mancs are pretending it's 1988. Look around the
> city and you're given constant reminders of Factory Records, The Haçienda,
> The Stone Roses, The Smiths, Acid House, New Order, Joy Division and…
> you get the idea. Our aim is to act as snipers to this relentless wave of bor-
> rowed nostalgia that continues to make stars of Madchester hangers-on and
> people steeped in yesteryear. We'll tear the memories to pieces, we'll show
> you where Manchester is getting it right, we'll harangue all that wallow in
> yellow and black hatchings and those that rifle the pocket of Wilson's corpse.
> (Anon, 2010)

While the content of the introduction is crafted with some humour, the
tone is distinctly serious, drawing out debates around heritage, nostalgia,
cultural value and 'bad' commerce. History, is seemingly, having an identity crisis. In this sense, we can see that retro-tours and reformations
alongside music city myths—have been, at least by some, looked back on
in anger, accused of either 'cashing in' or 'blocking' new creatives. In
addition, in the sphere of academia, the music revival trend as well as a
more general leaning toward the retro in the fields of fashion, art and
design has culminated in the production of various studies such as Svetlana
Boym's *The Future of Nostalgia* (2001), Elizabeth Guffey's *Retro: The
Culture of Revival* (2006), Simon Reynolds' recent *Retromania: Pop
Culture's Addiction to its Own Past* (2011) and Owen Hatherley's *The
Ministry of Nostalgia: Consuming Austerity* (2017). While these texts discuss and theorize ideas around retro and nostalgia in a variety of ways and
from a variety of different viewpoints, they have, alongside public
responses, worked toward producing a critical mass of information about
the intertwining of the recent past, the present and the future, determin-
ing more than ever that history is constantly 'in the making'.

Drawing on the work of Rupa Huq (2006), Keith Beattie (2008), Paul
Long and Jez Collins (2018), this chapter engages with broad questions of
representation and identity, particularly in relation to place, youth-culture,

gender and class. It also aims to consider specific issues in relation to the two documentary texts at its heart, thinking through questions such as: how does the medium of film work to position The Stone Roses and Oasis as 'authentic' Mancunian creatives? What cultural and social impulses align the directors of the documentaries and the bands that they chronicle? In what ways do the documentaries position the bands as relevant in and to the regional and national music scene of the present? How and via what aesthetic methods and modes do the films attempt to mythologise the recent past?

SITUATING THE BANDS AND SETTING THE 'SCENE': A BRIEF HISTORY

UK, and more specifically Manchester-based band The Stone Roses formed as a five-piece in 1983/1984 and released a number of singles prior to being signed in 1988/1989 to Zomba subsidiary, Silvertone Records on a famously exploitative eight-album deal. The release of their first self-titled album in 1989 was a success and their single, Fools Gold, reached number eight in the UK music charts. The same year the band won four accolades at the NME Awards, including Band of the Year and Single of the Year. 1990 saw The Stone Roses play at Spike Island and their status as authentic stars—articulate young Northern men who had something alternative to say or sing and who refused to 'know their place' in class terms—was seemingly cemented. Shortly afterwards, the band tried to withdraw from their contract and sign with Geffen Records. This action marked the start of a protracted legal battle with Zomba which blocked The Stone Roses from working on a second album for three years. Their next album, entitled *Second Coming*, was released in 1994 to a rather more muted reception. In 1995, Reni (the band's drummer) left the band. In 1996 the band finally broke up when John Squire (lead guitarist and songwriter alongside lead singer Ian Brown) left the band following a row with Brown. Sixteen years later The Stone Roses announced their resurrection—a second or indeed third coming. Two years later in 2013, the documentary *The Stone Roses: Made of Stone* was released, chronicling their reformation.

Established in 1991 and citing The Stone Roses and The Beatles amongst their musical influences, Oasis—a five-piece Mancunian guitar band—were signed to the independent label Creation Records in 1993.

Made up (initially) of Noel Gallagher (lead guitarist), Liam Gallagher (lead singer), Paul McGuigan (bass guitar), Paul Arthurs (rhythm and lead guitar) and Tony McCarroll (drums and percussion), Oasis worked incessantly, and 1994 and 1995 saw the release of two key albums, the first *Definitely Maybe* and the second, *What's the Story Morning Glory*. Both albums attained critical acclaim, and like The Stone Roses, Oasis's music spoke of British culture, difference, youth and class. Reaching the height of their fame in 1996 with two sell-out gigs at Knebworth attended by over 250,000 fans, the BBC recently described the concerts as 'era defining'.[1] Continuing to make music for a further 13 years, the band finally broke up in 2009 after a much-publicized spat between brothers—songwriter and front man respectively—Noel and Liam Gallagher. While Oasis have not reformed, both brothers have fuelled press speculation about the possibility, particularly amidst the reformation trend, and substantiating this, 2016 saw the release of *Oasis: Supersonic,* a documentary charting the band's rise to international stardom.

Narrative Openings

Despite their different temporal points of focus, both documentaries open with sensuous and visceral stylistic sequences. *Made of Stone* begins with a heady, slow-motion, black-and-white close-up of Ian Brown waving to fans, backed by an audio recording of Alfred Hitchcock defining happiness. Brown's face is clearly that of the present and thus the opening situates the time as 'now', documenting and dramatizing the emotional response of fans to Brown and his to them. In contrast, *Supersonic* opens with a question heard in voiceover: 'What's happened to the band in the last three years?' to which Liam Gallagher replies: 'It's a big question, and it deserves a big answer.' While indeed the question is still relevant in the present day (particularly in light of the revival trend), the crackle of the audio designates the interview as one from the past. This moment is then followed up with the distinctive voice of British radio DJ Jo Whiley designating Knebworth as the 'live gig of the decade', after which a male commentator notes that 'In three years Oasis have gone from being a new signing to being rock's true giants'. The visuals cut to helicopter footage of Knebworth, then to Oasis taking to the stage, then Liam singing/snarling the first lines of Columbia: 'There we were, now here we are. All this confusion, nothing's the same to me.' The lyrics here work to underscore the reflective nature of the rockumentary, playing with and vocalising the temporal shifts between the then and the now of Oasis. This schismatic opening operates both as an introduction to the contemporary confusion around Oasis's identity (provoking a 'What's the story?' now, question) and figuratively making a space in the present for past experiences and feelings to resurface. While the troubled contemporary status of the band implies a point of tension, the next cut—to an ecstatic Knebworth audience—serves to reinscribe the intense visualisation of fandom.

The highlighting of the visual attraction of bands is not unusual for rockumentary texts. Such spectacular openings are, particularly in the case of *Made of Stone*, further intensified by stylised slow motion, evoking a fantastical and hallucinatory visual quality for the viewer. What both texts make clear from the outset however is not only the importance of fandom to the evolving histories of the bands, but the importance of the *experience* of fandom as a cultural and dramatic high—a defining and intense moment in the making of identity. In both texts the openings (which function through foregrounding aesthetic tensions to highlight both the past as a moment in time and as a contemporary experience), underscore the capacities of visual images and sounds to compose identities in ways that not only perform, but also critique the processes of representation. It is in the same vein that I offer this chapter and the analysis that follows.

GENRE IDENTITY: WHAT'S IN A NAME?

The notion of identity is crucial to this chapter, and it is identity-work that I want to pick up on here to explicate and think through the geographical, generic and cultural labels assigned to the music of The Stone Roses and Oasis. As bands who emerged on the British music scene in the 1980s and 1990s, their music has been variously categorized as 'indie', 'baggy', 'Britpop' and 'Madchester'. In opposition to mainstream music, that which is 'indie', as Wendy Fonarow (2006, 66) notes, can be understood as 'intimate, personal, and modest, on a small scale and about specificity; it is authentic, lean and local.' While such a nuanced description befits much indie music, it is, arguably, 'out of place' when applied to the 1980s and 1990s bands that are central to this chapter—The Stone Roses and Oasis. Though, as Rupa Huq notes in *Beyond Subculture*, it is important to recognise the industry shift of the 1990s in which many indie bands were "poached' away from their earlier contractual homes' (2006, 155), another reason for the lack of fit between Fonarow's definition of 'indie' and the bands central to this chapter relates to the fact that while the style and ethos of The Stone Roses and Oasis may have started out as 'indie', their success on the indie scene worked to situate them as 'large-scale cool', providing them with subcultural capital that had significant commercial value. This coolness and the bands' success for the record labels Zomba and Creation gave them a new and precarious identity, somewhere between the indie/major label polarity, resulting in the situation that 'by the time Oasis became the UK's biggest band around 1996, the underground had become the overground' (Huq 2006, 155).

The 'baggy' label was one associated with the place of Manchester in the late 1980s and referred to both a sound and an oversized style of clothing. In general terms, the 'baggy' sound was made up of a combination of funk, psychedelia, house music and guitar rock.[2] The clothing style was more literal, encompassing a retro 1960s type of 'hippie' look, with baggy or bellbottomed jeans, oversized and brightly coloured t-shirts or casual style tops (frequently football shirts). Indeed, clothing and this 'look' or fashion style can be understood as an outward sign/symbol of association with the Mancunian music scene—and one through which working-class, masculinist identity is brought to the fore. Furthermore, the look can also be linked to the retro and nostalgic resurgence of both bands aided, for example, by the launch of the fashion chain Pretty Green, founded in 2009 by Liam Gallagher. As a brand, Pretty Green specialises in menswear, particular 1960s psychedelic shirts and 'casual style' tops—representing a look and feel associated with the band. This look is reproduced in the décor of the stores, which all feature neon 'stage' lighting signs and use guitars and vinyl LPs to adorn the walls. In terms of marketing, music identity heritage is pushed front and centre. The Pretty Green website states: 'Since the birth of rock 'n' roll in the late 1950s, British street culture has been influencing fashion and music worldwide. Pretty Green has an authenticity borne of a deep understanding of that culture and the things that make it relevant today.'[3]

Both the working-class identity and pluralism that can be understood as central to the 'baggy' label can also be extended to the political aims of The Stone Roses and Oasis. As Dave Haslam (2000, 180) notes: 'Ian Brown put a positive political spin on the spirit of the musical times. He was all for breaking down barriers and opening minds [...] In May 1988 The Stone Roses played [...] at an anti-Clause 28 benefit [and] two days later he went on the affiliated march and rally in Albert Square.' The baggy label was and still is particularly interesting in relation to both speaking of and to the pluralism of the music scene in Manchester.

Problematically, the music of The Stone Roses and Oasis has often been considered in identity terms as male, straight, white and aggressively British (more specifically English)—and therefore as limited, purposefully disengaged from both differing gender and sexual identities and what David Hesmondhalgh (2001, 278) refers to as 'a cosmopolitan interaction with other cultures'. Ian Brown, John Squire and the Gallagher brothers have been critical of such misunderstandings. In *Made of Stone*, Brown carefully explains that his decision to be a singer in a band was influenced by African-American R&B and rock singer Geno Washington, who, at a party in Brown's run-down flat in Hulme in 1983, told him "You're a star, you're a star. You should be a singer." Speaking to *Rolling Stone* in 1990 Brown, noting the importance of non-white and non-British music lamented: 'I think pop music was saved by the advent of acid house and rap because whites have done nothing for ten years.'[4] This clear engagement with non-white music, and Brown's refusal to be situated as a single type of musician influenced by a narrow array of white British heritage, speaks to an attitude of plurality.

The faux nationalist (and more specifically English) locating of The Stone Roses and their music can also be (albeit wrongly) extended to Oasis, whose music is commonly defined as 'Britpop'. In 2014 the BBC celebrated '20 years of Britpop' with a week of shows across UK television and radio including archived interviews, contemporary reflections, an online image gallery and a specially designated webpage featuring a new photography exhibition on Oasis announcing 'Britpop is Back'.[5] The tagline 'Britpop is Back' was of course specific to the BBC's timeline of 'Britpop', a genre to which they accorded a starting date of 1994 with Suede's Brett Anderson's appearance on the cover of *VOX*. What was not mentioned by the BBC in relation to this issue of *VOX* (Issue 42, 3rd March, 1994), which they pictured, was the other image that takes up space on the front cover—that of The Stone Roses, covered in grey, pollock style paint with the adjacent tag 'Return to MADCHESTER'. Indeed, this talk or title of return and of 'Madchester' seems particularly apt not only as a headline in 1994 (The Stone Roses second coming), but as a headline of the present. Arguably, the 'mad' in Madchester not only operates as an indicator of the hedonism associated with the Mancunian music scene in the late 1980s and early 1990s, but as a present form of protest, making visible the limitations and problematic appropriations of 'new laddism' in defining the Manchester scene. In addition, at the height of their Britpop fame in 1995, Oasis rejected claims that they would record a song for the England football team who were due to compete in Euro'96 with Noel robustly asserting, 'Over my dead body, we're Irish.'[6] **Mad**chester is not **Man**chester. It is, rather, a jumping off point, a place from which music can start to look beyond its immediate locale and value a new type of identity formation that embraces and acknowledges both its own roots and the place of others in creating new sounds, new vibes, new genres and new identities.

The problematisation of the term 'Britpop' has also been discussed by other cultural commentators. In his chapter on 'British Popular Music and National Identity', Hesmondhalgh notes that:

> Britpop has caused some confusion. The term was generated within one particular genre—indie/alternative rock—to describe a tradition of Britishness in popular music [...] Britpop was never, in any sense, a *movement* with common artistic aims. Nor can Britpop usefully be thought of as a musical genre [...] Britpop is best understood, instead, as a *discourse*: a group of utterances and statements that have a significant role in organizing understanding in the social realm. And what Britpop discourse did was to construct a tradition of quintessentially British and/or English music that distorted and simplified British musical culture. (2001, 276)

This British musical culture was however, as Huq (2006) suggests, already nostalgic for a past moment of glory even if it was enlisted to 'Cool Britannia'. Akin to Hesmondhalgh however, my aim here is to point to the politics and problems of labelling and think through the ways in which *Made of Stone* and *Supersonic* explore the nationalist discourses that have, at times, been associated with the bands that they represent. This sort of identity work seems particularly apt in the present moment as the 2016 British vote for Brexit and the rise of right-wing politics in Europe and beyond could make easy work out of suggesting that the revival of 1980s and 1990s music could be interpreted as part of a British, and more specifically English, resurgence of colonialist, euro-sceptic and/or hard-right attitudes. Though certain political commentators such as Conservative MP John Redwood sought in his 1996 article 'There's Always England' to affiliate Britpop music with right-wing values, I want to suggest that as in 1996, when this notion was popularly derided, the recent revival trend is part of a distinctly different cultural and political tack. The contemporary indie revival is not a return to white noise, but is rather an attempt to make visible a more authentic era *in* and idea *of* music and identity formation, prior to the digital music revolution.

That is not to say that the bands central to this chapter did not perform problematic rock/indie personas, but that these were primarily concerned with gender rather than race. While proclaiming their difference from UK Tory-led middle-class culture (Noel Gallagher, for example, caused controversy by noting that taking class A drugs was as common for young people as drinking a cup of tea), both bands exhibited behaviours that almost perfectly fit the traditional mould of the 'rock-star'. Both Ian Brown and Noel and Liam Gallagher cockily stated in various interviews that The Stone Roses and Oasis were 'the best bands in the world' and performed identities which, akin to the male-only makeup of their bands, pushed forward a type of aggressive masculinity. Again, this strand of hyper-masculine identity is not unusual within the scene of rock music. As Sara Cohen has noted, rock music is associated with 'a male history, [...] canon and legacy full of male bravado, male comradeship and collectivity' (1997, 30); it is, in short, premised on men 'making a scene'. Interestingly, while this is most dominantly the mode of masculinity associated with The Stone Roses's and Oasis's reputation formations, both documentaries work in interesting ways to simultaneously reinstate this performance of retrogressive masculinity, and revolt against it.

PUTTING WOMEN IN THE PICTURE

Supersonic begins by not only making female commentators on and in music heard (specifically Jo Whiley), but also reinscribes the male legacy of the band with two female-centred stories. The first relates to Noel and Liam's mother, Peggy Gallagher—an Irish immigrant who moved from Ireland to Manchester in 1962 before meeting Tommy Gallagher, getting married and going on to have three sons over the next eight years. The second retells the Oasis origins story focusing on the all-female indie band Sister Lovers, whose insistence that Oasis played at a gig in Glasgow (taking half of the Sister Lovers own designated set), led to the band getting signed.

In the first instance, the rockumentary screen makes visible family photographs of Peggy Gallagher and her young sons, starting with an image of Peggy and Liam, before making way for a montage of 1970s photos showing various pre-school and school-aged shots of Noel and Liam. Besides the soft Irish voice of Peggy talking about her sons and the difficult relationship between them, even as children, a second soundscape also serves to sonically situate the social background of the brothers: that of the unmistakable introductory guitar riff of The Stone Roses track 'This Is the One'. Soon afterwards, Noel begins narrating the story of Oasis getting signed:

> We were sharing a rehearsal room with an all-girl band called Sister Lovers. Unbeknownst to us, one of the girls in the band, Debbie Turner, God bless Debbie, was an ex-girlfriend of Alan McGee's, the head of the coolest record label in England. We were asking her what they were up to and they were saying "We're going up [to Glasgow] to do this gig [...] She said "Why don't you come with us?" [...] We all put £25 each in to hire a splitter van. We get there and we say "We're Oasis from Manchester." And the guy says "There's no band down here." I said "Yeah, yeah, it's all right, we're with Debbie." And he's like "No, no, no, no fucking way."

Debbie is then heard in voiceover, as the animated story plays out on-screen: 'I think we said "Well, if they're not playing, we're not going to play. We'll do a really short set." Then Oasis were allowed to play.' The rockumentary then prints the date and location on-screen 'GLASGOW, 31st MAY, 1993' before showing grainy footage of Oasis performing. The musical performance then gives way orally to the voice of Alan McGee noting how impressed he was with the punkish lyrics, style and raw sound of Oasis's tracks, noting in particular the lyrics 'You're the outcast. You're the underclass. But you don't care. Because you're living fast.' After the set, McGee notes he went straight up to Noel and asked him if the band wanted a contract with Creation Records.

The punkish spirit of the band is important to briefly consider here. As Haslam notes, 'Punk made Manchester a credible pop city, bred noncon-formist attitudes, nurtured indie labels and gave us a DIY tradition' (2000, 133). These aspects of identity are not only applicable to the city of Manchester, but to the attitudes of both the Sisters Lovers and Oasis as narrated in the story above. While McGee's words, particularly in relation to punk, serve to highlight the masculine heritage of punk rock power in the music industry, the clear recognition given to Debbie Turner by Noel as the facilitator of this opportunity—her willingness to lay herself on the line to ensure that Oasis's music was heard—is resounding. Indeed, the importance of women is further mined in the documentary with a longer section on Peggy Gallagher who notes how her husband beat her and Noel mercilessly before she found the courage to leave him. In response, Noel and Liam both note their anger at their father for his behaviour and praise their mother, with Liam saying: 'Mum was an angel, still is. I wanted to get her to stop doing like three fucking jobs and put her feet up [...] and have nice things.' Noel goes on to note: 'When I think of those times, she sort of brought us up on her own, really. And three lads, particularly one of them being Liam, it was very tricky. I mean, she gave it all up for us [...] I wanted to make her proud.' While other stories narrated in the documentary point to and serve to highlight the rock behaviour of the band (an animated VFX sequence produced by The Brewery retelling the story of the band's arrest on a ferry to Amsterdam, for example), the tender moments in which Noel and Liam acknowledge the importance of key women in their lives are represented in a continuum with their authenticity in which the family/softness is a balance to the hedonism/laddishness made visible elsewhere. These narrative fragments are not animated (indeed, they need no extra-textual elements to be brought to life), but instead are presented minimally, with Noel and Liam simply talking to the camera.

Peggy's Irish background—her status as an immigrant to England—is also highlighted in the documentary and is coupled with Noel and Liam's acknowledgement of their Irish heritage. As Paolo Hewitt notes in the rockumentary discussing a large gig that Oasis performed in Ireland: 'It's that immigrant thing, isn't it? It's that sense of identity. Ireland saw them as one of their own.' As a band whose music is often described as belonging to 'Britpop', this explicit recognition of the difference between English and Irish identity and the Gallagher brothers' acknowledgement of their Irish heritage serves to eschew the frequent elision between British and English identity that, as Hesmondhalgh notes, is a frequent problem of Britpop labelling and discourse, causing a 'constant slippage [...] and the presentation of a notion of Englishness that marginalized regional variation' (2001, 278). What we see in the Gallagher brothers' identity recognition and hear in their music, is an intercultural ethos with transformative potential for representing and understanding rich and multicultural identity.

AUTHENTIC MOMENTS

In terms of *Made of Stone*, the Roses rockumentary also brings to the fore authentic moments. However, it does so by concentrating on and making visible in the body of the film the *experience* of fandom rather than focusing on the talk or performances of the band themselves. In a sequence filmed outside Parr Hall in Warrington, Meadows positions his hand-held cameras in the street in order to capture the public response to The Stone Roses last-minute radio announcement of a reformation gig that evening at the intimate venue for people who could prove their historic fandom by bringing original merchandise—1980s and 1990s cassette tapes and LPs, gig tickets and other memorabilia. Capturing a single man running down the road in a formal suit with his mobile phone in his hand saying 'I've been fucking everywhere mate, there's nothing', then a trickle people in work clothes heading purposefully toward Parr Hall, then a swelling multitude of fans, young and old, a man's face fills the screen as he confesses: 'I've had to lie to my boss and tell him my father-in-law's had a heart-attack.' This dedication to seeing The Stone Roses play is further explored by Meadows in other grainy interviews. With the camera pointing at another male waiting in line in the Parr Hall queue, an interviewer asks him if he's meant to be working. The man, dressed in high visibility vest and with remnants of plasterboard on his hands and face says: 'Yeah, I've actually left. I've knocked through into the house and not even boarded up. So, if you're watching, Richard, sorry mate—I'll sort it out tomorrow.' Various interview crew then ask individual fans why they have come and what it is about The Stone Roses and their music that is so special. The fan responses are, for the most part, captured in low grade and at times with poor sound, yet this serves to make the replies and the moments themselves more affective. One fan notes:

> I was doing some work at home about half an hour ago. It came up on Facebook. Kecks on, van, here. You know and I know [why they're so special], but you can't write it down, can you? [...] There's a reason why I've still got my hair like this twenty years later, you know what I mean? There's a reason why I've never worn a tie. There's a reason why I still listen to that album once a week. And it still makes me tingle. There's a reason why I'm here and my childminder's looking after my baby somewhere.

These moments work to establish the depth of feeling of fans for the band, but more than that, they establish the importance of *being there* and experiencing the first reformation gig alongside The Stone Roses. In speaking of the band in these interviews, fans don't talk of music alone but of the way in which the Roses music has influenced and shaped their identities and lives. Indeed, these oral testimonies fulfil the typical oral history function of documentary and underline the authenticity of having been *there* and wanting to be *there* again.

The notion of being *there* that is stressed in the interviews can be understood as an indicator of the importance of presence in relation to music and identity formation in the pre-digital age. This nostalgic acknowledgement of the past is also mined in *Supersonic.* In the penultimate scene of the rockumentary, Noel, somewhat self-consciously, reflects on Oasis's 1990s success:

> It was the pre-digital age, it was the pre-talent show, reality TV age. Things meant more. It was just a great time to be alive, never mind a great time to be in Oasis. We were about to enter in to a celebrity-driven culture and I've always thought that [the 1990s] was the last, great gathering of the people before the birth of the internet. It's no coincidence that things like that don't happen anymore. Twenty years ago, the biggest musical phenomenon was a band that came from a council estate. I just think in the times in which we live, it would be unrepeatable.

THE DIRECTORS: ALIGNING SOCIAL IMPULSES

A further source of authenticity in the rockumentary case studies is an alignment between the bands and the directors of their documentary texts. I want to suggest here a set of shared cultural and social sympathies between The Stone Roses and director Shane Meadows and between Oasis and director Mat Whitecross. Shane Meadows, the acclaimed British film director of *A Room for Romeo Brass* (1999), *Dead Man's Shoes* (2004) and *This Is England* (2006), is widely known for his powerful, British, working-class, youth-orientated narratives. Writing of him in 2015, journalist Mark Lawson noted that Meadows was 'a chronicler of England's public and personal stories', comparing him to Ken Loach and Mike Leigh in terms of his ability and desire to interrogate the political through the personal. Like much of Loach and Leigh's work, Meadows films have hitherto been dominated by teen characters, growing up and struggling to come of age. In his films, adult identity and its emergence is a difficult process, yet is often helped by finding alignment with subcultural clans. *This Is England* (2006), Meadows' most successful film to date, is notably engaged with and explicitly rejects notions of white nationalism, looking instead (perhaps nostalgically) to subcultural clans such as skinheads and music such as ska to embrace and recognise new, more divergent and rich British identities. Via the narrative strand of mixed-race character Milky's (Andrew Shim) identity amidst a skin group, *This Is England* exposes the true horror of nationalist racism, situating Nazi-influenced character Combo (Stephen Graham), as a weak individual, who is so jealous of Milky's family and dual-heritage that he fails to contain his pathetic rage, beating Milky to the point of near-death. This clear engagement of Meadows with nationalist politics and indeed their deplorable consequences is, I suggest, a concern that is both authentic and clearly shared by The Stone Roses. In addition, having spoken on various occasions about the semi-autobiographical nature of his work and his love of music—particularly the music of his formative years including The Stone Roses—Meadows, a working-class male who came of age in the 1980s and 1990s and whose work has an explicit focus on class and subculture, shares a social impulse with The Stone Roses whose music speaks of many of the same issues. Both believe that their stories—stories of ordinary working-class people—matter, and both tell their stories through their art. Both are often and problematically characterised as 'rough' and uncultured, and neither had professional grounding in their respective areas of music or filmmaking. Yet, both acknowledge the often-harsh realities of working-class life but are not confined to merely documenting and reproducing them—instead, they share a commitment to a delicate and poetic transformation of the mundane and the familiar.

Interestingly, the director of *Supersonic*, Mat Whitecross, first came to public attention with the docudrama *The Road to Guantanamo* (2006), co-directed by Michael Winterbottom. The film tells the story of three British Muslims who travelled to Pakistan for a wedding and were taken to Guantanamo Bay in Cuba where they are held without charge, terrorised and tortured for two-and-half years. Deeply political, the film was followed by another collaboration with Winterbottom, *The Shock Doctrine* (2009)—chronicling what Naomi Klein calls 'disaster capitalism'. Next, Whitecross embarked on a singularly directed project *Moving to Mars* (2009)—a story that traced the journey of two Burmese families from a refugee camp on the Thai/Burmese border to the UK. It was at this point and after significant critical acclaim that Whitecross decided to take his work back to where it had first originated—the music video. Directing a video short for the Mancunian band Take That (who were embarking on a revival tour) and then another for Coldplay, 2010 also saw the release of *Sex & Drugs & Rock & Roll*, a biopic of Ian Dury, a British singer-songwriter and actor who, in the 1970s, became one of the founders of the domestic punk-rock scene. In 2012 this was followed by *Spike Island*, a comedy film following the journey of four youths determined to attend

The Stone Roses Spike Island gig—a narrative that ironically resonates closely to the real-life experience and desires of Meadows. Whitecross's documentary *Supersonic* came out four years later in 2016. This combination of the intensely political, the biographic, the musical and the personal—and moreover the complexities of exploring identity—are in clear congruence over Whitecross's oeuvre. As Oasis noted The Stone Roses amongst their key influences, Whitecross, in an interview with *IndieWire* in 2006, noted the importance of Meadows as a creative inspiration, as he 'always maintained that anyone could be a filmmaker, that everyone had stories to tell.' The social impulses that Whitecross and Oasis share are, I suggest, in part down to their social similarities. Both Whitecross and the Gallagher brothers were born of immigrant parents. Neither had formal musical or film training, and in both cases their work tends to focus on issues of displacement being overcome by collective effort. In the cases of The Stone Roses and Meadows and Oasis and Whitecross, the directors of these rockumentaries can be understood as more than collaborators—they are fans, critics and co-conspirators. While this makes for clear creative calibrations, such pairings also run the risk of lacking critical distance.

Conclusion

Keith Beattie, writing in the book *Documentary Display* notes that:

> Rockumentary maintains a commitment to the traditional documentary project within a focus on youth subcultures and music subformations—and attendant perspectives on personal identity—which constitute the informational core of the form. However, rockumentary motivates knowledge in ways different to nonfiction works [...] In the rockumentary the provision of information ('telling') operates within and through a mode which emphasises and exploits the representational capacities of the visual register ('showing'). The form of knowledge produced within this model is subjective, affective, visceral and sensuous. (2008, 60)

The subjective, affective, model of which Beattie speaks is in clear evidence in both *Made of Stone* and *Supersonic*. Indeed, both texts self-consciously acknowledge this, pushing front and centre via their directors and the dynamic visual and aural spirit of the work, their own fandom. This is most evident in *Made of Stone* in which Meadows notes that The Store Roses are his heroes and the film project is the fulfilment of a life-long dream. In an interview for *The Observer* newspaper, Meadows described *Made of Stone* as 'the closest thing to a love letter that I've ever made.'[7] Whitecross shared a similar story in relation to Oasis, noting in an interview with Tom Stroud that: 'There's no way you could grow up in the '90s and be the age I was and not have Oasis as part of your DNA.' This notion of the directors' own identities being so bound up with the bands and music that they sought to represent, makes visible and seeks to acknowledge a clear and conscious lack of objectivity in their record of the past and present. Rather than being understood as a failing however, both directors embrace the intimate intertwining of their emergent stories and transformed relationships with the bands, music and scenes at their heart, keying out and pushing forward their own place in the creation of new and renewed fan identities.

Whether viewed with optimism or as retrogressive, revival culture has encouraged a reconsideration of the power, point and cultural capital of the music, bands and fans under its lens. In relation to *Made of Stone* and *Supersonic*, while the former can be understood as a revival of the 'real thing', the latter operates as a mediated stand-in for a desired reunion. Both rockumentaries are clear responses to a particular, past cultural context—a pre-internet age when music was about being *there*, and above all it is this notion that links the texts to the past rather than any nationalistic resurgence.

Both texts do represent the past somewhat nostalgically at times, however, nostalgia here is not represented as a failure to imagine the future, but a recognition that the past, the present and the future are not separate spheres but are enmeshed through experience, feeling and memory, both visual and vocal. In short, the main message of the rockumentaries is that we should not look back in anger. The Stone Roses and Oasis are not 'bloated corpses', but, like the films that depict them, are very much alive: a living history, still in the making.

NOTES

1. As noted on 'Britpop at the BBC' (online): http://www.bbc.co.uk/programmes/profiles/1mpyWmdshwT3gGzhPwZ3JbR/britpop-at-the-bbc-whats-on.
2. See, for example, John Robb's description of 'baggy' in *The Stone Roses And The Resurrection of British Pop: The Reunion Edition* (2012).
3. Pretty Green. Accessed at: https://www.prettygreen.com/discover/timeline/.

4. Ian Brown in interview with *Rolling Stone*, accessed online: http://louder-thanwar.com/stone-roses-key-figures-talk-about-the-band/?relatedposts_hit=1&relatedposts_origin=241426&relatedposts_position=0.
5. 'Britpop at the BBC' (online): http://www.bbc.co.uk/programmes/profil es/1mpyWmdshwT3gGzhPwZ3JbR/britpop-at-the-bbc-whats-on.
6. Noel Gallagher cited in Eugene Masterson (1996) *The Word on the Street: The Unsanctioned Story of Oasis.* Edinburgh: Mainstream, p. 56.
7. Shane Meadows speaking to Miranda Sawyer in *The Observer*, 26th May 2013.

REFERENCES

Anon. 2010. FUC51: Manchester Deniers—Introduction (January 2010) Online at: http://fuc51.blogspot.co.uk/2010/01/fuc51-introduction-of-sorts.html Accessed 03.04.17.

Beattie, Keith. 2008. *Documentary Display: Re-viewing Nonfiction Film and Video.* London: Wallflower Press.

Boym, Svetlana. 2001. *The Future of Nostalgia.* New York: Basic Books.

Brown, Ian in *Rolling Stone* (1990) (online): http://louderthanwar.com/stone-roses-key-figures-talk-about-the-band/?relatedposts_hit=1&relatedposts_origin=241426&relatedposts_position=0 Accessed 17.12.16.

Cohen, Sara. 1997. "Men Making A Scene." In Sheila Whitely (ed.) *Sexing the Groove: Popular Music and Gender.* London & New York: Routledge, pp. 17–36.

Fonarow, Wendy. 2006. *Empire of Dirt: The aesthetics and rituals of British indie music.* Middletown, Conn: Wesleyan University Press.

Gallagher, Noel cited in Masterson, Eugene. 1996. *The Word on the Street: The Unsanctioned Story of Oasis.* Edinburgh: Mainstream.

Guffey, Elizabeth. 2006. *Retro: The Culture of Revival.* London: Reaktion Books.

Haslam, Dave. 2000. *Manchester, England: The Story of the Pop Cult City.* London: Fourth Estate.

Hatherley, Owen. 2017. *The Ministry of Nostalgia: Consuming Austerity.* London: Verso.

Hesmondhalgh, David. 2001. "British Popular Music and National Identity." In David Morley and Kevin Robins (eds.) *British Cultural Studies: Geography, Nationality and Identity.* Oxford: Oxford University Press. pp. 273–286.

Huq, Rupa. 2006. *Beyond Subculture: Pop, Youth and Identity in a Postcolonial World.* London and New York: Routledge.

Lawson, Mark. 'Shane Meadows: Chronicler of England's Public and Personal Stories' in *The Guardian* 7 August, 2015 (online): https://www.theguardian.com/film/2015/aug/07/shane-meadows-chronicler-england-public-personal-stories Accessed 02.06.16.

Long, Paul and Collins, Jez. 2018. "Another Uniquely Mancunian Offering?' Un-Convention and the Intermediation of Music Culture and Place." In Ewa Mazierska (ed.) *Heading North: The North of England in Film, Television and Popular Music.* London: Equinox.

Meadows, Shane. 2013. "Made of Stone: Interview", *The Observer*, May 26 (online): https://www.theguardian.com/music/2013/may/26/shane-meadows-interview-made-of-stone Accessed 12.12.16.

Redwood, John. 1996. "There's Always England," *The Guardian*, March 20.

Reynolds, Simon. 2011. *Retromania: Pop Culture's Addiction to Its Own Past.* London: Faber and Faber.

Robb, John. 2012. *The Stone Roses and The Resurrection of British Pop: The Reunion Edition.* London: Ebury Press.

Whitecross, Mat. 2006. "In Interview", *IndieWire*: http://www.indiewire.com/2006/06/indiewire-interview-mat-whitecross-co-director-of-the-road-to-guantanamo-76530/ Accessed 23.02.17.

Whitecross, Mat cited by Tom Stroud. 2016. "This is History: Mat Whitecross on directing *Supersonic*" (online): http://www.oasis-recordinginfo.co.uk/?page_id=1947 Accessed 12.12.16.

FILMOGRAPHY

A Room for Romeo Brass (Dir. Shane Meadows, 1999).

Dead Man's Shoes (Dir. Shane Meadows, 2004).

Moving to Mars (Dir. Mat Whitecross, 2009).

Oasis: Supersonic (Dir. Mat Whitecross, 2016).

Sex & Drugs & Rock & Roll (Dir. Mat Whitecross, 2010).

Spike Island (Dir. Mat Whitecross, 2012).

The Road to Guantanamo (Dirs. Michael Winterbottom and Mat Whitecross, 2006).

The Shock Doctrine (Dirs. Michael Winterbottom and Mat Whitecross, 2009).

The Stone Roses: Made of Stone (Dir. Shane Meadows, 2013).

This Is England (Dir. Shane Meadows, 2006).

PART III

Critical Theory and Subcultural Representations in Other Media

Figures in Black: Heavy Metal and the Mourning of the Working Class

Scott Wilson

MENTAL CASES

In 1965, fifty years after the height of the 'carnage incomparable' of World War One (Wilfred Owen, 'Mental Cases', 1917), and just twenty years after the even greater devastation of World War Two, anthropologist Geoffrey Gorer (1965) published a remarkable survey, *Death, Grief and Mourning*, which noted the profound decline in public mourning rituals in contemporary Britain. Gorer and his colleagues attributed this decline largely to the mass slaughter of these wars, their targeting of civilian populations and the teeming number of vanished, mutilated, unmarked and unknown dead. The excess of the dead—particularly among the working-class 'cannon fodder' at the front and the devastated cities at home—rendered the traditional, public mourning of communities redundant, or impossible. There were too many corpses, and too many communities razed to the ground.

Consequently in contemporary Britain, as Gorer shows, mourning has remained largely a matter of private grief constrained in discreet stoical funerals. Unlike in other cultures, in Britain there are no professional

S. Wilson (✉)
Kingston University, Kingston-upon-Thames, UK

© The Author(s) 2018   147
N. Bentley et al. (eds.), *Youth Subcultures in Fiction, Film and Other Media*, Palgrave Studies in the History of Subcultures and Popular Music, https://doi.org/10.1007/978-3-319-73189-6_9

mourners, no public displays, set dress code (other than to wear a black tie) or rituals, and certainly no outward manifestations of sorrow; no raging at the wickedness of the world and the 'war pigs', 'the evil sorcerers of death's construction'. Oh Lord, no, not in 1965. There is of course one day of national mourning for the war dead every year on 11th November held at the Cenotaph in London. The Cenotaph, significantly, is the tomb of the Unknown Soldier, and as such it is a monument to the impossibility of mourning. Individual members of the community can have no personal relation to the depersonalised and un-representable corpse that is hidden within the stone edifice; other than in a highly abstract way, he or she is nothing to them, nor were they anything to him or her.

It is well known that fans of heavy metal wear black, as do the vast majority of the very many subgenres of metal that now proliferate around the world: the darkest, blackest, doomiest, depressive, funereal, most satanic black the better. While it may be framed and supplemented by black leather, denim waistcoats and patches hinting at the style's proletarian roots in the bomber-jacketed garb of the biker gangs derived from itinerant ex-aircraft crew after World War Two, or indeed the combat pants and various other scraps of army surplus gear, the key garment is the black T shirt commemorating the name of one's favourite band. The necessity of black relates directly to the title track of the album *Black Sabbath* by Black Sabbath, the first heavy metal band. The enigmatic and frightening 'figure in black which points at me' summons all listeners through identification with the terror, doom and excitement of the singer, Ozzy Osbourne. It is the supreme instance of metal interpellation. We are 'hailed', as listeners, at the altar of the Black Sabbath where we must sacrifice, in a Satanic inversion, all prior identity to 'die' and become born again as a metalhead. Like Hamlet, confronted with the accusatory finger of the ghost of his father demanding revenge, the 'adolescent and funereal', nascent heavy metal fan must in turn don black mourning weeds, 'drawn to mirror and materialize the figure conjured in the music in himself'(Masciandaro 2015, 40).

As strange and unlikely as it may seem, Black Sabbath's lyrical and musical modality, their mise-en-scene in the late 1960s precisely addresses the problem of working class mourning in the most sensational way, in the form of a spectacular 'Electric Funeral' (*Paranoid*). On the first album, along with the central theme of death and sacrifice, references to doom and sorrow abound, 'bodies turning to corpses', the impossibility of 'people counting their dead' (*Black Sabbath*). Most famously, of course, in

Paranoid's 'War Pigs', perhaps Sabbath's most famous song, Osbourne rages explicitly against the 'Generals', the perpetrators of 'mass destruction', for whom Satan is waiting at Judgment Day. The title of the second album also broaches, like Wilfred Owen, the question of sanity and its relation to war, loss, mourning and psychotic forms of melancholia. 'People think I'm insane because I am frowning all the time' ('Paranoid'). Indeed Wilfred Owen's opening lines from 'Mental Cases' are pure metal: 'Who are these? Why sit they here in twilight?/Wherefore rock they, purgatorial shadows,/Drooping tongues from jays that slob their relish/baring teeth that leer like skulls' teeth wicked?' (1–4).

A retrospective review of Sabbath's *Paranoid* succinctly sums up the main elements or themes that became defined as heavy metal. The review states that *Paranoid* is:

the album that defined metal, musically, sonically and thematically. Hate mongers ('War Pigs'), lunatic robots ('Iron Man') and schizos ('Paranoid') dance a jig while Sabbath's four horsemen of the Apocalypse play instruments of mass destruction. The star of the show is Tony Iommi's detuned SG, which pukes the largest, loudest guitar sound known to man. Add Geezer Butler's sci-fi lyrics and Ozzy's prophet-in-the-wilderness vocals and you have the rock equivalent of the book of revelations. (Reviewer 1992 in Rosen 2002, 61–2)

Here we have a definition of heavy metal as a schizoid war machine wandering a divine wilderness divested of God but haunted by Satan or the cries of his invocation in what Osbourne described as 'an evil sound, a heavy doom sound' (Ozzy Osbourne in Rosen 2002, 46).

It is significant that this great panoply of war, destruction, religious transgression and doom is framed by a title referencing mental health, particularly 'paranoid' forms of mania and depression. Indeed, 'Black Sabbath', the title track of the first album sets the 'bi-polar' template for metal that alternates between the heaviness of gloomy atmospheres and the rush of power chords. Subsequently, the various subgenres of metal that have followed in Sabbath's wake will gravitate towards one pole or another: speed metal, thrash metal, power metal, battle metal and so on are nuanced and set off by doom metal, death metal, black metal, sludge metal, drone metal, funereal doom metal, depressive—and even suicidal—funereal doom metal.

For the clinical psychoanalyst Darian Leader (2009), the exponential rise in states of depression and depressive symptoms since the Second World

War is in large part due to the reduction and interiorisation of mourning noted by Gorer's study in the 1960s, such that mourning has become a problem increasingly posed to individuals distanced from the life of the community. In his clinical practice Leader sees that many apparent states of 'depression' actually indicate an underlying yet unacknowledged state of mourning or melancholia. The affect associated with some prior loss is triggered by an event such as a redundancy, divorce or blow to self-esteem that plunges a subject into a fathomless slough of despair and despondency. For Leader, depression is a blanket term for a variety of different types of symptoms related to an instance of singular loss and a failure of mourning since this original, defining loss is unacknowledged, disavowed or repressed.

In this chapter, I am going to suggest that Sabbath's initial template for heavy metal offers the form and structure for a *work of mourning* that, as Kleinian analyst Hanna Segal (1986) argues of art generally, allows artists and their fans, through processes of identification—in the case of metal supplanted through states of sonic ecstasy—to make 'something out of an inferred experience of loss', to create 'out of chaos and destruction' (Bataille et al. 1995, 86). I will look initially at Black Sabbath, but also at how fellow Midlands metal band Bolt Thrower creatively externalise loss so that it may be publicly registered, acknowledged and celebrated. In so doing they—perhaps un-deliberately if not unconsciously—work through various stages of mourning. According to Leader these are: first, the framing and representation of loss; second, the constitution and symbolic 'killing' of the lost object apprehended in all its ambivalence; third, the isolation of the place that the object has vacated and left empty; and fourth, the internalisation of that space as a conditioning absence, or void, out of which the artistic works of mourning can be created and publicly celebrated, as Hanna Segal suggests.

The representations of various lost objects that are brought to bear in heavy metal's characteristic tales of violence, destruction, doom, depression and death—representations that can be figured as popular cultural works of spectacular mourning—are predicated, I suggest, on one fundamental prior loss that has been characterised as both an absence and an impossibility. That is the notion of working-class culture itself.

THE FACTORY AND THE SLAUGHTERHOUSE

The first two albums of Black Sabbath are conventionally regarded as genre defining, but as we have seen, in laying down what retrospectively became known as heavy metal, Sabbath's sound is indelibly conjoined with doom in a sonic bi-polarity of mania and depression linked to an underlying sense of mourning and psychotic melancholy. Certainly a pall of doom did indeed hang over the Black Country, its metal industries and working class inhabitants in the late 1960s. Industrial Birmingham and its bleak environs, Aston in particular, home of the band's members, provided the background and milieu for the genre, adding an economic hue to the depressive set of features characterising its early iconography.

This association is supported by the metonymy connecting the term 'metal' with industry, a connection that is riveted together by the anecdote of Sabbath's lead guitarist Tony Iommi's industrial injury, caused when a piece of sheet metal that he was supposed to weld, sliced off the ends of his fingers. It is as if Iommi's doom-laden power chords are the groaning expression of this loss, the wound of those severed fingertips sacrificial victim of the clash between flesh and metal. With Sabbath's signature sound, scars moving on guitar strings bind with a violent, external force of sonic vibration. It is a sound born of a loss that is symbolic as well as real.

The day job of the band's singer, Ozzy Osbourne, also had an historical connection with death. He worked in the local slaughterhouse. Historically, slaughterhouses are institutions linked with religion; they were temples of sacrifice, serving 'a dual purpose of prayer and killing', that resulted in 'a disturbing convergence of the mysteries of myth and the ominous grandeur typical of those places where blood flows' (Bataille et al. 1995, 73). For example in the feast of Yom Kippur, on the Day of the Great Atonement, a bull is sacrificed at the bass mourning sound of the *shofar*, an instrument shaped from a ram's horn. Sacrifice makes the sacred, the death of the totem animal summoning the absent God. The demand leads, however, in the Judaic Christian tradition through a series of displacements, to the death of the Golden Calf, the death of the Son and even to the death of God himself, disclosing the void in which everything is consumed in a process of self-destruction. The secularisation that accompanies this displacement eventually eliminates the dimension of the sacred altogether. Slaughterhouses become industrialised, 'cursed and quarantined like plague-ridden ships' (Bataille et al. 1995, 73). Death is disavowed, and indeed like life and existence generally is homogenised, standardised and pre-packaged.

The deep groaning sound of Iommi's chords and Osbourne's wailing vocals, hail from teenage dreams of the slaughterhouse and the decaying factory. As if the sound echoed throughout the ages, through the debased medium of pulp Hammer horror films and Dennis Wheatley novels popular and prevalent at the time fuelling lyricist Geezer Butler's imagination. Metal resounds like the *shofar* not (or not just) in the absence disclosed by the death of God, but in the void of working-class culture. Just as God had to be summoned out of inexistence in order to be killed, so metal brings British working-class culture into existence for the first time in the sound of mourning for its 'death' that is predicated upon the impossibility of its birth. Heavy metal is not the first form to have noted this. In the eighteenth century, Thomas Gray's proto-black metal 'Elegy Written in a Country Churchyard', observes the 'mould'ring heap' of an unmarked, common grave and wonders if 'some mute, inglorious Milton here may rest'. In heavy metal the sound of mourning for the stillborn death of working class culture is developed through a weird appropriation and mutation of American blues that is completely reshaped and transformed in the name and sound—'metal' and industry—that precluded that culture in the drudgery of factory work. Heavy metal is not a form of the blues. It is a new form of music initially forged in Britain, but which eventually took on a global trajectory. Metal is no longer predominantly British: it is now in very different ways Norwegian, Finnish, Brazilian, Japanese, Chinese, Turkish, Lebanese and so on. Across numerous festivals and generic extremes, metal exists as an essentially empty *form* like a *shofar* or Viking drinking horn—the sign of the horns being of course the universal signifier of metal affirmation and kinship—that can take any ethnic or national content. Across Europe, old and new, national and regional varieties and subgenres of metal have tracked the expansion of globalised capital and the failures of nation states to sustain cultural differences, often providing the medium for a trail of discontents related to the loss of ethnic identities that are given voice in metal as a mourning sound through which sacrifice, loss and desire are articulated. For a discussion of how metal provides the positive reverse of the absence of any European popular culture in which could be located a political alternative to the 'globalatinisation' represented by institutions like the EU, see Wilson (2012). It is in this somewhat paradoxical way, as an empty vessel, that heavy metal can be described as a genuine product of working-class 'culture'. Heavy metal is a working-class 'Thing', in the terminology of Martin Heidegger. For Heidegger, the 'Thing's thingness', its authenticity, does not so much lie in the material of which it consists, but in 'the void that holds' (1975, 169). So while the origin may be British, there is nevertheless nothing necessarily inauthentic about Brazilian or Turkish metal, say, given the specificity of the active 'void' that shapes and resonates through it in the noise that it 'holds'.

CULTURAL STUDIES AND THE 'JUKE BOX BOYS'

Directly contemporaneous with the birth of heavy metal was the emergence of the discipline of cultural studies that was developed from the late 1960s at The Centre for Contemporary Cultural Studies (CCCS), Birmingham University. In its own way, the impetus for CCCS was also an effect of mourning for working-class culture. This movement grew from the founding assumptions set out in Raymond Williams's seminal text *Culture and Society* (1971). The main theme of the book laments the great severing of 'culture' from 'society' produced by the industrial revolution in which the former became the exclusive preserve of a largely leisured, ruling class. By contrast, the growing urban working class (or in Marx's term the proletariat) that was produced from the agrarian peasant workers who provided the labour for England's economic growth and industrial power in the eighteenth and nineteenth centuries had no time or inclination to produce any culture worthy of the name. Williams writes, 'the traditional popular culture of England was, if not annihilated, at least fragmented and weakened by the dislocations of the Industrial Revolution' (1971, 320). It is a view reiterated by cultural studies' most commanding figure, Stuart Hall, writing even in the 1980s that 'there is no separate, autonomous, "authentic" layer of working-class culture to be found' (Hall 1981, 227). Williams's project in the book is to advocate the reintegration of culture and society in an understanding of culture as 'a whole way of life'. It was not evident, however, that this more holistic notion of culture could be produced in the context of the capitalist mode of production. Indeed, the culture actually enjoyed by the working classes of the twentieth century—cinema, television and popular music for example—he regarded as essentially a mode of alienation that reinforced the separation of culture and society. Williams writes, 'we cannot fairly or usefully describe the bulk of the material produced by the new means of communication as "working-class culture". For neither is it by any means produced exclusively for this class, nor, in any important degree, is it produced by them' (1971, 319–20). Even The Beatles, a broadly working-class group from Liverpool who would go on to write all their own songs and redefine American popular music for Britain and the world, were regarded with disdain by the New Left. 'Beatles culture' wrote Terry Eagleton in 1966, 'is created largely by a complex of agents, composers and businessmen who are part of a system which creates a culture from above' (Eagleton 1966, 122). The Beatles, of course, were originally 'rock 'n' rollers', teenagers who dreamt of Elvis Presley and America. In *The Uses of Literacy*, cultural studies founder Richard Hoggart is disapproving of the 'peculiarly thin and pallid form of dissipation' represented by teenage boys in 'drape suits, picture ties, and an American slouch' listening to rock 'n' roll on juke boxes. Living in 'a myth world compounded of a few simple elements they take to be American life', they are suffering from 'a sort of spiritual dry rot' (1957, 248).

This kind of assessment judges cultural activities according to a notion of authenticity that is informed by a national, essentially literary culture— endowed no doubt with the English oak of spiritual sturdiness. A hugely influential text, Hoggart's book informed academic critiques of popular culture subsequently. At the same time, Williams's nostalgic desire for a future in which culture can be understood as 'a whole way of life', and his non-elitist understanding of culture as 'ordinary' in *Keywords* and else-where, began to shape the understanding of subcultures as expressions of ways of (working-class) life in a manner that was not quite so dismissive. The subcultures that emerged from working-class cultural practices that necessarily engaged with commercial, consumer culture were both acknowledged and assessed politically, becoming valued according to the degree of 'resistance' they offered to 'dominant culture'. They might also be valued evidentially if such subcultures, their products and activities could be interpreted in a Marxist analysis to see what 'contradictions' they either disclosed or concealed in the dominant culture and society (see for example Hebdige 1981). What was important for the cultural studies tradition ultimately was not popular culture itself and its specific forms and qualities, but its potential as a political 'site of struggle' and a 'sphere [...] where socialism might be constituted.' As Stuart Hall emphasised: 'that is why "popular culture" matters. Otherwise, to tell you the truth, I don't give a damn about it' (Hall 1981, 239).

Heavy metal was supposed by sociologists and cultural studies academ-ics not to provide congenial ground for socialist revolution or progressive social movements, and its fans were not considered worthy of attention as a subculture. While 'mods' are the cornerstone of British academic accounts of subcultures, rockers are assumed to have disappeared. In fact they became metalheads and subsequently, following the various forms of metal subgenres, have along with rap and hip hop the largest fan base in the world. It is true social scientists did not neglect metal entirely. As Andy Brown (2011) documents, metal came to academic attention in the disci-plines of psychology or sociology because it was assumed to be associated with delinquency and deviance, or 'non-normative behaviour'. Heavy metal was placed on the same plane as drug taking and juvenile crime. It would be much later in the history of cultural studies, in the 1990s and early decades of the twenty-first century, before metal would be afforded any kind of sympathetic academic attention. Yet even here, assumptions regarding conservative or 'hegemonic' representations of masculinity, for example, metal's so-called 'politics of gender' (ignoring the innumerable female metal bands), and the presumption of 'whiteness' (ignoring the innumerable metal bands from South Asia, South East Asia, South America, the Middle East and so on) informed even those academics who were more favourably inclined—or who were even fans themselves—in moments of awkward bad conscience. The voices of Hoggart and Williams still speak powerfully in this discourse such that art is reduced to social behaviour leading, in the case of metal criticism, to an imperative to con-jure-up ever more monstrous instances of male or 'paternal' authority, or fantasies of control, 'mastery', 'masculinity based on a fear of feminine weakness', or in the case of black metal 'misanthropic elitism' (Harris 2006, 31–48). Metal continues to be subject to sociological show trials that have no other purpose it seems to me than to justify the violence— not of the art of metal—but of academic discourse itself, in its bio-political pursuit of social inclusivity in the form of normalisation.

But perhaps none of this is very surprising. Metal emerges in part in reaction to the progressivism of the late 1960s that informs academic dis-course in the human sciences. No doubt, the sound of metal can provide support to negative attitudes and emotions. At the time, certain frustra-tions and suspicions informed a rejection of the perceived continuity between the conventional sensibility of pop romance and the 'peace and love' mantras of 'hippie' politics. As Sabbath drummer Bill Ward recalled, 'we got sick and tired of all the bullshit—love your brother and flower-power forever, meeting a little chick on the corner and you're hung up on her and all this' (cited in Rosen 2002, 31).

Alongside the apparent bad attitude and alleged political incorrectness, the other aspect of heavy metal that meets with scorn and disapproval is the prevalence of occult and satanic symbolism, which is regarded as naïve and irrational, if not infantile. For the progressive materialism of the human sciences, to be divested of God is all well and good, but not when it is replaced by the antithesis of the Good God, the bad Devil. This point has been addressed elsewhere by myself and others. In 'Introduction to Melancology' (2014), for example, I argue that black metal constitutes a radical if paradoxically divine atheism that loathes God and embraces Satanism in order to open itself to a world of transcendent imagination that secular atheism and scientific realism precludes. But to keep within the context of this chapter, I would contend that the elaboration of a supernatural domain—no matter how 'pulpy' and artificial—is a necessary step in representing and mourning the dead. This is for two reasons: first, because recourse to the domain of the supernatural is a means of acknowledging that the dead do not die that easily. The dead haunt the living that struggle to mourn, their presence registered in guilt and resentment at being abandoned, in hatred, remorse and self-hatred, the elements of melancholy that so often accompany mourning: the afflictions of 'the minds that the Dead have ravished' in the words of Wilfred Owen ('Mental Cases'). Second, the fictional life of the undead that haunt the present in the pulp fictional forms of vampires, zombies, ghouls and all the occult paraphernalia that populate the iconography of the metal subgenres testify to the need to kill the dead for a second time, so that one might be finally free of them. But in order to kill them, one must occupy their domain symbolically. Thus, while the mourning 'black of the metalhead is adolescent and funereal' it communicates 'a problematic immersion in the world' of the dead rather than the 'elite transcendence' of it represented by the critically distanced, mature gaze of the social scientist (Masciandaro 2015, 40).

Of course one is never entirely free of the dead, so the third and fourth aspects of mourning concern constituting the lost object more precisely and our relation to it. The lost object is not necessarily identical to whom or what has died. Citing Freud from *Mourning and Melancholia*, Leader writes, 'there may be a difference between whom we have lost and what we have lost in them' (2009, 128). The nature of this object must be further considered in relation to the uncertainty that we have concerning what we ourselves might have meant to the person who has died. Or what indeed the lost object, the dead 'thing', might expect from us. There is at the core of the lost object a point of nonknowledge or 'sense of alterity and of a register beyond' all forms of representation (Leader 2009, 163). It is in relation to this sense of alterity that lies the possibility for creativity and a new beginning. In the next section I shall reiterate the first two aspects of mourning in order to progress to the third and fourth by turning to Bolt Thrower. Bolt Thrower articulate, similarly through the means of 'trash' consumer culture, a quasi-medieval (a 'bolt thrower' is a medieval weapon) pre-industrial, mytho-poetic barbarism with futurological, dystopian visions of mass slaughter and sacrifice. Defining this vision, however, is the twentieth-century history of the disenchantment of war in the industrialised carnage of working-class soldiers and populations. The band are from Coventry, a city devastated by carpet bombing that is dominated by a huge Cenotaph, the title of one of their most powerful tracks.

CENOTAPH

The word cenotaph derives from the Greek κενοτάφιον/*kenotaphion* (*kenos*, one meaning being 'empty', and *taphos*, meaning 'tomb'). The word Cenotaph then literally means '*empty tomb*', or a monument erected in honour of a person or group of people whose remains are elsewhere. It can also be the initial tomb for a person who has since been interred somewhere else. Or again, as in typically 'The Tomb of the Unknown Soldier', it can be the tomb of remains that are unnamed and unrecognisable; the mortal remains that mark the absence of identity. The essential thing is that the Cenotaph contains a central absence or emptiness that is both symbolic and real. As such, it is an object that has the dignity of the 'Thing' in Heidegger's terms. In this instance, the central emptiness symbolises death, and the suffering that led to it. The construction of an edifice built symbolically around a monumental emptiness also provides a means of acknowledging that such suffering and death is impossible to imagine or represent.

Bolt Thrower's 'Cenotaph' (*War Master*, 1991) seems to reiterate this sense of the monument as a 'Thing' in Heidegger's terms, but in an ambiguous way. While the tomb stands alone, destined to silence in its commemoration of mortality, it is also described as a 'parody'. Is the Cenotaph commemorating the unknown remains of a nameless victim, or commemorating the death of death itself? Is this the final death, 'mankind's oblivion', or the overcoming of death in a hyper-mechanised universe? 'Cenotaph' sits slightly uneasily as the centrepiece of *War Master*. Not musically where it provides a point of continuity between *War Master* and particularly 'World Eater' from *Realm of Chaos* (1989) that plunges the band's sound into something more like full-blown death metal. Musically, 'Cenotaph' performs 'World Eater's' vision of bomb-blasted carnage with crushing riffs, pulsing bass and punishing drums like banks of artillery and a hail of bullets. The pulsating sonic force of 'World Eater' is accompanied by growling lyrics declaiming on the wounded and the dead, on carnage and the devastation of bodies melting in blasts of white hot metal, bodies screaming in agony. In 'Cenotaph', however, the verses slow down into a doom mode appropriate to the idea of the monument. It is well known that Bolt Thrower take their visual imagery and much of the inspiration for their lyrics from the Games Workshop and the Warhammer games, particularly *Realms of Chaos* and no doubt much of *War Master*. However, as far as I am aware, players are not offered a Cenotaph alongside the action figures to deploy in the game. 'Cenotaph' seems to be an attempt to provide a link between the fantasy wars in Warhammer and Warhammer 40k and the reality of twentieth-century war, most notably World War Two and the devastation of Bolt Thrower's hometown. Coventry possesses its own formidable Cenotaph in Memorial Park. A magnificent, futuristic art deco construction designed by T.F. Tickner, it was ultimately completed in 1927 but opened in 1921 in order to honour the dead of the 'Great War' of 1914–1918. However because Coventry remained home to many metal-working industries and munitions factories, it was famously subjected to an intense Blitz from July to August 1940, culminating in an attack, on 14 November, from 515 German bombers that devastated the city in firestorms affecting every building in the city centre. The lyrics from 'World Eater' that evoke melting flesh in the face of white-hot bomb blasts could easily have been written about that event.

In *War Master* then, Bolt Thrower adopt with their Warhammer imagery something highly artificial, such that their 'Cenotaph' becomes the representation of the representation of the monument in Coventry, in order for it to commemorate the death of death. The sense of 'parody' that is mentioned in the first line suggests that it is neither an Unknown Soldier nor a particular pile of corpses that is commemorated: it is the corpse of war itself. Bolt Thrower's 'Cenotaph' is a memorial to mortality and memory, to mankind's oblivion and ultimately 'war's terminal conclusion'. And this is catastrophic—more catastrophic than war is the death of war since it involves the sacrifice of the sacrifice that establishes the social bond. 'Cenotaph's' place in the context of Bolt Thrower's oeuvre evokes the worst possible dystopian outcome that is inextricably linked to the overcoming and obliteration of mankind: that war itself would come to a terminal conclusion at the hands of a war 'master'. Does this have a contemporary reference to something outside the Warhammer-esque mythology?

World War One was not the only war that threatened to end all wars, or at least the sacrifice necessarily inherently to war. Bolt Thrower's *War*

Master was released in 1991, the year of the first Gulf War, which began in January, the war that, notoriously, Jean Baudrillard declared 'did not take place' (1995, 2). America, he writes, Saddam Hussein and the Gulf Powers are fighting over the corpse of war. 'Since this war was won in advance' between a Western cyborg army run by an inhuman machine intelligence and an Iraqi human army that were obliterated in the sand, it did not take place. Not even the 10,000 tonnes of bombs that were dropped on the Iraqis per day could make this a war. It is possible that *War Master* contains an implicit Baudrillardian critique. Certainly it anticipates the present and future of drone warfare driven by artificial intelligence that threatens humanity according to Steven Hawking, Elon Musk and Bill Gates (Sainato 2015).

Warhammer 40k is set in a universe in which humanity is enslaved by an alien intelligence bedecked in the semi-generic accoutrements of futurist medieval techno-barbarism. The cinematic reference is to some of Arnold Schwarzenegger's movies from the 1980s such as *Conan the Barbarian* inflected with the *Terminator* franchise. This conjunction is symptomatic of a particular concern of the early 1990s that is clearly thematised by *The Terminator* movies. On the one hand, the explosion of new technological innovations and the exponential rise of the machines render war, on a human scale, redundant. It is post-industrial war involving third-generation machines, a question of machines against machines in which humanity is surpassed. This is the theme of 'Profane Creation', of course, of *War Master*, the album in which 'technology's progression' results in the enslavement of mankind. Human life is rendered worthless in an 'automated living hell'. War is dead because humanity just does not have the capacity to compete with the machine's new revolution in military affairs. The Conan-the-Barbarian-style Medievalism, then, is a phantasmatic attempt to imagine the re-enchantment of war on something like a human scale, or on the scale at least of techno-sapiens, or cyborgs. This is the cyborg fashioned on the idea of a pre-modern warrior rather than the cyborg 'consoldier': the soldier or pilot fighting war in the comfort of a sealed cockpit with an onboard simulator, or the operator in a console in Nevada at the heart of a nexus of networked computers commanding drones.

The 'war master' of the Gulf War was the consoldier pilot or drone operator, remote from the consequence of his or her actions. The sound of Bolt Thrower is forged in the furnace that burns the corpse of war, simultaneously simulating war and mourning it in their characteristic combination of death and doom metal. Of course it is ironic but also significant that death metal became the music of choice ten years later as US soldiers sought to supplement the lack of war's reality in the second war on Iraq, with pilots flying missions with Hatebreed in their helmets (see Pieslak 2009).

The 'lost object' for Bolt Thrower is evoked by war. Bolt Thrower actually *mourn war*. But what is it in war that 'points' to them, like Sabbath's enigmatic 'figure in black'? What are they to war? *War Master* represents a culmination of a number of themes marking their writing from the beginning. 'Concessions of Law', for example, is concerned with the lawlessness of war, but as a figure for something else. War is not lawless, as the very notion of a 'war crime' suggests. It is not just that there are always rules of engagement that one may bend or twist or transgress. War may be a locus of transgression, but the ecstasy of transgression depends upon and sustains the law as its condition. For Bolt Thrower, however, the invocation of the lawless chaos of war is to suggest the idea of a force hostile to humanity that is located outside all human law, rule, norm. It is a force that can only be imagined in terms of all too human atavistic crimes and cruelties, killer instincts, sadism, but which is entirely other and alien. For Bolt Thrower, war is the name of cosmic trauma, war as the force of the Outside; war as means towards a figure for some Other Thing. In this sense Bolt Thrower's death metal is a practice that is oriented entirely towards contact with the unknown that requires engagement with an alternative, transcendental medium heterogeneous to language. This heterogeneous medium is of course music, or rather metal, in this instance death metal whose sonic pulverisation of the brain and solar plexus seeks to hollow out the body of its organs in intense reveries reminiscent of the experience of schizophrenia—a recurrent theme and affect of metal going back, as we have seen, to Sabbath's *Paranoid*.

One of the problems with deploying forms of analysis that reference lyrics and themes drawn from them is that it implies that the music is just there to support and enhance these lyrics and themes, as if they were some kind of movie soundtrack, nuancing lyrical feeling and emotion. But this is not the case. On the contrary, it is completely the other way around. More often than not, the function of lyrics is simply to enhance the music in an untenable commentary on its sonic *force* that is inaccessible to any system of linguistic meaning. For the most part inaudible in the case of death metal, sung or rather growled lyrics provide an improper, catachrestic, objective correlative to an in-human sonic system designed to impact the sensorium with the unsettling force of cenaesthetic schizophrenic symptoms, the symptoms of 'mental cases' in the words of Wilfred Owen: weird voices in the cerebellum, growling, indistinct yet threatening beneath sonic explosions of violent percussion and blood-curdling bass. These sounds ultimately evoke the shattering of normal existence in cosmic trauma caused by 'unknown powers', 'Unleashed (Upon Mankind)'; or 'An unseen force' that tears through body and soul, ('What Dwells Within'); or a 'force' that strives to gain control of 'your mind' that 'burns you deep inside' ('Shreds of Sanity'). With the latter, 'Shreds of Sanity', schizophrenia is used as a trope to evoke bodily events and the sonic reorganisation of the sensorium and a reordering of psychic cathexes in relation to an extraterritorial vastness yet to be discovered.

In Bolt Thrower's death metal, schizophrenia is not a specifiable defect of human central nervous system functioning. It is not a medical condition but a *schizosonic*, transhuman vector of exteriority heading towards 'regions of the unknown' ('After Life'), cutting across and opening out the effects of the (de)tonalities that mark the singular life of sonic beings. With Bolt Thrower, death metal is not about war, rather, war is about death metal (an inversion they share with the Italian Futurists for whom the cacophony of war was an art of noise). In the work of Bolt Thrower, working-class mourning takes the form of the creative deployment of the sound and fury of war and madness, 'snatching after' those 'that smote them, brother' (Owen, 'Mental Cases'). Black Sabbath, Bolt Thrower, and metal at its best, shapes out of chaos and destruction a sonic war machine that courses through the void of Culture as its scourge.

REFERENCES

Bataille, G., Leiris, M., and Griaule, M., 1995. "Slaughterhouse" in the *Encyclopaedia Acephalica* assembled by Alastair Brotchie, London: Atlas Press.
Baudrillard, J. 1995. *The Gulf war Did Not Take Place*. Sydney: Power Publications.
Black Sabbath. 1970a. Black Sabbath. Vertigo.
Black Sabbath. 1970b. Paranoid. Vertigo.
Bolt Thrower. 1989. Realms of Chaos. Earache Records Ltd.
Bolt Thrower. 1991. War Master. Earache Records Ltd.
Brown, A. 2011. 'Heavy Genealogy: mapping the currents, contraflows and conflicts of the emergent field of metal studies, 1978–2010' in special issue 'Metal Studies? Brown, A., Harris, K.K. and Spracklen, K. (eds.) Cultural Research in the Heavy Metal Scene', *The Journal for Cultural Research* 15.3: 213–42.
Eagleton, T. 1966. *The New Left Church*, London: Facet Books.

Gorer, G. 1965. *Death, Grief and Mourning in Contemporary Britain*. New York: Doubleday.

Hall, S. 1981. "Notes on Deconstructing 'the Popular'" in *People's History and Socialist Theory*, Samuel, R. (ed.). 227–242. London: Routledge & Kegan Paul.

Harris, K.K. 2006. *Extreme Metal*, London, Berg.

Hebdige, D. 1981. *Subculture: The Meaning of Style*. London, Routledge.

Heidegger, M. 1975. *Poetry, Language, Thought*. London: Harper and Row.

Hoggart, R. 1957. *The Uses of Literacy*. London, Transaction Publications.

Leader, D. 2009. *The New Black: Mourning, Melancholy and Depression*. Harmondsworth: Penguin.

Masciandaro, Nicola, 2015. 'Black Sabbath's "Black Sabbath": A Gloss on Heavy Metal's Originary Song' in *Floating Tomb: Black Metal Theory*, edited by Edia Connole and Nicola Masciandaro, 35–52. Mimesis International, pp. 40.

Owen, W. 1994. The War Poems of Wilfred Owen. London: Chatto & Windus.

Rosen, S. 2002. *Black Sabbath*, London: Sanctuary,

Segal, H. 1986. "A Psychoanalytical Approach to Aesthetics" in *The Work of Hanna Segal*, 185–205. London: Free Association Books.

Wilfred Owen. 1994. The War Poems of Wilfred Owen.

Williams, R. 1971. *Culture and Society* 1780–1950. Harmondsworth: Penguin.

Wilson, S. 2012. "From Forests Unknown: "Eurometal" and the political/audio unconscious" *The Metal Void: First Gatherings*, Scott, N. (ed.): 149–159. London: Inter-disciplinary Press.

Wilson, S. 2014. *Melancology: Black Metal and Ecology*. Winchester: Zero Books.

Sainato, M. 2015. 'Steven Hawking, Elon Musk and Bill Gates Warn about Artificial Intelligence' in *The Observer*. 08/09/15.

Pieslak, J. 2009. *Sound Targets: American Soldiers and Music in the Iraq War*. Bloomington: Indiana University Press.

Shock Rock Horror! The Representation and Reception of Heavy Metal Horror Films in the 1980s

Nedim Hassan

In histories of the development of the heavy metal music genre in the United States, the 1980s has been considered a hugely significant period. Not only did heavy metal become a 'dominant genre of American music', it became the locus of a moral panic and accordingly, as Walser puts it, 'a site of explicit social contestation' (Walser 1993, 24). This moral panic has been discussed at length by various scholars who have identified how during the mid-1980s the Parents' Music Resource Center (PMRC), a powerful pressure group with links to US politicians, pursued a highly visible media campaign that effectively served to demonise heavy metal as a genre that allegedly promoted violence, suicide, Satanism, involvement with the occult and other deviant activities to America's youth (Brown 2011; Wright 2000; Chastagner 1999).

As Wright (2000) and Brown (2011) suggest, major factors in amplifying the moral panic during this period were the accessibility and authority of the groups making claims about the destructive influence of heavy

N. Hassan (✉)
Liverpool John Moores University, Liverpool, UK

© The Author(s) 2018
N. Bentley et al. (eds.), *Youth Subcultures in Fiction, Film and Other Media*, Palgrave Studies in the History of Subcultures and Popular Music, https://doi.org/10.1007/978-3-319-73189-6_10

163

metal. Politicians, religious organisations, police, probation and mental health services were all articulating concerns about the negative influence of metal on youth to parents and families via mass media. This construction of metal culture as deviant had implications for fans' notions of self-identity, with some feeling that they were treated differently by authorities and that they had to defend their musical tastes (Weinstein 2000; Friesen 1990). Furthermore, in the light of debates about metal's influence on youth, mental health facilities in Southern California were willing to hospitalise adolescents on the basis of parental concerns about their children's preference for the music (Rosenbaum and Prinsky 1991). Therefore, it is apparent that the moral panic had an impact upon the regulation of young peoples' behaviour in the 1980s.

The prominence of these claims within the mass media ensured that even though articles that challenged such ideas did appear within academic research and niche media such as heavy metal magazines, they were largely ignored in broader media debates. Consequently, Brown (2011) concludes that fans in the 1980s had limited means to counteract the development of the moral panic. However, while much has been written about the above moral panic and its impact, hitherto there has been relatively little attention paid to how it influenced popular film in this period. Taking as a starting point Andrew Tudor's emphasis on the importance of scrutinising the sociocultural moment when attempting to understand the potential appeal of genre texts at a particular place and time, this chapter examines a relatively short-lived cycle of films that may be termed 'heavy metal horror movies' (Tudor 2002). Films like *Trick or Treat* (1986), *The Gate* (1987) and *Black Roses* (1988) explicitly portrayed aspects of heavy metal culture and were released at a point when debates about metal's influence on youth were at their most acute. This chapter contends that consideration of these films as products released during a climate of moral panic is crucial. It illustrates that the broader media debates mentioned above, which were motivated by the purpose of controlling America's youth, influenced both discourses about heavy metal music and discourses relating to the heavy metal horror films. However, through analysis of these films and an assessment of audiences' interpretations of them, this chapter demonstrates that these texts are ambivalent and had the potential during this vital historical moment to constitute resources of resistance for youth audiences and metal fans in particular.

Heavy Metal Horror Films as Exploitation Movies

Shary depicts the heavy metal horror films as a 'short-lived phenomenon' (2002, 147) that constituted a generic subcategory in its own right and existed alongside other more established horror subgenres such as the slasher film. However, as Deighan (2016) points out, the heavy metal horror film has a longer history that complicates definitions of it as a distinctive subgenre. This is because earlier films like *Terror on Tour* (1980) and *Rocktober Blood* (1984) were essentially drawing upon motifs from the slasher horror subgenre but featured protagonists who were associated with metal and hard rock bands (either as victims or killers). Deighan goes on to point out that the heavy metal horror trend stretches into the 1990s with low-budget films such as *Shock 'Em Dead* (1991) and *Dead Girls* (1990). This chapter will focus upon the films that were released in the immediate wake of the PMRC media campaign and the congressional hearings of 1985 when the moral panic relating to metal music culture was at its most acute. Consequently, analysis will be confined to a consideration of *Trick or Treat* (1986), *The Gate* (1987), *Rock 'n' Roll Nightmare* (1987) and *Black Roses* (1988).

In a sense, then, these films can also be defined as exploitation movies in that they were produced in order to capitalise on both the success of the heavy metal musical genre and to exploit the controversy surrounding it. Commenting on the development of the exploitation movie in the 1950s, Doherty notes that such movies were 'triply exploitative, simultaneously exploiting sensational happenings (for story value), their notoriety (for publicity value), and their teenage participants (for box office value)' (1988, 8). The heavy metal horror films, as will be illustrated below, all match this description to a large extent.

As Cherry asserts, horror films are adept at being able to 'tap into the cultural moment by encoding the anxieties of the moment into their depictions of monstrosity' (2009, 11). It will be demonstrated below that these heavy metal horror films achieved this by primarily connecting iconography and events associated with metal culture to notions of monstrosity, Satanic ritual, possession, deviance and violence. Crucially, they all accomplish this articulation through narratives that centre on the experiences of young people. Thus, in one sense they can also be seen as part of a broader trend which saw the growth of teen-centred horror films, particularly after 1985, a year in which teen horror film releases had doubled compared to the previous one (Shary 2002). Shary argues that the teen horror of this period, exemplified in slasher films such as the popular *Nightmare on Elm Street* and *Friday the 13th* series, worked as what Feuer terms a kind of 'cultural problem-solving' device in that it served to 'Other' youth characters in specific ways, featuring monsters that punished adolescent transgression (Feuer 1987, 144; Shary 2002).

This ritual approach to the study of the horror genre is valuable because it enables us to explicate how horror film texts can become part of a 'cultural forum [...] involving the negotiation of shared beliefs and values, and helping to maintain and rejuvenate the social order as well as assisting it in adapting to change' (Feuer 1987, 144). Consequently, horror films in this period that depicted the activities of youths had the potential to become part of the negotiation of shared cultural values, contributing to understandings of 'normal' and 'abnormal' youth behaviour by directly confronting anxieties about 'Otherness' (Wood 2002).

However, Neale (2000) and Tudor (2002) point out that this approach needs to be adopted with care because there is a tendency for analysts using it to be somewhat selective when choosing films that are exemplars of cultural problem-solving, ignoring texts that may contradict their theories. Moreover, scholars employing the ritual approach have sometimes tended to lack an appreciation of the potential complexity of film audiences. Consequently, it is vital to consider the 'appeal of a genre in a particular socio-temporal context' and to appreciate that audiences 'conceive genres variably, taking divergent pleasures from them' (Tudor 2002, 49). Thus, the analysis that follows attempts to maintain a consideration of Tudor's key question: 'why do *these* people like *this* horror in *this* place at *this* particular time' (2002, 54). Consequently, the sections that follow, whilst analysing the generic conventions of heavy metal horror, will also connect these with issues emerging from the aforementioned moral panic and will consider the reception of these films by audiences.

CONVENTIONS OF HEAVY METAL HORROR

In terms of their use of generic conventions, the heavy metal horror films of the mid-to-late 1980s utilised elements that featured in wider youth-oriented films of the period. Sharing similarities with texts like *976-EVIL* (1988) and *The Lost Boys* (1987), as well as with earlier texts like *Carrie* (1976), several of the films depict alienated teen characters who are struggling to deal with a dysfunctional family life, the loss of a parent or the pressures of high school. *Black Roses* and *The Gate* in particular establish problematic relationships between key characters and their parents from early scenes onwards. For instance, both John (*Black Roses*) and Terry (*The Gate*) live in single-parent households with their fathers, who are portrayed as either distant (John's father hardly looks at him and is mainly depicted staring at his newspaper) or absent (we never see Terry's father, but we see a note left on the refrigerator door that he is away 'on business' and Terry is left to eat cold pizza). While Eddie, the central character in *Trick or Treat*, has a caring single mother, he spends the majority of his time in his bedroom and, moreover, his status as an alienated teen is established from the outset of the film when we learn that he is being bullied by jocks at his high school.

In a highly effective opening sequence, not only does *Trick or Treat* establish Eddie as a victim of bullying, it alludes to the notion that this has led him to contemplate suicide. We see Eddie in his bedroom writing a letter to his rock star idol, Sammi Curr, and we hear the content of this in the form of a monologue that continues to unfold whilst we witness high-school-based incidents of harassment that provide visual testimony to some of his words. In this sequence we learn that Eddie has had 'radical' thoughts of ending 'it all' but that 'the one thing that kept me going' was his rock idol.

Trick or Treat's broaching of the issue of teenage suicide is distinctive. It is the only heavy metal horror film to allude to the connections between metal and suicide that were being made during some of the debates in this period. Weinstein (2000) and Brown (2011) make clear that this was a connection that was articulated during testimony given at the Senate hearing organised by the PMRC in 1985, as well as during subsequent media reports. However, *Trick or Treat*'s immediate refutation of Eddie's suicidal thoughts through the affirmation of his fandom—'the one thing that kept me going was you'—provides a striking contrast to the wider media discourse of the period. Rather than suggest that metal music fandom can cause or promote youth suicide, which was an allegation that became central to discourses denouncing metal, *Trick or Treat* implies that metal fandom can offer salvation from suicidal thoughts. Indeed, to an extent, both this film and *The Gate* construct metal music as a positive communicative force that can become a medium for the empowerment of young people. Ironically when Eddie first listens to backwards messages on a Sammi Curr record, (an act associated with controversy because Christian groups were alleging that backward masking on records often promoted pro-suicide or Satanic messages), he is given instructions on how to stand up to his high school tormentors (Ladouceur 2016). In *The Gate* it is the album sleeve notes and lyrics of the fictional band Sacrifyx that provide Terry and Glenn with the specialist knowledge they need to understand and eventually close the gateway to the Hell-like world that they have inadvertently opened, saving Glenn's sister and his family home.

What complicates the construction of music culture as a potential source of youth empowerment in the heavy metal horror films is the way that metal music and musicians are to varying degrees located within the realm of the occult and the Satanic. In *The Gate* Sacrifyx possess knowledge of the 'Old Gods' and have performed occult rituals that their album sleeve implies enabled them to open the gate and led to their destruction. Rock star Sammi Curr in *Trick or Treat* ritually sacrifices himself in flames in order to be eventually reincarnated as a demon by the devoted Eddie. The Satanic Black Roses of John Fasano's 1988 film are masquerading as a metal band in order to convert the youth of Mill Basin into murderous demons. While in *Rock 'n' Roll Nightmare*, although the band Tritonz and their followers are ultimately revealed as 'mere shadows' designed to enable the Archangel Triton to entice and do battle with Satan, it is still telling that it is a metal band that is depicted as being suitable to lure 'old Scratch' himself.

In *Trick or Treat* and *Black Roses* the articulation of metal with Satan and the occult is compounded by a narrative device employed in earlier films such as *Children of the Corn* (1984), namely the inclusion of a false God or prophet who brainwashes youths, attempting to turn them against adults and carry out murderous deeds. This is manifested most explicitly in *Black Roses* when the band plays a series of concerts in Mill Basin. After each show the town's youth become enchanted by the band's power, becoming increasingly alienated from school and their families. This then leads them to carry out acts of delinquency before eventually murdering their parents. In this instance, the metal band Black Roses are a malign, corrupting influence, who, like Isaac, the deranged child preacher in *Children of the Corn*, indoctrinate the town's youth into committing murderous acts on adults in order to serve an evil deity. In *Trick or Treat* despite the warnings of his DJ friend Nuke (played by hard rock band Kiss's Gene Simmons) that Sammi Curr 'wasn't a God', Eddie's idolising of Sammi is ultimately revealed as dangerous when his continued playing of backwards record messages helps to reincarnate Curr as a powerful demon capable of controlling electricity. Once the source of a more empowered and assertive sense of identity for Eddie, idolatry of a metal star is revealed as misguided once Eddie realises that Curr is a 'false God'.

All of the films discussed above feature, to varying degrees, iconography associated with metal music culture. This includes: album sleeves and artwork; clothing such as denim and leather jackets, bandanas, patches and rock T-shirts; other markers of subcultural style and affiliation such as long hair styles and dance styles such as head banging and air guitar; electric guitars and amplifiers. Furthermore, each of the films features metal music that is often deployed for both diegetic and extra-diegetic purposes during the soundtracks. Yet it is the portrayal of music technology in these texts that is another significant factor to examine in order to further explicate how they work as horror texts and resonate with wider social anxieties. Each film posits the notion that musical artefacts such as recording studios (*Rock 'n' roll Nightmare*), speakers (*Trick or Treat* and *Black Roses*), personal stereos and hi-fi systems (*Trick or Treat*), or else vinyl records themselves (*Trick or Treat*, *The Gate* and *Black Roses*) can act as conduits for evil.

This notion is most prevalent in *Trick or Treat* when playing an album backwards facilitates the eventual reincarnation of the demonic Sammi Curr. Although even prior to Curr's full appearance, one of the most striking scenes in the film is when, following instructions from Curr's backwards messages, Eddie plants a tape recording with Tim, the jock who leads the bullying against him. Tim's girlfriend, Jeannie, then listens to the cassette on her personal stereo in Tim's car after he momentarily leaves her alone whilst they are 'making out' by a lake. A ghostly green essence slowly emanates from Jeannie's headphones and proceeds to sexually arouse her by stimulating her breasts and vagina, before a monstrous salivating apparition is manifested, causing her to scream and faint. When Tim arrives back at the car Jeannie's headphones are smoking and appear to have melted the flesh of her ear lobes.

This scene and later ones, such as when Sammi Curr emerges from Eddie's bedroom speakers or attacks people at the high school concert by firing bolts of electricity from his guitar, blends fears concerning the threat of the occult with technophobia. In his essay on technology and the Satanic film, Ferguson argues that films like *976-EVIL* (1988) and *Evilspeak* (1981) foreground anxieties in 1980s USA over 'controversial communication technologies' such as 976 and 900 premium rate phone lines that parents were concerned about their children accessing from the home because they 'posed threats to traditional family structures' through the way that they potentially made pornography available (Ferguson 2016, 97). In the heavy metal horror films such anxieties about the control of communication technologies are (at times literally!) amplified. Not only is metal music a source of fear, this genre is portrayed as ubiquitous and mobile in that it can attack from hardware within the home and outside of it. Indeed, towards the end of *Trick or Treat* Eddie's car stereo possesses his car through the broadcast of Sammi Curr's music.

Given that radio had by the 1930s become a domesticated medium for music that as Moores (2000, 48) puts it 'was passing from the miraculous to the taken-for-granted', these representations of music technologies that had by the 1980s become naturalised within everyday American life are striking. Although there were some concerns about personal stereo usage and its potential to be socially disruptive or cause hearing damage, it had become a central leisure activity for many Americans by the mid-1980s (Du Gay et al. 2013). The transistor radio had enabled music to be heard 'on the move' since the mid-1950s (Peterson 1990). Yet in these texts such everyday media technologies were implicated in the potential destruction of youth and the family.

While the domestication of music technologies within the family home is a process that historically involved contestation and negotiation between men and women (Keightley 1996; Moores 2000), in the heavy metal horror films the construction of this domestication as uncanny can be linked with parental anxieties over their children's use of such technologies. In Freud's (2003 [1919]) influential work on the uncanny he examines the relationship between the German terms *heimlich* (which roughly translates as meaning something familiar and home-like) and *unheimlich* (which translates as the opposite—something unfamiliar) in order to discuss how certain fictional depictions or real situations can foreground uncanny thoughts or feelings that human subjects have repressed. Drawing on this concept, it is apparent that films like *Trick or Treat* and *Black Roses* articulate the notion that familiar, domesticated, everyday *heimlich* music technologies located in living rooms, bedrooms and cars have become *unheimlich*: de-familiarised and uncanny. Freud makes clear that the uncanny is 'something familiar [...] that has been repressed and then reappears' (2003 [1919], 152); in these films, an older sense of the 'miraculous' (Moores 2000, 48) and undomesticated, rather than the everyday aspect of music technologies, is being foregrounded.

Moreover, this foregrounding takes place in order to emphasise a loss of parental control over their children and over musical commodities that have been appropriated by youth. Nowhere is this anxiety over the loss of control more effectively summed up than in a scene in *Black Roses* where efforts by a paternal figure to control loud metal music are met with a deadly attack by music technology. Tony's father chastises him in the living room, telling him to 'turn this [metal] music off!' before switching off the record. Sending Tony out of the room to help his mother with the dishes, his father sits down on the sofa only for the stereo system to switch itself back on and continue blasting out metal. When he inspects the record turntable he finds that the spinning vinyl disc has distorted into a monstrous form with bulging black flesh. Glancing up he realises that the speaker has undergone a similar transformation and he is powerless to prevent a spider-like alien monster from attacking him, wrapping its jaws around his head and devouring him through the speaker.

The generic conventions of these heavy metal horror films, therefore, need to be understood not only in relation to broader horror texts of the period, they need to be situated in relation to broader sociocultural anxieties about the control of youth cultural activities. As the above examples illustrate, these were ambivalent texts that exploited moral panics about metal culture in order to suggest that this was something firmly linked with the occult and uncanny, yet they also suggested that this culture could offer salvation as well as damnation. For the remainder of this chapter issues with the reception of these texts will be considered by paying particular attention to more contemporary audience evaluations of *Trick or Treat*. This will then enable an exploration of the impact of the aforementioned discourses and representations.

'Most of Us Metalheads Thought She Was Full of B.S.': The Reception of *Trick or Treat*

The production notes of *Trick or Treat* are revealing in that they clearly portray the film as having been produced with the satirical intention of 'poking fun at the forces and individuals on all sides of the controversy' surrounding metal music (*Trick or Treat*: production notes 1986, 5). As the main scriptwriter Rhet Topham (who was also a metal fan) explained in an online interview with a fan website, the debates led by the PMRC were: 'definately [sic] the seed for the film. At that time Tipper Gore [...] was running around screaming about something called 'Rock-Porn.' Most of us metalheads thought she was full of B.S.' (cited at SammiCurr.com, online 2016b). Indeed, *Trick or Treat* features a scene near the beginning of the film that parodies the congressional hearings into music lyrics that were instigated by the PMRC, with fictional rock star Sammi Curr raging against what he sees as attacks on free speech in much the same way that rock musicians Dee Snider and Frank Zappa had attacked the PMRC at the actual hearings. That the film was satirising the controversy being generated is also suggested by its ironic casting of heavy metal icon Ozzy Osbourne. Osbourne plays an evangelical preacher, the Rev. Aaron Gilstrom, who is featured on television ranting against 'sick' and depraved metal music.

This satirising of the moral panic about metal could be seen as a kind of folk devil reaction (Griffiths 2010) that was disseminated in a popular media form. Griffiths defines a public folk devil reaction as one that would be understood by members of a subculture but is designed to 'to be seen or heard by people who are not already involved or familiar with the group, community, or subculture that has triggered the moral panic in question' (2010, 410). Such reactions are designed to defend the subculture that is being demonised. Although not all of the producers of the above films may have set out to achieve this, it is interesting that some comments of fans of *Trick or Treat* interpret it in this manner.

For instance, a prevalent position articulated in the Internet Movie Database (IMDb) reviews of the film is a recognition that the film engages with the controversies surrounding heavy metal in the 1980s, with 35 out of the 65 reviews indicating some acknowledgement of the debates referred to earlier. Some of these comments demonstrate an awareness of the impact of the film's parodying of the moral panic. This is made evident in comments such as: 'What is also great about TT is how funny it is when [it] mocks and pokes fun at the controversy and criticism Heavy Metal went through at the time especially with Tipper Gore, the PMRC, playing Metal records backwards and probably hearing subliminal messages. It takes all those things that are mentioned above and makes laughs out of them' (jcbutthead86, Internet Movie Database 2016).

The significance of these aspects of *Trick or Treat* is augmented when we consider its dissemination to a mass market. It was the thirteenth most popular horror film watched in the US during 1986, a year that saw big blockbuster horror franchises like *Aliens, Poltergeist II* and *Friday the 13 Part VI*, doing good business at the box office. The film grossed $6,797,218, and it was likely that it was watched by a healthy audience on home video given that the film was released during the boom in video recorders and movie rentals (Box Office Mojo 2016 [online]). The soundtrack to the film, which was performed by Fastway, stayed on the US album charts for 11 months (Larkin 1995, 131). *Trick or Treat* was, therefore, watched and listened to (and potentially discussed and reflected upon) by a substantial number of people in the US.

If we accept James Twitchell's argument that the primary audience for horror in this period was adolescents, then consideration of the reception of this film becomes even more pertinent (Twitchell 1985, 68). In a period when it is apparent that some heavy metal audiences found it difficult to defend their cultural practices in the face of a sustained mass-media campaign by the PMRC, a different popular media form watched in the cinema and at home may have helped them to legitimate their self-identities in spite of marginalisation elsewhere. Indeed, as was discussed above, *Trick or Treat* in particular articulates anxieties about teenage marginalisation in that its central character, Eddie Weinbauer, is a heavy metal fan who is struggling to cope with high school life. The significance of this representation of Eddie and its potential impact on audiences within this specific historical context will now be considered further.

Eddie's victimisation by characters that are portrayed as jocks positions him as a 'burnout', which as Eckert (1989) has made clear in her ethnographic study of high school social roles was a prominent social category during the 1980s. Whereas jocks embody an attitude of conformity to the US high school's corporate hierarchical structure, burnouts represent the opposite end of the spectrum and are more alienated from this structure (Eckert 1989, 4). In a telling scene from early in the film, Jeanie, the girlfriend of the main jock character who bullies Eddie, confronts him and asks him why he is so 'creepy' and why he is not interested in who is 'running for school council'. Hence, from the outset *Trick or Treat* suggests to us that Eddie is connected with the burnout category in that he rejects the corporate hegemony of the high school. Yet, burnouts were not usually considered as targets for bullying; indeed as Eckert pointed out in personal communication, they were often considered 'tougher' than jocks and they usually had strong friendship networks (personal communication, 20th June 2014). By portraying Eddie as marginalised from any strong friendship networks, especially at the start of the film, but foregrounding the notion that he is (like burnouts) alienated from the high school system, *Trick or Treat* emphasises that this character is vulnerable. Furthermore, by largely isolating Eddie but maintaining a 'jocks versus burnouts' dialectic that would have been highly familiar to high school students, the film might have provided some in the audience with an opportunity to reflect upon personal anxieties about their position within school hierarchies.

The potential for this is demonstrated in online responses to the film on both IMDb and also fan websites devoted to *Trick or Treat*. Eleven out of the 65 IMDb reviews discuss identifying with Eddie, and some of these feature revealing reflections upon personal experience. One reviewer in particular elaborates on the significance of the fact that Eddie is portrayed as a victim of bullying and notes that 'The way Eddie is being bullied in the film is timeless and real and it will always be relevant because it happens all the time' (jcbutthead86, Internet Movie Database 2016). Another reviewer directly relates to Eddie's experiences, writing that 'I am a lot like the Eddie character as I was constantly bullied in school for loving heavy metal music and being different. So much so I now have post-traumatic stress disorder because of it and to see a movie where the lead character refuses to put up with the bullies anymore is inspiring' (cradleoffilth-fan777, Internet Movie Database 2016).

The theme of identification with Eddie is also suggested in contributions to the fan-created guestbook of a website devoted to the film. Guests on SammiCurr.com left messages such as: 'me and my life'; 'Can totally relate to Ragman [Eddie's nickname in the film]. I was [i]n high school when this came out. I was a metalhead. And still a metalhead.' (SammiCurr.com 2016a); 'this movie grabbed a part of myself that will forever be' (SammiCurr.com 2016a). While these online testimonies should not be read as a straightforward 'reflection' of the reception of *Trick or Treat* in the 1980s, what they do indicate is the potential for such texts to be empowering for some youth audiences at a time when other media, political and institutional discourses were constructing metal and other forms of youth culture as illegitimate and deviant.

Conclusion

In his seminal book on the cultural contexts of horror fiction, Grixti argues that magical beliefs become dominant in societies where humans have gaps in their knowledge and in their *powers of control* (Grixti 1989, 153). The power of horror is therefore connected with the way that it often plays with uncertainties that stem from anxieties about a lack of control over different aspects of life. Thus, it is not surprising that in *Trick or Treat*, as well as in other heavy metal horror films, the occult is often explored by adolescents. This is because as Twitchell points out, the concerns of adolescents are 'fraught with inarticulated [often sexual] anxiety' (1985, 68). It is significant that the specific use of the occult in *Trick or Treat* enables Eddie to control aspects of his life that he otherwise finds difficult (including getting a girlfriend). He accesses dead rock star Sammi Curr's occult powers (through playing a record backwards) in order to get back at the bullies who are making him feel powerless. The increased (magical) power that he obtains through engaging with Curr also gives him the confidence to present a more assertive self-identity in front of Leslie, the main love interest in the film.

Conversely the theme of helplessness and a lack of control dominated the discourses of those who claimed that metal music was a pernicious influence on youth in this period. The PMRC, as well as organisations like California-based Back in Control that delivered workshops to parents advising them of the dangers of their children's involvement with heavy metal and advocated 'de-metaling', articulated anxieties about the vulnerability of adolescents under the influence of metal and about the subsequent loss of parental control (Rosenbaum and Prinsky 1991). In the face of a national crisis over the condition of US youth evidenced by higher levels of child poverty and teenage suicide, it is striking that pressure groups like the PMRC partly attributed the causes of these problems to cultural artefacts like heavy metal albums (Giroux 2002, 172). For here too, as in heavy metal horror films, we have an example of magical beliefs about popular music's influence being invoked when groups of people lacked knowledge and had anxieties about control over others. Anxieties about control, particularly control over adolescents' life experiences are, therefore, a central thread for understanding the cultural impact of heavy metal horror films like *Trick or Treat* in mid-1980s USA. Yet, as this chapter has shown, these films were not only able to lay bare these anxieties. They offered youth audiences potential opportunities to reflect upon their own sense of control over their cultural practices when faced with wider discourses that denied them any agency.

REFERENCES

976-EVIL. 1988. Directed by Robert Englund. USA: Cinetel Films.
Black Roses 1988. Directed by John Fasano. USA: Shapiro-Glickenhaus Entertainment.
Box Office Mojo 2016. *Trick or Treat* [online] Available at: http://www.boxofficemojo.com/movies/?id=trickortreat.htm [accessed 20th October, 2016]
Brown, A. R. 2011. Suicide solutions? Or, how the emo class of 2008 were able to contest their media demonization, whereas the headbangers, burnouts or 'children of ZoSo' generation were not. *Popular Music History*, 6 (1–2): 19–37.
Carrie. 1976. Directed by Brian De Palma. USA: Red Bank Films.

Chastagner, C. 1999. The Parents' Music Resource Center: from information to censorship. *Popular Music*, 18 (2): 179–192.

Cherry, B. 2009. *Horror*. London: Routledge.

Children of the Corn 1984. Directed by Fritz Kiersch. USA: Angeles Entertainment Group.

Dead Girls. 1990. Directed by Dennis Devine. USA: Bovine Productions.

Deighan, S. 2016. Trick or Treat: Heavy metal and devil worship in '80s cult cinema. In *Satanic Panic: pop-cultural paranoia in the 1980s*. Janisse, K. and Corupe, P. (eds.) 201–215. Surrey: FAB Press.

Du Gay, P., Hall, S., Janes, L., Madsen, A. K., McKay, H. and Negus, K. 2013. *Doing Cultural Studies: the story of the Sony Walkman*. Milton Keynes: Open University.

Doherty, T. 1988. *Teenagers and teenpics: the juvenilization of American movies in the 1950s*. London: Unwin Hyman.

Eckert, P. 1989. *Jocks & Burnouts: Social Categories and Identity in the High School*. New York: Teachers College Press.

Eckert, P. (eckert@stanford.edu) 20th June 2014 *Re. A Question about Jocks and Burnouts*. Email to Nedim Hassan (n.a.hassan@ljmu.ac.uk).

Evilspeak. 1981. Directed by Eric Weston. USA: Leisure Investment Company, Coronet Film Corporation.

Ferguson, K. L. 2016. 'Devil on the Line: technology and the satanic film.' In *Satanic Panic: pop-cultural paranoia in the 1980s*. Janisse, K. and Corupe, P. (eds.) 97–125. Surrey: FAB Press.

Feuer, J. 1987 'Genre Study and Television.' In: *Channels of Discourse*. Allen, R. C. (ed.) 138–160. London: Methuen.

Freud, S. 2003. *The Uncanny*. London: Penguin Books.

Friesen, B. K. 1990. 'Powerless in Adolescence: exploiting heavy metal listeners.' In *Marginal Conventions: popular culture, mass media and social deviance*. Sanders, C. R. (ed.) 65–77. Ohio: Bowling Green State University Popular Press.

Giroux, H. A. 2002. *Breaking into the movies: film and the culture of politics*. Oxford: Blackwell.

Griffiths, R. 2010. 'The gothic folk devils strike back! Theorizing folk devil reaction in the post-Columbine era.' *Journal of Youth Studies*, 13 (3): 403–422.

Grixti, J. 1989. *Terrors of Uncertainty: The Cultural Contexts of Horror Fiction*. London: Routledge.

Internet Movie Database 2016. Reviews & Ratings for *Trick or Treat* [online] Available at: http://www.imdb.com/title/tt0092112/reviews?ref_=tt_ov_rt [Accessed 24th October 2016]

Keightley, K. 1996. 'Turn it down!' she shrieked: Gender, domestic space, and high fidelity, 1948–59. *Popular Music*, 15 (2), 149–177.

Ladouceur, L. 2016. 'The Filthy 15: When Venom and King Diamond met the Washington wives.' In *Satanic Panic: pop-cultural paranoia in the 1980s*. Janisse, K. and Corupe, P. (eds.) 159–171. Surrey: FAB Press.

Larkin, C. (ed.) 1995. *The Guinness Who's Who of Heavy Metal.* London: Guinness Publishing.

Moores, S. 2000. *Media and everyday life in modern society.* Edinburgh: Edinburgh University Press.

Neale, S. 2000. *Genre and Hollywood.* London: Routledge.

Peterson, R. 1990. Why 1955? Explaining the advent of rock music. *Popular Music,* 9 (1): 97–116.

Rock 'n' Roll Nightmare 1987. Directed by John Fasano. USA: Thunder.

Rocktober Blood. 1984. Directed by Beverly Sebastian. USA: Sebastian International Pictures.

Rosenbaum, J. L. and Prinsky, L. 1991. 'The Presumption of Influence: Recent Responses to Popular Music Subcultures.' *Crime & Delinquency,* 37 (4): 528–535.

Sammi Curr.com 2016a. *Guestbook* [online], updated 31st October 2016 Available at: http://sammicurr.123guestbook.com/ [Accessed 20th November 2016]

Sammi Curr.com 2016b. *Interview with Trick or Treat screenwriter Mr Rhet Topham* [online] Available at: http://sammicurr.com/mrtopham.htm [Accessed 20th November 2016]

Shary, T. 2002. *Generation multiplex: the image of youth in contemporary American cinema.* Texas: University of Texas press.

Shock 'Em Dead. 1991. Directed by Mark Freed. USA: Noma Productions.

Terror on Tour. 1980. Directed by Don Edmonds. USA: Four Features Partners.

The Gate 1987. Directed by Tibor Takács. Canada: New Century Entertainment.

The Lost Boys. 1987. Directed by Joel Schumacher. USA: Warner Brothers.

Trick or Treat 1986. Directed by Charles Martin Smith. USA: De Laurentiis Entertainment Group.

Trick or Treat: Production Notes 1986. De Laurentiis Entertainment Group.

Tudor, A. 2002. Why Horror? The Peculiar Pleasures of a Popular Genre. In *Horror: the film reader* Jancovich, M. (ed.) 47–55. New York: Routledge.

Twitchell, J. B. 1985. *Dreadful Pleasures: An anatomy of modern horror.* Oxford: Oxford University Press.

Walser, R. 1993. *Running with the Devil: Power, gender and madness in heavy metal music.* Hanover, NH: Wesleyan University Press.

Weinstein, D. 2000. *Heavy Metal: The Music and its Culture.* Boston: Da Capo Press.

Wood, R. 2002. The American Nightmare: Horror in the 70s. In *Horror: the film reader.* Jancovich, M. (ed.) 25–32. New York: Routledge.

Wright, R. 2000. 'I'd sell you suicide': pop music and moral panic in the age of Marilyn Manson. *Popular Music,* 19 (3): 365–385.

Youth, Hysteria and Control in Peter Watkins's *Privilege*

Rehan Hyder

INTRODUCTION: THE PITFALLS OF THE BRITISH POP MOVIE

The twin releases on DVD and Blu-ray of Peter Watkins's *Privilege* in 2010 by New Yorker Video and the BFI was a significant moment of rediscovery for those interested both in post-war British film and also for students of the pop music movie. Not only did this release reintroduce a key film in the oeuvre of one of Britain's most gifted and controversial directors, it also filled an important gap in the development of a particular strand of film-making exploring the avenues and byways of the popular music industry. Watkins's film is key to the development of the subgenre of British films that focus on the exploitative aspects of the popular music industry. Whilst many films have explored the manipulative and dehumanising forces brought to bear on the figure of the pop star, it is only Watkins's film that attempts to explore such a narrative within a broader political context. The framing of the narrative within *Privilege* around post-Marxist ideas of media manipulation as practised by the forces of the culture industry marks out his film as a unique provocation, one that reflects not only

R. Hyder (✉)
University of the West of England, Bristol, UK

© The Author(s) 2018
N. Bentley et al. (eds.), *Youth Subcultures in Fiction, Film and Other Media*, Palgrave Studies in the History of Subcultures and Popular Music, https://doi.org/10.1007/978-3-319-73189-6_11

179

the tumultuous period in which it was made but also is prescient in its representation of pop music as a means of pacifying the vulnerable masses.

The framing of the pop music industry as devious and unscrupulous was a theme first established in British film in the 1950s. The focus on the machinations of commercial pop has retained a grim fascination for generations of film-makers and their audiences. Following early attempts to chart the rise of the nascent rock 'n' roll star, films such as *The Tommy Steele Story* (1959), which reflected a celebratory and optimistic quality, British film-makers soon began to explore the pitfalls of the music industry and adopt a much more cynical tone.

Films like *Expresso Bongo* (1959) and *A Hard Day's Night* (1964), whilst capturing the energy and excitement of the burgeoning post-war pop industry, began to reflect a more sceptical and cynical approach. This tendency focused on the machinations of the commercial aspects of the industry and emphasised the exploitation of the individual artist at the heart of the narrative. These often-disparaging and always-knowing accounts of the commercial pop world began playfully, satirising the self-serving operations of unscrupulous managers and promoters, but later gave way to darker and more disturbing tales of burnout and decline. Such was the dominance of this particular narrative that the decades following the 1960s gave rise to such films as *Stardust* (1974), *Flame* (1975), *Breaking Glass* (1980) and *Brothers of the Head* (2005) which developed more sinister takes on the 'rise and fall' story. The sleazy and cruel nature of the music industry depicted in these films gives little credence to the hope and optimism of the early British pop film, instead charting the protagonist's exposure to the dehumanising forces of organised capital.

In these films all of the potential and artistic creativity of the central figure of the singer/musician is all but smothered by an industry that treats them as little more than slaves,[1] ultimately reducing them to obscurity, madness and even death. These dramatic narratives are informed by a critique that contrasts the youthful energy and artistic potential of the titular star against an unfeeling and manipulative capitalist system that chews up and spits out these tragic protagonists. These films share an approach which views the industrial side of pop music in a negative light; any overtly political analysis tends to be dissipated and distributed by focusing on the individual roles played by managers, promoters and businessmen—the evil baddies that seek to thwart the naïve ambitions of the creative artist.

It is really only Peter Watkins's film that attempts a wider examination of the political and ideological implications of producing pop. Drawing on a post-Marxist critique of mass cultural production and reflecting the rise of the global pop star in the 1950s and 1960s, Watkins was able, in *Privilege*, to create one of the most overtly politically charged films to be produced by a major motion picture company. The largely negative critical response to *Privilege* and its subsequent obscurity was to have a profound effect on Watkins's approach to film-making, so much that he not only turned his back on the studio system but never made another film in his own country. Despite the many years that the film languished in obscurity, rarely viewed or discussed by audiences and critics alike, the re-emergence of *Privilege* nearly fifty years after its initial release reveals a work of uncommon passion and polemic, with the themes of mass-media and ideological manipulation both prescient and provocative for our times.

THE SOCIAL CEMENT: POP MUSIC AND THE CULTURE INDUSTRY

The imaginary setting of 'Britain in the near future' that provides the backdrop for *Privilege* presents a world where the production and consumption of popular culture has become fully integrated with the dominant political and ideological framework. Whilst clearly influenced by the recent developments in pop music culture represented by the rise of the international pop star—as epitomised by Beatlemania in the mid-late 1960s—the overriding concerns of Watkins's film owe much to the theories and ideas developed by post-Marxist writers and thinkers of the twentieth century. In particular, Watkins evokes the work of the Frankfurt School, especially Max Horkheimer and Theodor Adorno whose ideas about what they coined 'the culture industry' (Adorno and Horkheimer 1997) helps to frame the dramatic narrative of *Privilege*. Focusing on the internal logic of advanced capitalism and the rise of factory production, Adorno and Horkheimer emphasised that standardisation was becoming central to understanding this system. Their contention that cultural products such as movies and music could be produced in the same way as other consumer durables like cars and refrigerators was supported by examples such as the Hollywood studio system and Tin Pan Alley. The passivity of the audience/consumer implicated in this analysis reflects the wider ideological ramifications produced by this system of cultural production. Adorno and Horkheimer suggest not only that the culture industry ensures a predicable cycle of production and profit, but also that they propagate the political values that underpin the continuation of a system of inequality:

there is an agreement—or at least the determination—of all executive authorities not to produce or sanction anything that in any way differs from their own rules, their own ideas about consumers, or above all, themselves [...] (Adorno and Horkheimer 1997, 33)

A central facet within this argument is the notion that the mass ranks of ordinary people are both vulnerable and passive in their reception of the endless reproduction of standardised cultural forms. Taken together with the full panoply of mass-produced cultural forms, standardised popular music has the ability not only to generate repeatable profits but also to ensure that the masses are given the safe means of escapist relief:

Together with sport and film, mass music and the new listening helps to make escape from the whole infantile milieu impossible. The sickness has a preservative function. (Adorno 2001, 47)

Music, then, acts as a kind of 'social cement' (Adorno 1990) that is able to offer some temporary relief to the individual within the masses so that they are effectively distracted from the unequal and oppressive systems of economic and political control.

The vision of Britain presented in *Privilege*, then, effectively develops the themes outlined by Adorno and Horkheimer by focusing on the fictional career of the pop star Steven Shorter, 'the most desperately loved entertainer in the world'. We are introduced to Steven Shorter (portrayed by real-life pop star Paul Jones) as he is heralded in a US-style ticker-tape parade in his home town of Birmingham in celebration of his triumphant global tour. This is followed by footage of his homecoming live performance in front of a packed house of adoring and often hysterical fans. The bizarre stage show that focuses around Shorter's incarceration and attempted escape from brutal prison guards is inflected with violence and provocation, providing the backdrop for the film's first musical number *Free Me*.[2] This intense pantomime ends in a wilfully orchestrated near riot over which the film's deadpan narrator (voiced by Watkins himself) makes clear the ideological function of the performance;

The reason given for the extreme violence of the stage act that you are about to see is that it provides the public with a necessary release from all the nervous tension caused the state of the world...

Polemical statements such as this set Watkins apart from other British pop films which, although sharing elements of critique with

YOUTH, HYSTERIA AND CONTROL IN PETER WATKINS'S *PRIVILEGE* 183

Privilege, focus exclusively on the personal narrative of the manipulated pop star with little consideration of the wider political context. It is clear from the outset that Watkins's narrative has clear allegiances with the ideas of Horkheimer and Adorno. Whilst the character of Steven Shorter is afforded a demi-god status amongst his followers that is replicated in other British pop movies, the placing of the music star at the centre of wider political control and manipulation is unique. As we learn more about the central protagonist of *Privilege*, we realise that not only is he a purveyor of successive pop hits[3] and concerts but also the figurehead of Steven Shorter television stations, consumer 'dreampalaces' and discotheques. Watkins, then, establishes from the outset the key role that Shorter plays in binding together the various aspects of the culture industry in order to help maintain the political status quo:

> Britain in the near future. There is now a coalition government in Britain which has recently asked all entertainment agencies to usefully divert the violence of youth. Keep them happy, off the streets and out of politics.

During an interview in 1978, Watkins reflected on this articulation of the ideological function of popular music as represented in *Privilege*, claiming that 'The media uses so-called counter-revolutionary movements, methods and songs, and then simply repackages them and regurgitates them to the young' (Friedman 1983, 238).

Watkins emphasis in *Privilege* goes beyond the idea of pop simply as commercial manipulation extending this idea to encompass the broad range of media present in consumerist culture. In the aftermath of the histrionic opening performance the story moves first into one of Steven Shorter's branded discotheques, 'specially built (to) spread happiness throughout Britain', and then to a gaudy showroom where images of the compliant pop star are used to promote the sale of a range of household goods and easy credit:

> You are now in what is called a Steve Dream Palace. There are 300 of these in Britain each designed to keep people happy and buying British [...] A full range of consumer products bear the pop star's name including various items badged 'Steve's Electrics' (washing machines, refrigerators and TV sets) and even 'Steve Chunk Dog Food'. Once within the dream palaces, all goods and services are promised and as a piped in advert declares, 'If we haven't got it, Steve will get it for you'.

Placing the charismatic pop icon at the centre of the capitalist mode of production allows Watkins to develop the earlier notion of the culture industry by focusing on the increasing centrality of the star performer in stimulating and shaping patterns of popular consumption. The opening scenes of hysterical fan worship bordering on riotous display clearly evoke the recent phenomena of Beatlemania that had spread from Britain into Europe and America during the 1960s. The intensity of such fan behaviour, particularly when articulated by seemingly 'vulnerable' young people, lends itself then to the portentous narrative of centralised control and media manipulation at the heart of *Privilege*.

ONWARD, STEVEN SHORTER: THE MONOFORM POP STAR

Privilege, then, played an important part in the development of Watkins's overall critique of contemporary mass media and helped shape many of his subsequent projects, particularly *The Gladiators* (1969) and *Punishment Park* (1971). Both of these films develop the themes of mass manipulation and control first introduced in *Privilege* and helped to advance Watkins's critical approach to mainstream film-making and media which he himself sought to challenge as a film-maker. *Privilege* was the only time that Watkins worked with a major studio (Universal funded the film to the sum of £700,000, allowing the film-maker a remarkably free reign on the narrative and final cut). The effect of the largely negative critical and commercial response to *Privilege* (particularly in the UK) combined with his previous falling out with the BBC over the refusal to broadcast his controversial documentary *The War Game* in 1965, convinced Watkins that his future works should only be produced outside of mainstream media institutions.

Watkins's wider philosophy about film-making and his critique of mainstream media production focus on many of the issues foregrounded in *Privilege*. Watkins suggests that contemporary 'mass audio visual media' (MAVM) (Watkins 2016) seek to 'shape, distort, manipulate, control, fragment, isolate, blur and change our perception'. The term he uses to describe increasingly standardised media productions is 'MONOFORM' and this is characterised as

an instantly recognisable highly fragmented, rapidly cutting, endlessly tracking, zooming and fidgeting method of using images, accompanied by densely packed, noisy, restless and constantly interrupting soundtracks. (ibid.)

These techniques, argues Watkins, have saturated much of our contemporary media landscape, and, again reflecting notions akin to that emerging from the idea of the culture industry, he suggests that this has a damaging and stultifying effect on audiences:

> a consistent use of the Monoform—with its total absence of time for reflection, its apparently seamless (and thus unquestionable) narrative thrust, its constant monolinear direction forward (denying flexibility of memory, and complexity of human experience)—has had both obvious and incalculable long-term effects on our feelings. It has desensitized us to many of the things that occur both on the screen, and everywhere around us (particularly to violence, and the fate of others). (ibid.)

In *Privilege*, it is the figure of Steven Shorter that is at the apex of this MONOFORM culture so that not only is he an adored pop singer and arch advertiser of consumer goods, but also that his presence dominates all mainstream broadcast media. The drama in *Privilege* centres on the rebranding of Steven Shorter from rebel to conformist in order to maximise the pacifying potential of the pop icon. This change in image is introduced into the narrative at a board meeting of Steven Shorter Enterprises Limited, chaired by the merchant banker Andrew Goddard Butler (William Job). The proposed change of image is presented not merely in order to promote further sales but also to use the popularity of the star to help subdue and manage the unruly and youthful masses. As government expert, Professor Tatham (James Cossins) explains to the gathered members of the board:

> we must of necessity subdue the critical elements in the country's youth. Gentlemen, in accordance with our planned campaign and because we've reached commercial saturation point. In 10 days' time we're going to make Steven Shorter repent. We're going to make him say, I'm sorry for what I've done.
>
> > We're going to make him say, Now I want to go back into society.
> > Now I will accept law and order.
> > No longer will I criticize or rock the boat.
> > We're going to make Steven Shorter say these things because we want, as we've always wanted, the youth of Britain to say them also.

In order to ensure the widespread success of this campaign, Shorter's management team are closely aligned with a veritable array of establishment institutions. Also present at this crucial board meeting are representatives from the Central Office of Information, the Board of Trade, the Ministry of Defence, the British Tourist Board, the Foreign Office, the Air Ministry, the Inland Waterways Board and the Commonwealth Office. The full range of governmental and industry bodies included ensuring the success of this campaign demonstrates Watkins dystopian vision of the near future where the interests of government and the cultural industries are inextricably melded together. In Watkins's film, any notion of political difference—let alone dissent—has all but been erased with the UK being governed by the coalition government of Britain—'formed because of the complete lack of difference between the policies of the Conservative and Labour parties'—whose aims of control and consumption are shared by those producing both consumer durables and consumer culture. The final piece in this ideological jigsaw is provided by the Church of England, who in an opportunistic and timely move (partly to stem the sharp decline of church attendance) add their support to the remodelling of Shorter's image. With all of the various components and adherents to establishment ideology in place, a concerted and coordinated campaign is put into place so that every element of the pop star's image and influence can be carefully brought on message. The climax of this campaign is represented in the film's dramatic finale: a live performance (supported by blanket media coverage on television and radio) at the National Stadium by Steven Shorter himself, the 'establishment event' that will ensure the youthful masses follow their idol and in doing so will ultimately fall in line.

FORGIVE US ALL!: THE POP STAR AS IDOL

One aspect that *Privilege* shares with other British pop movies is the central focus on the star icon to illustrate the negative workings of the industry. In Steven Shorter, Watkins focuses on a pop star who is vulnerable and almost childlike in his acceptance of the role placed upon him by the various instruments of establishment self-interest. Watkins's emphasis here is on the pop star as unwitting puppet[4] of the dominant forces of self-interest that permeate the landscape of near-future Britain. Once again there are echoes of Adorno's writings on popular music which also stresses the important role of the star figure in ensuring the continued existence of the status quo:

Its ideology above all makes use of the star system, borrowed from individu-
alistic art and its commercial exploitation. The more dehumanized its methods of operation and content, the more diligent and successfully the culture
industry propagates supposedly great personalities and operates with heart-
throbs. (Adorno 2001, 101)

The gradual increase in the anxiety and resentment exhibited by
Steven Shorter throughout *Privilege* is reflected in several small acts of
churlish and ineffectual protest, such as his request that his retinue
drink hot chocolate instead of wine during a lavish meal. On the brink
of the biggest (and what turns out to be his ultimate) performance
where he is to publicly repent, Shorter tentatively attempts to express
his unease to Andrew Butler, the head of Steven Shorter Enterprises and
asks what would happen if he were to 'stop all this'. In response, Butler
ushers Shorter to the concrete balcony of his penthouse suite and deliv-
ers a chilling monologue, emphasising the ideological importance of
the star's role:

There are millions of people down there. Millions of little people. First we
must be quite clear in our minds about one thing: that the liberal idea that,
given enough education these millions will grow into self-aware creative
human beings is nothing but an exploded myth. It can never happen.
They're stunted little creatures with primitive emotions that are, in themselves, dangerous. They've got to be harnessed, guided ... we've got a
chance to make it work for their own good. You... You're our chance,
Steven. They identify with you. They love you. Steven, you can lead them
into a better way of life ... a fruitful conformity.

During the subsequent performance at the National Stadium where
Steven Shorter's redemption is revealed to mass audience of adoring fans,
the themes of ideological control and manipulation via the medium of pop
music and stardom become fully realised. The staging of this combination
of pop performance, religious assembly and nationalistic rally evoke the
images of Leni Riefenstahl's Nazi-era documentaries and anticipate the
mass gatherings of the Christian Nationwide Festival of Light movement
that emerged briefly in the Britain towards the end of the 1960s. Ranks of
military personnel, police and Boy Scout groups are framed by huge
murals of Steven Shorter's contrite visage and more forthright Christian
iconography, most pointedly the huge crucifix put to flame alongside the
lofty stage. The event is broadcast live to the entire nation and as Watkins's

sardonic voiceover declares, 'What you are now watching is the largest staging of nationalism in the history of Great Britain.'

Even before Steven Shorter has taken the stage, the ideological function of the event, framed by echoes from the totalitarian past, is made abundantly clear. After a disarming blessing by a young choirboy, Shorter's warm-up act appears in the shape of the charismatic Reverend Jeremy Tate (Malcolm Rogers) who makes clear the underlying purpose of the evening. Exhorting against the forces of moral decline and immortality the Reverend focuses on the three words inscribed on the 'pledge cards' that have been handed out to all of the gathered throng. 'We will conform' is written on the card, demanded by Tate and reciprocated in the roar of the crowd. This conformist call to arms is followed by a rousing Mersey-beat inflected version of *Jerusalem* by Shorter's backing band The Runner Beans. Garbed all in black and wearing red and white armbands, the band end their routine with a coordinated Nazi salute to the huge crowd. Once Shorter reaches the stage, resplendent in his stylishly tailored red redeemer suit, the atmosphere has reached fever pitch, with the front rows of disabled fans falling into chaos as fans, nurses and even policemen lose themselves in a fervour of religious, nationalistic star mania. The reprise of *Free Me* that follows has undergone some significant changes. The dirty-sounding rock instrumentation of the original has now evolved into an orchestration of lush strings and heavenly choirs and the lyrics now speak of peace and religious redemption rather than violence and rebellion.[5] Shorter, rechannelling his rebel angst into an earnest display of contrition and religious euphoria, gives his most convincing performance yet, ensuring that both his change of image and the 'establishment event' is an overriding success. As the voiceover declares, 'In one evening in the National Stadium 49,000 people gave themselves to God and Flag through Steven Shorter'.

I'M A PERSON! I'M A PERSON!: SYMPATHY FOR THE POP STAR

In the aftermath of what appears to be his greatest triumph, Steven Shorter quickly moves towards his ultimate demise as he finally kicks back against the very system that has given him almost godlike status. The mounting anxiety and alienation reflected throughout the film comes to a head at a music awards ceremony where Steven Shorter, inspired by his burgeoning romance with his official portrait painter, Vanessa Richie (Jean Shrimpton), finally cracks in front of a packed audience of industry bigwigs. Upon receiving his curious spinning, silver award—given to our 'platinum boy' on behalf of 'the staff and executives of Federated Records and its overseas subsidiaries in Germany, France, Japan, United States'—Shorter does the unthinkable and speaks his mind. After a somewhat stilted attempt to reassert his own sense of selfhood—crying out, 'I'm a person, I'm a person, I'm a person'—the disaffected star underlines his protest by telling those who have so long pulled his strings what he really thinks of them screaming, 'I hate you!', and thereby sealing his fate. According to the omnipresent voiceover, Shorter has doomed himself by momentarily breaking away from the totalising force of the status quo:

> All that Steven Shorter has just done has been to express the wish to become an individual. But that, in an age of conformity, can become a social problem.[6]

The consequences of Shorter's short but impassioned speech are swiftly felt, with the star quickly falling from grace. This motif of an almost inevitable decline is characteristic of several British films focusing on the music industry, and in *Privilege* this fate is severely administered. In *Flame*, the musical protagonists walk away from fame to presumably fade into obscurity, in *Breaking Glass* madness overcomes post-punk singer Kate, and the stars depicted in both *Stardust* and *Brothers of the Head* end up tragically dead. Although none of the latter outcomes are served upon Steven Shorter, his fate is arguably the most bleak and complete as he is all but erased from history in a united front presented by the culture industry that had previously supported and benefitted from his efforts. The following day after his sensational outburst,

> with public endorsement... Steven Shorter is barred from this and any further appearance on television just to ensure that he does not again misuse his position of privilege to disturb the public peace of mind.

Watkins presents a downfall that is as swift as it is complete; not only do the ideological forces of the state and industry turn against Steven Shorter, but so do the legions of fans that had so slavishly followed and adored the charismatic pop star for so long. According to Watkins's voiceover, 'The public knows what it feels. Its love for Steven has turned to hate'.

Presumably the public will move on to follow another well-packaged and more acquiescent star figure, with the eventual fate of the former icon Steven Shorter left uncertain and ambiguous. We are never told what happens to the disgraced star, reflecting the cold efficiency of the culture industry that seeks to completely remove all trace of his former status:

> Within about a year all that remained of Steven Shorter were a few old records and a piece of archive film ... with the sound, of course, removed. It's going to be a happy year in Britain this year in the near future.

A FRUITFUL CONFORMITY? RETHINKING THE AUDIENCE

Whilst it can be argued that the cynical and polemical narrative of *Privilege* sets the film apart from other British films about the music industry, it does however share one of the key failings of this genre as a whole. In emphasising the corrupt nature of the industry by focusing the drama on the narrative of the manipulated pop star, Watkins fails to consider the potential agency of the audience. Throughout the film, it is made clear that Steven Shorter's fans are merely passive dupes; mindlessly following their icon's changes of image and ravenously consuming all that the culture industry provides. This tendency to portray the masses as vulnerable, passive and easily manipulated by the producers of disposable popular cultural artefacts reflects a wider trend within left-leaning narratives about the spread of advanced capitalism throughout the twentieth century. Such a notion was key to the arguments made by many of the writers of the Frankfurt School, including Adorno who considered fans of popular jazz music to be 'childish' and 'childlike', even referring to them on occasion as 'insects' (2001). In this light, fans of popular music function act simply as cogs in the capitalist machine, unquestioningly amplifying and supporting the very system that exploits them;

> There are [...] the enthusiasts who write fan letters to radio stations and orchestras, at well-managed jazz festivals, produce their own enthusiasm as an advertisement for the wares they consume. (Adorno 2001, 52)

This representation of young fans as mindless and easily manipulated dupes of the music industry is consistent across most British films set in this area, where audiences are portrayed either as a hysterical mass or as expendable groupies and hangers-on. In Watkins's film, the unquestioning and passive nature of the pop audience is stretched to its fullest extent. Not only do the fans of Steven Shorter eagerly consume all of his music and various associated branded products, they unproblematically accept and embrace his ideological transformation from sinner into saint. The hysterical images of fans witnessed during Shorter's 'rebel' performance at the outset of the film are mirrored and intensified as the star presents his new redemptive image at the National Stadium. Even more striking than this is the abrupt and absolute way in which Shorter's entire fan base is persuaded to denounce and abandon their adoration of the pop star following his ill-advised outburst at the Federated Records award ceremony. The very fans who have slavishly followed every word and change of image of the object of their adoration reject Shorter en masse, helping to ensure that all memory of the star is expunged from the popular imagination. This provides a stark and sudden conclusion to the film's narrative and emphasises the lack of agency afforded to fans throughout the narrative.

Looking back on *Privilege*, over a decade later, Watkins recognised the failings of his portrayal of the fans of Steven Shorter which he felt reflected 'a certain dismissal of the public which I very much regret now' (Gomez 1979, 84). Watkins was not alone in portraying fans as passive consumers; most other film-makers adopted this approach which arguably reflected widespread attitudes to fandom encompassing both popular culture and academic debate (Lewis 1992). It is only in the wake of groundbreaking studies focusing on subcultural youth and fan cultures (Hall and Jefferson 1976; Jenkins 1992 etc.) that there has been a recognition of the cultural agency—and potential 'resistance'—exhibited by those participating in music cultures. Watkins himself later echoed such ideas, suggesting an alternative to the portrayal of fans as entirely compliant in *Privilege*:

> many young people are aware of this manipulation process. They may not be quite sure how to stop it but are conscious of it and in one way or another may be trying to break that pattern. (Friedman 1983, 238)

This recognition of the potential agency of young audiences to recognise and resist the forces of ideological control led Watkins to reflect on how he might alter the film's ending with the benefit of hindsight:

> I would probably add something which deals with the way the public, in a rather complex way, feels about this young gentleman and what he has done, showing that there is already an ambivalence in attitude towards him because

there obviously is a tension. While the public may watch television or appear to be manipulated, at the same time most of us don't, of course. *Privilege* is guilty of not dealing with that tension. (Friedman 1983, 239)

Whether such an approach would be successful is debatable, and a film attempting to reflect on the tension that Watkins identifies might undermine the powerful polemic of *Privilege*. There have been very few films that have successfully combined a critique of the music industry with notions of fan agency and resistance. Although there are many films that have focused primarily on the experience of fans rather than artists, often these replace cynical critique of the industry with an emphasis on nostalgia and sentimentality. Whilst recent British examples like *Spike Island* (2012) and *Northern Soul* (2014) celebrate the everyday vitality and creativity of music fans from various eras, they tend to adopt nostalgic, coming-of-age narratives that all too often lapse into clichéd storyline populated with familiar stereotypes of youthful self-discovery.

CONCLUSION: BRITAIN IN THE NEAR FUTURE...

Given the subject matter of the film and also the social and historical context in which it was made, it is perhaps inevitable that certain elements of *Privilege* appear somewhat dated. Such is the veracity of the scenes of hysterical fan mania—clearly inspired by the rise of Beatlemania—that the film at first glance appears firmly rooted to its particular historic moment. Whilst Johnny Speight's original story can be seen as just the latest of a line of British 'rise-and-fall' pop films produced since the 1950s, the radical reworking of the narrative by Peter Watkins and his co-writer Norman Bognor created a film whose pertinence and relevance continues to resonate some forty years after its inception. Although previous films had attempted to throw a cautionary spotlight on the sharp practices of the music industry, none had explicitly linked these to wider processes of political and cultural control. Watkins followed the well-trodden path of focusing on the figure of the pop star, but he also placed his protagonist at the centre of an institutionalised web of economic, cultural and political control. This focus on the ideological function of mass-produced popular culture marks out *Privilege* as unique in the pantheon of mainstream film. No other film produced by a major studio has attempted such an explicit political polemic attacking the very machinery of the culture industry from which it emerged. It may well be that the circumstances surrounding the genesis of Watkins's project represent a perfect convergence of factors that are unique to the time and context in which *Privilege* was able to emerge. The phenomenal rise of pop music and youth culture in Western Europe and the US in the post war years undoubtedly opened up new ground for those seeking to produce and profit from this new youth 'market' and for others seemed to represent the latest development in the pacification and exploitation of the masses. The emergence of the pop music film—a new sub-genre cynically aimed at tapping into the economic potential of the youth market—nevertheless allowed both writers and directors of these projects to question the motivations and machinations of the marketplace. Building on some of the themes established by writers and directors in the previous decade, Watkins was able to bring his unique sensibility to a subsection of British cinema that had already been grappling with the rapid rise of this new, exciting and, for some, alarming brave new world. By the end of 1965, at the same time that Beatlemania was sweeping the globe, Peter Watkins's career had reached something of a crossroads. Disillusioned with his former patrons at the BBC, Watkins was looking for new opportunities to develop his distinctive themes and methods. At the same time, Universal Pictures—attracted by the favourable tax breaks offered by the British government to film-makers working in the UK—were searching to mimic the critical and commercial success of films like The Beatles *A Hard Day's Night*. The combination of these economic and cultural factors ultimately persuaded the major Hollywood studio to invest a sizeable budget in *Privilege* and to take a calculated risk on a controversial but undoubtedly gifted British director on the rise.

Privilege then in many ways can be seen to represent something of an experiment which, on the basis of both the initial critical response and box office, ended in failure. The innovative structuring of the narrative and clever blend of generic conventions, allied with the satirical polemic overlaying the entire film, undoubtedly made *Privilege* hard to categorise and also to place within the marketplace. When presented with the finished film, Universal were clearly perplexed by the work, stating in an article in the *Daily Express* (April 1967) that 'This is an unusual film, interesting and problematic. We are not sure how to sell it' (Glynn 2013, 122). As a result *Privilege* suffered from a lack of backing as it attempted to reach its audience, with national UK distributor Rank refusing to distribute a film that they felt 'mocked the church, defied authority, and encouraged youth in lewd practices' (Glynn 2013, 122). The film also

received some particularly savage reviews with critics deriding the performances of the film's two lead actors and dismissive of *Privilege's* unique
blend of generic styles and conventions.[7]

For Watkins these responses to his completed film were both bruising
and affecting. After the experience of working with Universal Pictures,
Watkins never worked with a major studio again, instead pursuing many of
the ideas explored in *Privilege* with independent producers of both film
and television. By the time of the release of the film on DVD and Blu-ray
in 2010, *Privilege* has become recognised as an important and innovative
film that not only captures a key historical moment of change, but whose
themes continue to provoke and resonate in relation to the contemporary
political, economic and cultural landscape.

Whatever the shortcomings of Watkins's film, in particular the inability
to recognise the potential agency in the pop audience, *Privilege* nevertheless
stands out from the crowd. The inventive and sometimes playful innovations of style and structure mark out the film as one of the most original
of its period, and the angry and incisive political critique that *Privilege* so
passionately conveys ensures a legacy that is unique in the annals of mainstream cinema.

NOTES

1. The musician as slave to the industry is usually metaphorical, whilst *Brothers
   of the Head* takes this one stage further as the conjoined Howe twins have
   their lives signed away to an ambitious pop impresario by their unfeeling
   father.
2. The film's music, written and arranged by Mike Leander, is a particular
   strength of *Privilege*, helping to add to the film's documentary feel and
   sense of veracity. Leander most famously arranged The Beatles *She's Leaving
   Home* on their influential *Sgt Pepper's Lonely Hearts Club Band* (1967) and
   went on to write and produce most of Gary Glitter's chart-topping hits of
   the 1970s.
3. In one sequence Shorter is asked to change the channel on his wrist bound
   radio which is playing his latest hit 'I've been a bad, bad boy' (also a top five
   hit in the actual UK charts) but he finds that whatever station he tunes into,
   it is playing the same ubiquitous tune.
4. Some posters for the film and the original soundtrack album depict an image
   of Steven Shorter represented as a puppet hanging on controlling strings.
   This design later reappeared as the cover art for the New Yorker DVD
   release.

5. The initial version of *Free Me* include the lines;

> My spirit's broken
> No will to live
> My body's all aching
> My hands are tied
> I need my freedom
> Not your sympathy

These are later changed to;

> I kneel before Him
> My time has come
> O Father, Father
> Your children call
> Defend our mothers
> Forgive us all

6. Again this seems to echo the work of Adorno who stated:

> In the culture industry the individual is an illusion not merely because of the standardisation of the means of production. He is tolerated only so long as his complete identification with the generality is unquestioned. (Adorno and Horkheimer 1997, 38)

7. The British Film Institute Monthly Film Bulletin wrote that

> 'What hangs around Watkins' neck is sheer lack of professionalism: his film is a mass of poor scripting, inept acting, and directionless, irrelevant camerawork and editing [...] the television-vérité style that Watkins has clung to so obsessively throughout his short career has now reached its ultimate condemnation [...] Everything in 'Privilege' goes wrong, and one can do little but catalogue the failures [...] For 'The War Game' the technique was just about as hollow, but the film's subject gave it the compulsive fascination of a nightmare; with 'Privilege, the result is mere farce'. (Watkins 2016)

REFERENCES

Adorno, T. W. 1990. "On popular music." In *On record: rock, pop and the written word*. Simon Frith and Andrew Goodwin (eds.) London: Routledge.

Adorno, T. W. 2001. *The Culture Industry: Selected Essays on Mass Culture*, London: Routledge.

Adorno, T. W. and Horkheimer, M. 1997. *Dialectic of Enlightenment*, London: Verso.

Friedman, L. 1983. "The Necessity of Confrontation Cinema: Peter Watkins interviewed" *Literature/Film Quarterly*, 11.2: 237–48.

Glynn, S. 2013. *The British Pop Music Film: The Beatles and Beyond*, Basingstoke: Palgrave Macmillan.

Gomez, J. A. 1979. *Peter Watkins*, New York: Twayne Publishers.

Hall, S. and Jefferson, T. (eds.) 1976. *Resistance through rituals*, London: Hutchinson.

Jenkins, H. 1992. *Textual poachers: television fans and participatory culture*, London: Routledge.

Lewis, L. 1992. *The Adoring Audience: Fan Culture and Popular Media*, London: Taylor and Francis.

Watkins, P. 2016. *Peter Watkins: Filmmaker/Media Critic*. Available from; http://pwatkins.mnsi.net/. Accessed 15/01/17.

FILMOGRAPHY

The Tommy Steele Story (Hudis UK 1959).
Expresso Bongo (Guest UK 1959).
A Hard Day's Night (Lester UK 1964).
Privilege (Watkins 1967).
The Gladiators (Watkins SE 1969).
Punishment Park (Watkins US 1971).
Stardust (Apted UK 1974).
Flame (Loncraine UK 1975).
Breaking Glass (Gibson UK 1980).
Brothers of the Head (Fulton & Pepe UK 2005).
Spike Island (Whitecross UK 2012).
Northern Soul (Constantine UK 2014).

Representing Subcultural Identity: A Photoessay of Spanish Graffiti and Street Art

Andrzej Zieleniec

INTRODUCTION

Graffiti has a long history. Writing on walls was practised by our distant ancestors as they represented themselves and the animals they shared their environment and lives with through cave paintings. On ancient Greek and Roman buildings, on Meso-American temples, signs, symbols and messages from the past are found scratched and drawn on walls. Explorers as diverse as Viking marauders and colonists and Victorian grand tourists have left their marks on walls to signify 'I was here' (see Lovata and Olton 2015). Abel and Buckley (1973) demonstrated that the fascination that exists for writing messages and leaving names on the private space of public toilets, 'Latrinalia', is a common imperative for many. In this way we can perhaps view graffiti as exhibiting a universal human tendency to 'leave signs of our passing', to make marks of existence and symbols of our being and presence in the places that we inhabit and occupy, even if only for a limited time.

A. Zieleniec (✉)
Keele University, Newcastle-under-Lyme, UK

© The Author(s) 2018
N. Bentley et al. (eds.), *Youth Subcultures in Fiction, Film and Other Media*, Palgrave Studies in the History of Subcultures and Popular Music, https://doi.org/10.1007/978-3-319-73189-6_12

197

The origins of modern graffiti reside in the creative expression associated with and located within the disadvantaged and deprived communities of US inner-cities in the late 1960s and early 1970s. The innovative and imaginative explosion associated with hip-hop also included graffiti as a fundamental backdrop and signifier of a new cultural field of expression. This was, at least in part, a demand for the recognition and acknowledgement of the lives and experiences of an urban population who were discriminated against, disenfranchised, alienated and ignored except in negative representations in popular and political discourse. The opportunity to give voice and to paint, draw and write provided marginalised urban youth a means to express their identity, creativity and worth through signs and symbols of a cultural politics that expressed the inhabitation and colonisation of the city that demonstrated and celebrated existence and being. The development of modern graffiti, particularly within New York, has been documented and illustrated by a number of authors (see Cooper and Chalfant 1984; Chalfant and Prigoff 1987; Cooper 2009a, b, 2013; Felisbret 2009; Stewart 2009), reflecting its increasing popularity and appreciation as a form of urban cultural practice. From the walls of the ghetto, subway and transit systems of the city (Austin 2002; Gastman and Neelon 2011), graffiti has spread to become an almost universal urban phenomenon. Graffiti is now a feature of towns and cities across the globe (see Chmielewska 2007; Valjakka 2011; Benavides-Venegas 2005; Best 2003; Ferrell 1993; Manco et al. 2005; Brighenti 2010; Schacter and Fekner 2013). It has grown and developed in style, sophistication, complexity and form as it has been adapted by new writers in new urban geographies using new methods and media, with new influences and aesthetics.

Modern graffiti was and is associated with the use of permanent marker pens and aerosol spray paint to adorn the city with a mainly calligraphic or text-based writing based on 'the tag' and its expansion into throw-ups, blockbuster and wildstyle as well as large scale murals, sophisticated and skilful (master)pieces. However, graffiti remains embedded as a street-based embodied practice, writing without permission or approval. It is made on and in the streets as unsanctioned and illegal embellishment, adornment and decoration of the city by predominantly young people who write for a variety of reasons and audiences, not least each other, and the recognition and status to be achieved amongst fellow writers. However, since the late 1990s new means and methods of adorning the streets and walls of cities have developed. Street art employs a variety of techniques and methods that includes stencils, stickers ('slaps'), the pasting up or gluing of pre-prepared posters ('wheatpastes') and the placing of objects in the public sphere. Whilst for some this reflects an extension of graffiti, for others there are clear distinctions (see Catterall 2010; Bengsten and Arvidsson 2014; Young 2012, 2014; McAuliffe 2012; Iveson 2010a). Street art may not only be more varied in terms of methods and means, it may also be considered as more 'legitimate'—attracting paid commissions for work, and appreciated more as 'art' by the public, policing authorities and the art market. It has also become the focus of growing public attention as 'urban art' and has become popular and of interest as a form of creative practice (Jaka 2012; Schacter and Fekner 2013) that is collectible and saleable. Banksy may be the best-known example of a graffiti artist whose work is regularly bought and sold in auctions houses as well as appearing in galleries. However, there are many more writers and artists who are now recognised and promoted as having 'value'. This acknowledgement of graffiti and street art and its commodification has led to criticism that the original meanings and values associated with graffiti have been diminished (Dickens 2010; Bengsten 2013, 2014).

Nonetheless, both graffiti and street art remain as embodied practices oriented towards a clear association with the writing and painting, adornment and decoration of the physical urban environment (see Schacter 2008, 2014) and which makes claims on the right to occupy, colonise and 'create' urban space (Nandrea 1999; Zieleniec 2016). It is supported, promoted and promulgated as a subculture through the increasing use of social media. There are any number of digital repositories (see for example Art Crimes: The Writing on the Wall https://www.graffiti.org/), open and closed Facebook groups, Instagram posts, forums and blogs for making and developing contacts, swapping tips, techniques, warnings and advice as well as publicising work and creating a sense of subcultural group identity and collective endeavour associated with the painting of the urban.

Graffiti and street art have been subject to a range of academic research that has explored their diversity and practice, the people and places associated with these practices as well as the conflicts and governance strategies that have been employed as a means to control or combat them. There have been studies that reflect the use of graffiti as associated with territoriality and gangs (Ley and Cybriwsky 1974; Phillips 1999), and those who consider graffiti as a pedagogical tool to promote identity, learn about culture, and explore and understand the city (see Calvin 2005; Civil 2010; Iveson 2010a; Nandrea 1999; Burnham 2010; Schacter 2014). There are also a range of ethnographic studies that have sought to document the lived experiences of graffiti writers and the meanings, values, aesthetics, risk and excitement they encounter in their mainly nocturnal adornment of the urban landscape (see Ferrell 1993, 1996; Halsey and Young 2006; Snyder 2009; Young 2014; McDonald 2001; Schacter 2008, 2014). This has been extended by graffiti writers and street artists speaking for themselves about their motivations for writing (see Banksy 2002, 2006, 2012; City 2010; Desa 2006; Jaka 2012; Schacter, and Fekner 2013; Gastman and Neelon 2011; Martin 2009; Monsa 2013; Puig 2008; Scholz 2003; Madrid Revolutionary Team 2013; Uys and Uys 2013; Ruiz 2008).

Graffiti and street art employ means and methods by practitioners to make claims on or colonise urban space through their creative interventions, the production and circulation of a symbolic and aesthetic realm of signs, symbols, meanings and messages. It is a practice which often raises conflicted reactions. On the one hand it reflects an active engagement with the world and provides opportunity for expressing meanings and values as a practice that sees, reads and writes the world in ways meaningful to not only the individual but to a community of other practitioners engaged in similar activities. It can be considered as a creative, artistic and aesthetic urban practice that colonises, subverts or adorns often-subjugated and commodified space. It represents a number of embodied practices (your body has to be there to do it) that challenge the delineation, regulation and policing of the urban as a social and public cultural sphere. These may be considered as everyday acts and experiences for those who practise graffiti writing but also can be associated with resistance during particular events such as riots, protests, occupations, strikes and sit-ins. As such, it can be understood as a form of colonisation, appropriation and reflection on and representation of alternate readings and uses of community and space.

Whilst academic research and graffiti writers own words reflect a range of motivations and reasons for writing, it is possible to identify a number of themes. These include territoriality, the marking and claiming of space, whether or not it is associated with gang affiliation. Engaging in graffiti may also be a reaction to the boredom and frustration experienced by urban youth. Whether this is explicitly deviant or criminal there is a sense of excitement, adventure and danger in leaving your mark, sign or art in public that has an obvious thrill and appeal to many. Writing graffiti can also reflect the need for individual and/or group recognition and status. Having your art/writing seen by peers and fellow practitioners is a means to achieve 'fame' or notoriety for both the quantity and/or quality of work produced. Similarly, graffiti provides a means for personal expression, social and subcultural kudos and reputation building, the expansion and development of techniques, skills and abilities portrayed and advertised as a form of everyday art and practice in a very public gallery.

Graffiti and street art represent 'signs of passing', fleeting presence or symbols of existence as well as (self)identification and (self)publicity within a group of practitioners who assess, critique and comment on each other's works. Various ethnographic studies and the self-expressed meanings and motivations of practitioners provide evidence of graffiti and street art as subcultural forms of practice which, as Hebdige (1979) argues, use form, style and symbolism as an intentional and signifying communication and meaning system, that is, a homology. Thus there are ideological or political values, beliefs and meanings, codes of conduct and practice amongst graffiti writers and street artists. For example, where it is or is not appropriate to paint or write. Such codes of conduct and evidence of being in the know function as means to bind or include members, however loosely, within a group. Similarly, one can also reflect on the subcultural career of writers/artists as they progress from being novices ('toys') to experts ('kings') and as discussed above, how subcultural activity, style and material objects can be subsumed and commodified by the market. What is evident is that there are a range of identifiable styles or types of graffiti as well as abilities and skills, from the simple, quickly done to the very elaborate and often breathtaking full-wall creations. There is a language and vocabulary as well as a complicated hierarchy involved in graffiti that reflects an internal communication between practitioners as well as its display and promotion to a general urban public. Thus graffiti and street art can be associated with the definition of a subculture. What is created is an urban (sub)cultural aesthetic that uses the streets of the city as a gallery, notice board and medium for display, conversation and communication.

On the other hand, graffiti is often portrayed as antisocial and criminal behaviour, a symbol of community breakdown and decline, symptom of urban blight, a lack of direction, discipline and deviance in youth. Wilson and Kelling's (1982) 'broken windows' thesis argued that examples of low-level criminality such as graffiti are precursors or indicators of community decline and causally linked to serious violent crime. Whilst Harcourt (2005), Harcourt and Ludwig (2006), and Bowling (1999) have undermined such claims as flawed, the broken windows thesis and zero-tolerance policing used in the US was supported by politicians and policymakers around the world (see Waquant 2006). Iveson (2010b) refers to the policing strategies and criminalisation of writers as a 'War against Graffiti' that has led to the use of new technologies, innovations in urban design and the securitisation of urban public space as a state-sponsored response (see also Ferrell 1993, 1995, 1997, 2001; Young 2010; Dickinson 2008). This reaction to graffiti and street art reflects how such practices and performance conflicts with the values and priorities of property holders, developers, the state, the police and courts (see Bengsten and Arvidsson 2014) that view it as a threat to law, order and security, and have sought to purge it from the public urban realm. Graffiti thus also represents conflicting ideas about who and what the city is for and punishes with fines, confiscation of property and, in some cases, jail sentences those who are caught.

Graffiti has become an omnipresent feature of the urban in recent years, eliciting as discussed above a number of responses, reactions and analyses. It has spread and developed to become a global phenomenon, one that has not bypassed Spain. There is an established and prevalent culture and practice of graffiti in towns and cities across the country. As is common elsewhere, there is a network of actors and communication within and between practitioners as well as competition over locations or 'spots' and demonstrations of skill and ability. The history of Spain's flourishing and developed graffiti and street art scene is evident both on the streets of its cities as well as in publications (see Madrid Revolutionary Team 2013; Martin 2009; Monsa 2013; Puig 2008; Scholz 2003). This is supported and promulgated by a variety of websites (for example, *Valencia Street Art, Spanish Graffiare, Ultimate Guide to Barcelona Street Art and Graffiti*). What follows will develop aspects of the varied approaches and analyses discussed above to explore how, using a variety of styles and methods, graffiti writers and street artists in Spain represent themselves, exhibit their work, illustrate the means and methods of their practice as well as promote the scene and the activity as a subculture. The explicit focus will be on the material object of their work. It will use examples collected from the street during a research project in Spain, as opposed to its existence in virtual or digital reality, to illustrate aspects of the performed practice of graffiti as a subcultural activity and to demonstrate the self-reflective way graffiti writers represent themselves, their work and their practices in what they produce. It will explore, illustrate and analyse the way in which graffiti writers represent their identity, practices and themselves through their work in the public arena of the streets, walls, public places and spaces of the urban they inhabit.

The following commentary and analysis uses the author's own photographs, collected as part of a research project, supported by a small grant from the Santander Research Fellowship Scheme. The photographs were taken by the author engaged in a visual ethnographic research project (Ward 2014; Pink 2013; Harper 2012) conducted in Spain's three largest cities of Valencia, Barcelona and Madrid during multiple visits between August 2012 and May 2013. The methodology employed was a form of directed psychogeography (see Coverley 2010; McDonough 2009; Ford 2005; Knabb 2006) in which specific areas of each city were identified through online research and contact with graffiti practitioners who advised on locations/areas to investigate. Fieldwork consisted of multiple trips to each city where 'walking' the area in a non-directional manner permitted investigation of the locale; the collection and collation of the types, forms and prevalence; and the photographing of graffiti and street art found in the streets and public spaces of each area. This was coupled with other qualitative research methods such as a small number of semi-structured interviews with practitioners and scholars in each city to extend and deepen not only the meanings, values and intentions behind their practice, but to elicit a situational understanding of the practice of writing/painting within their experience of the city as well as within the graffiti/street art community. The following illustrated commentary and analysis will demonstrate how graffiti and street art practitioners reflect on and represent themselves and their activities as part of processes of associative identity making which forms part of, or is constitutive of, their subcultural community.

GETTING YOUR NAME UP AND KNOWN: TAGS

The most prevalent type of graffiti to be found in most cities in Spain and elsewhere is the tag. This is a writer's signature made with permanent marker pen or spray paint. It can be simple or more complex and is the unique identifying mark of an individual writer that indicates participation in the practice of graffiti writing. In Spain there are a plethora of tags to be found in towns and cities. They can appear on almost any surface from walls, doors, windows, street signs and furniture as well as on public and private transport. Tags are relatively easy to do and quick to accomplish. It is an individual writer's identifying graffiti signature that acknowledges being in place as well as being and belonging to an active, if amorphous and non-constituted community of graffiti writers. It is akin to making a statement that 'X was here'. As the photographs below demonstrate the colonisation or occupation of particular sites by multiple tags is common.

The concentration of tags in a single site (see Figs. 1, 2, and 3) may reflect an ease of access and/or a means to mark a particular spot that has significance or importance for writers. It may also mark out a common ground and meeting point for writers to clearly demonstrate their pres-

Fig. 1 Tags on unoccupied shops—Madrid

Fig. 2 Tagged doorway—Barcelona

Fig. 3 Tagged abandoned shop—Madrid

ence and active participation in the scene and on the street. Whilst for some the tag is evidence of vandalism and anti-social behaviour making public space ugly and inscribed with visual dirt, the use of multi-coloured markers and paints can lend a kaleidoscopic and phantasmagoric aesthetic to what, in some cases appears abandoned or closed premises. Such tagging is evidence of an active population engaging in a form of practice that represents an urban street culture that gives a sense of life to the street in contrast to a lack of activity in the premises or buildings tagged.

Tags can also be used to mark an individual's territory or, as in Fig. 4, to signal a group identity. This is an example from a 'gang' was found across a wide geographically dispersed area of Madrid. The 'crew' responsible were clearly mobile, active and keen to be 'seen' in the city, publicly announcing their existence and presence. Similar examples of multiple tagging by individuals or gangs/crews are common features across many areas and cities in Spain. They represent attempts to ensure visibility that advertises or publicises the existence of a group as active practitioners. Tagging, whether by an individual or group, is a simple way of 'getting up', being seen and known and ensuring visibility amongst peers. It can be linked to 'bombing', which is tagging a lot of areas/places over a short period of time. Similarly, tagging can develop into other practices such as the throw-up (a name painted quickly with one layer of paint and outline), and those who develop their skills to include more detailed writing styles such as block-type lettering known as 'blockbuster'.

The idea of claiming space and colonising areas reflects an aspect of graffiti subcultural identity making. Where sites or 'spots' provide opportunities they are often ones which become collectively owned and made by multiple use. Whilst there may be competition between individuals and groups and over-writing does take place, there is also the possibility for a

Fig. 4 Crew/gang tag—Madrid

mutual experience of being in a communally shared writing-place that offers a concentration of activity and reflects a vibrant and active graffiti scene. This allows writers to share tips and methods and to copy and develop the skills and methods of more experienced or skilled writers. This embodied practice where individuals act in what at times are often dangerous conditions and in the dark, these sites of multiple writing provide the possibility for a collective practice and sense of belonging to a group that exists in physical space as well as through shared digital media communication. This can be related to other practices such as squatting where the 'claim' to a building is often publicised in its external adornment by a variety of graffiti writers and street artists using a range of style, techniques and sophistication. Figure 5, shows abandoned offices whose ownership was disputed in Plaza Espana, a major public square in the capital of Spain. It demonstrates how unused buildings can be appropriated or colonised and become an important, if albeit temporary, location for writers to make their mark. What is also clear in this image is how graffiti writers and street artists go to extraordinary lengths and dangers to get their name, tag or work in places where it is not only highly visible, but also difficult to remove. Such spots are referred to as 'heaven' and are usually high above the street in elevated locations. This involves writers and artists negotiating not only access to buildings that may have material barriers in place, security personal and systems, but also the inherent hazards that accompany operating in the dark, and being vulnerable to a range of hazards and risks in the form of physical dangers from dilapidated or unmaintained buildings as well as from other people, whether fellow writers competing for prime 'spots' or from those who occupy empty buildings as temporary homes or shelters or for drug and drink use. What is clear is that the extremes to which some artists and writers will go, whether hanging out

Fig. 5 Squatted abandoned office buildings 'claimed' by graffiti—Madrid

of windows or from roofs, as exemplified in Fig. 5, are inherently dangerous but apparently worth the risk to have one's work on high and in front
of peers and the public.

SELF-REPRESENTATION

Graffiti writers also represent themselves and the practices and activities
they engage in through what they leave on the walls of the city. This is
done by 'self' portraits, figurative and idealised self-representations, showing not only themselves 'at work' but also the tools and methods they use
to write and paint. Whilst this can appear as a hyper-inflated or romantici-
sation of the practice of writing and painting, it is also informative of how
writers and artists see and represent themselves, giving insight into graffiti
and street art as a subculture as well as reflective of processes of associative
identification within a community of active and like-minded practitioners.

Barcelona SM172 (Fig. 6) shows a representation of a 'writer in action'
using the ubiquitous spray can to adorn the walls of the city with their
work. In Fig. 7 the same artist, this time in Madrid, shows not only another
figure engaged in the 'act' of making street art but also how the ladder is
another 'tool of the trade' to reach places and take opportunities where
they are found. The inclusion of a figure in both cases can be viewed as a
form of self-depiction as well as a self-conscious attempt to reflect their
practices, techniques and means by which their art is achieved. Similarly in
Fig. 8, YCN2 in Madrid depicts a figure, face covered and holding a paint
roller—a necessary tool and part of the process of preparing a wall for art
work. In all of these images the depiction of figures and their equipment
are integrated into the art itself, showing the act as a form of praxis as well
as the means and methods used to achieve it.

Fig. 6 SM172—Barcelona

Fig. 7   SM172—Madrid

Fig. 8   YCN2—Madrid

Fig. 9   Wheat paste—
Noche Crew, Valencia

At other times, street artists depict themselves as a 'heroic' group of mostly unseen, invisible night-time contributors to the creative culture and aesthetic of the street. For example, in Fig. 9 the faint image of the 'Noche Crew' in Valencia reveals how one shadowy group leave not only their marks but traces and representations of themselves on the walls of the city that they stalk by night. As in Fig. 8 the faces of those depicted are

Fig. 10 'Stick-Up Kids'—Valencia

Fig. 11 Zone—Barcelona

mostly covered. This may signify that graffiti writers and street artist have to operate not only anonymously undercover with pseudonyms as signatures/tags, but also that their identification may lead to prosecution and sanction by policing and legal authorities.

Other examples of street art demonstrate this sense of reflective self-portraiture, perhaps reflecting a somewhat humorous and tongue-in-cheek sense of self and what they do. In Fig. 10 the cartoon images of the self-styled 'Stick-Up Kids' in Valencia is an ironic allusion to the nefarious activities of bandits, highwaymen and women, street hustlers, muggers and robbers replayed in numerous fictional accounts in film and literature. Whilst these 'stick-up' merchants don't take your money they do paste up and paint on your walls and your imagination, arresting your attention and making you stop and think. Other portraits such as by Zone in Barcelona (Fig. 11) paint a somewhat heroic Che Guevara-esque figure complete with bomb to represent both the practice of 'bombing' (hitting an area with multiple tags or graffiti in a short space of time) and perhaps, given the somewhat stereotypic explosive held in the hands of the figure, a nod

Fig. 12   'Hello sorrow'—Fromthetree,
Valencia

to the anarchic practices of past 'revolutionaries'. However, these 'bombers' detonate their ideas, messages and values through images and text that 'explode' on the streets and walls of the city and impact on the imagination and senses rather than causing physical damage to those caught by them. These examples provide insight into the self-referential representation of actors in the subculture and the means they employ as well as their experience of themselves as fleeting figures, anonymous but ever-present, in the creative culture of adorning, embellishing and decorating the city.

Whilst all of the images discussed so far are relatively small in size and completed or 'put up' quickly, other work is of a far larger scale that requires much more planning, equipment and time to implement. The work by 'Fromthetree' in Valencia (Fig. 12) not only demonstrates the size and scale of some street art it also depicts some of the means and equipment used to access sites and produce such large 'masterpieces'. In Fig. 12 the scale of the work is contextualised by the presence of cars below the wall that is being used as a large canvas. Whilst the potential dangers and extreme lengths that writers can go to get their work in 'heaven' or to access dangerous locations, sites or 'spots' has been discussed above, this image shows that some work requires planning and the use of more sophisticated equipment. The depiction of barriers to keep the public at a safe distance from the work in progress as well as the use of a scissor lift demonstrates not only that some street artists work is on a grand scale but also that the means and methods, the care and consideration for health and safety (of the artist and the public), requires planning and implementation that is both complex and potentially expensive. Whilst some large-scale pieces are commissions in which permission and payment may provide a sense of security from prosecution and safety in using appropriate equipment. However, not all large pieces are commissioned or approved. There is a clear sense that many writers and artists put their health and safety in jeopardy, working high up on buildings that may be in disrepair and fundamentally unsafe. Such commitment to getting their art and craft to the public and their peers reflects how participation in the world of graffiti and street art has inherent dangers, but which is nonetheless considered as worth the risk.

REPRESENTING AND PROMOTING THE 'SCENE'

Some graffiti and street art is explicit in making connections to a recognised community or subculture. Thus practices, events, messages and meanings can be explicitly conveyed in some works reflecting a self-aware belonging to and promotion of a scene with a collective sense of identity. This represents and reflects various aspects of graffiti and street art activity, practice and culture. Whilst there may be at times competition, sometimes violent, between writers and street artists over spots and/or status and authenticity, there is also the sense of connecting with and contributing to a graffiti/street art scene. This is clear in the ways in which individuals represent what they do in their art, but also how they are part of a wider scene. Thus it is not only individual self-promotion that is on offer, but also a clear identification with others who are not only or necessary competitors but who participate in the creation of a an alternate urban aesthetic through their practices. For example, the Madrid collective of Yippi Yippi Yeah (Fig. 13) use humour as they 'flash' passers-by with images to 'advertise' the Madrid Street Art scene as well as themselves as practitioners operating within the city.

More explicit perhaps is the work of Julietta xlf, which illustrates the sense of collective identity and a culture of practice that is shared and pro-

Fig. 13 Yippi Yippi Yeah, Madrid

Fig. 14 Julietta xlf—
street art advertising
graffiti festival, Valencia

moted within the street art and graffiti subcultures, that is, the ways in
which graffiti writers and street artists use the walls of towns and cities not
only to promote themselves, but as advertising spaces for collective or
community events. Figure 14 is an example of wall art that explicitly is
used to inform the public as well as other artists and writers of a specific
event. *Mislatas Representan* is a biennial graffiti and street art festival held
in a neighbouring Valencian municipality with the support of the local
authority. This promotional piece has a resemblance to advertising industry techniques and aims but uses street art, and the particular skills and
influences of this artist, to paint space, to signal a meeting point, time and
event for fellow writers and artists as well as the general public who may
be interested in such creative practices. It is a clear sign of a collective
practice celebrated as a 'Festival of Graffiti'.

Graffiti and street art practitioners are aware and appreciate that in part
what defines their work, creations and contribution to an urban aesthetic
is not only the media and methods that they use, but also the spaces and
places that they practise. That is the street. It is a performed aesthetic and
creative practice that is inextricably connected to the urban and the city. As
Escif in Fig. 15 shows in the depiction of two animated brick walls using a
paint roller under the banner '*Otra Pared es Possible*/Another Wall is
Possible' there is a self-conscious awareness and promotion of the possibilities and potentialities of graffiti and street art to change the way we see
and understand the city as a creative space. Those who do it share through
their experience and their works collective meanings and values, a form of
associative community that reflects a do-it-yourself culture of practice,
learning, belonging and identity formation that has some correlation to
better-known and studied youth subcultures.

Fig. 15   Escif: another wall is possible'—Valencia

CONCLUSION

Graffiti and street art can be understood as a demonstration of a process of associative identity making. By inscribing, painting and decorating the physical environment of the city with signs, symbols and markers of subcultural activity, graffiti writers and street artists are directly engaged in the creation and promotion of an urban aesthetic that reflects individual identity, a collective sense of belonging to a group of similar practitioners, as well as a wider public. This public appeal and value is recognised by the sale of prints, gallery exhibitions and a market in original works by well-known writers and artists for most practitioners. However, it is primarily the community of graffiti writers and street artists who promote and perpetuate activities and practices that reinforce a sense of belonging, often supported by digital and social media, as well as funded, for some, by commissions and the sale of prints and original artworks. This is representative of subcultural identity making, affiliation and projection through praxis. Graffiti and much street art remains an embodied activity that necessitates the writer/artist to have intimate knowledge of the world on which they write/paint as well as putting their bodies, safety, security and liberty at risk.

The images presented in this chapter were collected from three Spanish cities in 2012–2013. Whilst they are a very small sample of the hundreds taken during the research project, they give some indication and illustration not only of the skills and abilities but also the practices, means and methods of a variety of graffiti writers and street artists. They demonstrate a sense of collective identity associated with the practices of writing/painting and the scene of which they are a part as well as their active colonisation and use of urban space. Like most graffiti and street art, it is on the whole ephemeral and temporary. It is expected by those who do it that it will be covered over by other writer/painters or that it will be 'buffed' by private or municipal cleaning crews who remove much if not most of what appears on the walls and streets of our cities. As such, these images may no longer exist in the places and spaces that they were seen and photographed.

Nonetheless the photographs used here illustrate a number of interrelated themes to demonstrate that graffiti and street art practices and material objects are indicative of subcultural identity making and promotion. These include the use of individual writers' tags or group or 'crew' tags as signifiers of collective belonging and identity, the self-representation of writers, and the 'tools' and methods of 'writing' they use, as well as the promotion of the graffiti and street art scenes themselves. Graffiti can be and remains for many the relatively simple act of getting out there and getting your name, tag or reputation recognised by your peers. However, the world of graffiti and street art is increasingly complex and sophisticated, using styles, methods and locations to promote activities and practices in the very public forum of the public spaces, streets and walls, and they remind us that subcultures not only exist and flourish but have the potential to change the way we see and read the city. They are practices and objects, art and aesthetics that reflect and represent ways of being and doing that support and promote subcultural identity and belonging.

REFERENCES

Abel, E. and Buckley, B.E. 1973. *The Handwriting on the Wall: Contributions to Sociology*, Greenwood, Westport, Conn.

Art Crimes: *The Writing on the Wall* https://www.graffiti.org/

Austin, J. 2002. *Taking the Train: How Graffiti Art Became an Urban Crisis in New York City*, Columbia University Press.

Banksy. 2002. *Existencillism*. London: Weapons of Mass Distraction.

Banksy. 2006. *Wall and piece*. London: Century Press.

Banksy. 2012. *You are an acceptable level of threat*. London: Carpet Bombing Culture.

Benavides-Venegas, F.S. 2005. "From Santander to Camilo and Che: Graffiti and Resistance in Contemporary Colombia", *Social Justice* Vol. 32. No.1 (2005) pp. 53–61.

Bengsten, P. 2013. "Beyond the Public Art Machine: a critical examination of street art as public art", *Journal of Art History*, Vol. 82 Issue 2, pp. 63–80.

Bengsten, P. 2014. *The Street Art World*, Almendros de Granada Press.

Bengsten, P. and Arvidsson, M. 2014. "Spatial Justice and Street Art", *nordic journal of law and social research* (NNJLSR) No.5 pp. 117–130.

Best, C. 2003. "Reading Graffiti in the Caribbean Context", *Journal of Popular Culture* Vol. 36 Issue 4, pp. 828–852.

Bowling, B. 1999. The rise and fall of New York murder: zero tolerance or crack's decline? *British Journal of Criminology* 39 (4): 531–554.

Brighenti, A.M. 2010. "At the Wall: Writers, Urban Territoriality and the Public Domain", *Space and Culture*, 2010 13: pp. 315–332.

Burnham, Scott. 2010. The call and response of street art and the city. *City* 14 (1–2): 137–153.

Calvin, L.M. 2005. "Graffiti, the Ultimate Realia: Meaning and Standards through an Unconventional Cultural Lesson", Hispania, Vol. 88. no. 3 (Sept. 2005) pp. 527–30.

Catterall, B. (ed.) 2010. "Graffiti, Street Art and The City", *City: analysis of urban trends, culture theory, politics, action*, 14: 1–2.

Chalfant, H. and Prigoff, J. 1987. *Spraycan Art*, Thames & Hudson, London.

Chmielewska, E. 2007. "Graffiti and Place", *Space and Culture*, 2007, 10, no.2, pp. 145–169.

Civil, Tom. 2010. Learning the city. *City* 14 (1–2): 160–161.

Cooper, M. and Chalfant, H. 1984. *Subway Art*, Henry Holt, New York, 1984.

Cooper, M. 2009a. *Tag Town: The Origins of Writing*, Dokument.

Cooper, M. 2009b. *Subway Art: 25th Anniversary Edition*, Thames and Hudson, London.

Cooper, M. 2013. *Hip Hop Files: Photographs 1979–1984, From Here to Fame* Publishing; Revised edition.

Coverley, M. 2010. *Psyhcogeography*, Pocket Essentials, London.

Desa. 2006. *Million dollar vandal: The life and crimes of Desa*. New York: AKA Projects.

Dickens, L. 2010. "Pictures on Walls? Producing, Pricing and collecting the street art screen print", *City: analysis of urban trends, culture theory, politics, action*, 14: 1–2, 63–81.

Dickinson, Maggie. 2008. The Making of Space, Race and Place. *Critique of Anthropology* 28 (1): 27–45

Felisbret, E. 2009. *Graffiti New York*, New York, Abrams.

Ferrell, J. 1993. "Moscow Graffiti: Language and Subculture", *Social Justice*, 20:13 (Fall Winter 1993) 188.

Ferrell, J. 1995. "Urban Graffiti: Crime Control and Resistance", *Youth and Society* 1995: 27 pp. 73–92.

Ferrell, J. 1997. "Youth, Crime and Cultural Space", *Social Justice* 24.4 (Winter 1997).

Ferrell, J. 1996. *Crimes of Style*, Boston, Northeaster University Press.

Ferrell, J. 2001. *Tearing Down the Streets: Adventures in Urban Anarchy*, Basingstoke, Palgrave.

Ford, S. 2005. *The Situationist International: a user's guide*, Black Dog Publishing, London.

Gastman, R. and Neelon, C. 2011. *The History of American Graffiti*, London HarperCollins.

Halsey, M., & Young, A. 2006. Our desires are ungovernable: Writing graffiti in urban space. *Theoretical Criminology*, 10(3), 275–306.

Harcourt, B. E. 2005. *Illusion of order: The false promise of broken windows policing*. Cambridge, MA: Harvard University Press.

Harcourt, B. E., & Ludwig, J. 2006. Reefer madness: Broken windows and misdemeanor marijuana arrests in New York City, 1989–2000. University of Chicago Public Law & Legal Theory Working Paper No. 142. Available at http://ssrn.com/abstract=948753.

Harper, D. 2012. *Visual Sociology*, Routledge, London.

Hebdige, D. 1979. *Subculture: The Meaning of Style*. London: Routledge.

Iveson, K. 2010a. "Graffiti, Street art and the City, Introduction *City: analysis of urban trends, culture theory, politics, action*, Vol. 14, nos. 1–2, February–April 2010, pp. 26–32.

Iveson, K. 2010b. "The Wars on Graffiti and the new military urbanism". *City: Analysis of Urban Trends, Culture, Theory, Policy, Action*. Vol. 14, nos. 1–2, pp. 115–134.

Jaka, 2012. *The Mammoth Book of Street Art*, Constable and Robinson, London.

Knabb, K. (ed.) 2006. *Situationist International Anthology*, Bureau of Public Secrets, Berkeley.

Ley, D. and Cybriwsky, R. 1974. "Urban Graffiti and Territorial Markers", *Annals of the Association of American Geographers*, Vol. 64 No 4 (Dec. 1974) pp. 491–505.

Lovata, T.R. and Olton, E. (eds.) 2015. *Understanding Graffiti: Multidisciplinary Studies from Prehistory to the Present*, Routledge London.

Madrid Revolutionary Team, 2013. *Madrid Revolution: The History of the Capital*, Hardcore/MTN, Madrid.

Manco, T., Lost Art, and Neelon, C. 2005. *Graffiti Brasil*, Thames and Hudson, London.

Martin, L.A. 2009. *Textura: Valencia Street Art*, Mark Batty Publishing, Brooklyn, NY.

McAuliffe, C. 2012. "Graffiti or Street Art? Negotiating the Moral geographies of the Creative City": *City Analysis of Urban Trends: Culture, Theory, Policy, Action*, 2012, 34, no 2 pp. 189–206.

McDonald, N. 2001. *The graffiti sub-culture: Youth, masculinity and identity in London and New York*. London: Palgrave Macmillan.

McDonough, T. (ed.) 2009. *The Situationists and the City*, Verso, London.

Monsa. 2013. *Urban art: Made in BCN*. Barcelona: Instituto Monsa de Barcelona.

Nandrea, L. 1999. "Graffiti Taught me everything I know about space: Urban Fronts and Borders", *Antipode*, 31.1 1999, pp. 110–116.

Phillips, S. 1999. *Wallbangin': Graffiti and Gangs in L.A.* Chicago, University of Chicago Press.
Pink, S. 2013. *Doing Visual Ethnography*, Sage, London.
Puig, R. 2008. *Barcelona 1000 Graffiti*, Gustavo Gill, Barcelona.
Ruiz, M. 2008. *Graffiti Argentina.* New York: Thames & Hudson.
Schacter, R. 2008. "An Ethnography of Iconoclash: An investigation into the Production, Consumption and Destruction of Street Art in London", *Journal of Material Culture*, Vol. 13(1): pp. 35–61.
Schacter, R. and Fekner, J. 2013. *The World Atlas of Street Art and Graffiti*, London, Aurum Press.
Schacter, R. 2014. *Ornament and Order: Graffiti, Street Art and the Parergon*, Farnham, Ashgate.
Scholz, A. 2003. *Scenes, Graffiti in Barcelona*, B Index Books, Barcelona.
Snyder, G. J. 2009. *Graffiti lives: Beyond the tag in New York's urban underground.* New York University Press.
Stewart, J. 2009. *Graffiti Kings*, Melcher Media/Abrams, New York.
Spanish Graffiare http://www.spanishgraffiare.com/
Uys, S., & Uys, D. 2013. *Street art of Santiago: Walls that talk.* Kindle Electronic Book, Amazon Media EU.
Valencia Street Art http://www.uv.es/fvillar/graffiti/
Valjakka, M. 2011. "Graffiti in China—Chinese Graffiti?" *The Copenhagen Journal of Asian Studies* 29(1) pp. 61–91.
Ward, K. (ed.) 2014. *Researching the City*, Sage, London.
Waquant, L. 2006. The "scholarly myths" of the new law and order doxa. *Socialist Register*, 42, 93–115.
Wilson, J. Q., & Kelling, G. 1982. Broken windows: The police and neighborhood safety. Atlantic Monthly, March, 29–38.
Young, Alison. 2010. Negotiated consent or zero tolerance? Responding to graffiti and street art in Melbourne. *City* 14 (1–2): 99–114.
Young, A. 2012. "Criminal Images, The affective judgement of graffiti and street art", *Crime, Media, Culture*, 2012, 8(3): pp. 297–314.
Young, A. 2014. *Street Art, Public City*, London, Routledge.
Zieleniec, A. 2016. "The Right to Write the City: Lefebvre and Graffiti", Urban Environment, Vol. 10. http://eue.revues.org/1421

From Wayward Youth to Teenage Dreamer: Between the Bedroom and the Street

Jo Croft

The dreamer is set adrift. (Gaston Bachelard, *Air and Dreams* 1943)

INTRODUCTION: 'SHOULD I STAY OR SHOULD I GO NOW?'

The Undertones' 'Teenage Kicks' (1978) echoes down the decades as an anthem of exuberant yet frustrated youth, inextricably associated with a punk iconography of urban decay—of brick walls, graffiti, shuttered shop fronts, alleyways and, of course, the street itself. And yet when we listen a little more closely to the lyrics, and try to decipher the song's pent-up, frenetic energy, it is clear that the narrator is addressing us from what is, to all intents and purposes, an *inside* space. He seems to *contemplate* rather than *participate* in life outside, gazing out at a girl as 'she walks down the street'—whilst he is 'all alone' and not yet able to act on his desire ('I'm gonna call her on the telephone'). In other words, The Undertones' song encapsulates the tension between inside and outside space, and these teenage dreams seem to be as much about individuated masturbatory fantasies as they are about collective thrill-seeking: this dreamer who 'wishes' and

J. Croft (✉)
Liverpool John Moores University, Liverpool, UK

© The Author(s) 2018
N. Bentley et al. (eds.), *Youth Subcultures in Fiction, Film and Other Media*, Palgrave Studies in the History of Subcultures and Popular Music, https://doi.org/10.1007/978-3-319-73189-6_13

'wants' may well be filled with desire for encounters in the outside world, but he is also still lingering on the threshold between bedroom and street, enchanted and transfixed, not yet part of the action.

My starting premise, then, is that the delinquent loitering in the street can also be the dreamer in the bedroom, and that subcultural narratives are often shot through with ambivalent spatial identifications or, as Sian Lincoln puts it, young people can 'often find themselves caught in the blur between the public and the private' (Lincoln 2012, 187). In this chapter, I trace lines of connection between the 'wayward youth' and 'teenage dreamer'. I consider how each of these categories occupies a contradictory subject position, conjuring up a peculiarly unanchored state, hovering somewhere between imagination and action, and shaped not only by 'kicks', but also by 'fantasy' (MacInnes 1959, 12).

My analysis is underpinned by the assumption that the words 'adolescent', 'youth' and 'teenager' may well mean almost (but not quite) the same thing, but that they also seem to cast quite different shadows (See for example Croft 1992; Savage 2007; Lesko 2001). It perhaps helps to picture the relationship between these subject positions as a Venn diagram which throws into relief their overlapping discourses, whilst also foregrounding the tensions between them. The 'wayward youth' and 'teenage dreamer' are categories that accentuate these discursive intersections, and which therefore seem to accrue an overdetermined borderline status. Key to my approach here is to consider how these iterations of in-between-ness come to be associated with intensely liminal spatialities, and how the fraught yet dynamic movements, exchanges and tensions between inside and outside space can be related to psychic processes of identification.

In my readings of three very different texts—August Aichhorn's *Wayward Youth* (1925), Frederic Thrasher's *The Gang* (1927) and Richard Kelly's *Donnie Darko* (2001)—I set out to show how the problem of 'being in-between' is often most intensely articulated through complex, ambivalent registers of feeling associated with fugue-like movement, a distracted drifting that has no clear destination (Hacking 1998). All of the borderline subjects that I write about, whether they are 'wayward youths', 'suggestible gang-boys' or 'teenage dreamers', seem torn between hesitation and recklessness—half wanting to be somewhere else, but unable to pursue a linear version of worldly progression. In other words, these teenagers waver on the brink, fending off the narrative closure that we expect from the Bildungsroman's purposeful trajectories towards fully individuated development (Moretti 1987), and mirroring the indecision expressed in another teenage anthem, The Clash's 'Should I Stay or Should I Go? (1981).

'WAYWARD REALITY'

August Aichhorn was an early pioneer of youth work, and his seminal text *Wayward Youth* bears witness to an unusual encounter between psychoanalytic and pedagogic approaches to 'delinquent youth' (Aichhorn 1925 [1936], 11). In his therapeutic practice with 'dissocial' young people in Vienna between 1918 and 1930 (Houssier and Marty 2009), Aichhorn deploys psychoanalytic techniques in contexts that might otherwise be regarded as the domain of criminology or pedagogy, and he sets out to synthesise Freudian analysis with what he calls 're-education'. There is something both optimistic and potentially radical about Aichhorn's mission to wrest psychoanalysis away from the genteel confines of the consulting room, extending its reach into the corridors of the courthouse, or even into the street (Danto 2005; Eissler 1949). For example, in *Wayward Youth* he describes how he counsels his patients while walking along, or even while riding on trolley-cars—'As we talked, we walked slowly along the street' (Aichhorn 1925 [1936], 106), 'he walked all the way home with me' and 'He went on the streetcar with me' (1925 [1936], 110). It is also striking that in his ambulatory version of the clinic, Aichhorn sometimes pictures his patients in a state of reverie—'We walked along in silence; he was lost in thoughts and I was busy watching him.'(1925 [1936], 108). And as Aichhorn lays claim to the roles of educator and analyst, he also maps out a different kind of clinical space, one which is transformed by movements which blur the boundaries between public and private: a space in which the daydreamer has a key stake.

The original title of Aichhorn's *Wayward Youth* is *Verwahrloste Jugend: Die Psychoanalyse in d. Fürsorgeerziehung; 10 Vorträge zur ersten Einführung*, and the editors of the 1936 English edition comment on the particular problems presented by the German term '*Verwahr*', which is translated in the title as 'wayward' but 'is also rendered interchangeably as "dissocial" and "delinquent"' (1925 [1936]: xi). While the German term 'Verwahrloste' itself suggests pathological resonances, with synonyms including abject terms such as 'seedy', 'depraved', 'mangy' and 'dilapidated' (http://en.bab.la/dictionary/german-english/verwahrlost), the

English word 'wayward' usually seems to have more positive, perhaps even romantic, connotations. More often than not, 'waywardness' makes us think of dislocated movement—i.e., movement away from where you're supposed to be. Indeed, in the 1935 edition of *Roget's Thesaurus*, 'wayward' is listed alongside adjectives such as 'unsteady', 'vagrant', 'wavering', 'afloat', 'alterable', 'plastic', 'mobile', 'fleeting' and 'transient'. Another entry in the same edition of the thesaurus links waywardness to obduracy, and nowadays, a more likely equivalent German term to 'wayward' would be 'eigensinnig'—a word which suggests both obstinacy and free will. Thus, as we thread our way through this list of supposed synonyms, the 'wayward youth' seems to become more and more entangled with ideas of both distracted movement and rebellion. This is in turn suggests a close link with another borderline adolescent category—the fugueur. In French this word refers, literally, to a runaway or absconder and, more often than not, is linked with adolescence. Crucially, though, 'fugueur' also tends to be associated with the related terms, 'fugue state' and 'dissociative fugue', which describe supposedly psychopathological states of amnesiac travel or 'bewildered wandering' (American Psychiatric Association 2013, 298).

In *Mad Travellers* (1998), Ian Hacking describes the case of Albert Dada, the so-called 'first fugueur' (Hacking 1998, 7). According to Hacking, Albert made 'obsessive and uncontrollable journeys' which 'were systematically pointless, less a voyage of self-discovery than an attempt to eliminate self' (1998, 30). Perhaps most significantly, though, Hacking suggests that the diagnostic category of 'fugueur' is premised on the *shape* of the subject's movement, which he characterises as both 'aimless' and 'compulsive' (1998, 198). Like Albert Dada, several of Aichhorn's runaways and truants seem to occupy a borderline position, somewhere between aimlessness and compulsion. For example, Aichhorn describes a case of 'vagrancy' in a 16-year-old boy, who runs away from home and from his apprenticeship because he cannot stop thinking about the death of his mother,

> I was apprenticed to a mechanic in July and was there for two months. I couldn't enjoy anything. I couldn't help thinking all the time about my mother and how awful she must have looked after her accident, and then I ran away from my work. (Aichhorn 1925 [1936], 44)

In this example, supposedly delinquent movements are set in motion by a train of distracted yet intrusive thoughts. The boy runs away in order to pursue his feelings, and also to avoid them. Or, to put it another way, he moves in order to 'eliminate self' (Hacking 1998, 198).

Aichhorn also tells us about young people who have failed to leave home, and who consequently end up being targets of their family's resentment. Whether they 'escape' or are 'stuck', these delinquents often seem to act in ways which are distracted or fugue-like, hesitating on the threshold between inside and outside. This, then, may be how best to understand Aichhorn's use of the term 'wayward': the frequent representation of spatial ambivalence in his study suggests that Aichhorn's 'wayward youth' has the potential to be both day-dreamer and fugueur. For example, he describes a case of 'waywardness' in a boy who, seeing cherry stones on the sill as he looks out of the window, steals his mother's money, and then runs away to pick cherries for her. But then he eats the cherries himself and returns home, washes and puts on clean clothes. The boy's mother cannot 'explain his running away', and she is keen to stress that 'his only friend was a boy of a nice family, and he was hardly ever on the streets.' Yet despite vouching for her son's respectability, she also insists that 'He belongs to a reform school' (Aichhorn 1925 [1936], 13). Aichhorn's narrative of the cherry-stealing youth thus seems fraught with confused movements and muddled identifications, experienced both by the boy himself and his mother. There is a complex interplay here between personal pleasure-seeking and familial duty, and an overwhelming sense of ambivalence, played out in bizarre to-ing and fro-ing movements, and contradictory gestures. In other words, the subliminal plea from both mother and son seems to be: 'I love you. I can't bear to be without you. I resent you. I can't bear to be with you.'

According to Aichhorn, the wayward youth also communicates ambivalence through the specific prism of class. Most of the case studies that Aichhorn cites are not conventionally bourgeois, and the typical protagonists of his wayward narratives are serving apprenticeships, perhaps leaving school early in order to support families, but also expressing dissatisfaction with their class position. For example, Aichhorn tells us about a boy who 'declared that he did not want to be a burden to his mother since he was strong and healthy, but he refused to be a common labourer as his mother wished.' (Aichhorn 1925, 66). This boy apparently refuses to leave home and, like the 'cherry-picking' delinquent, he is resented by his mother who declares, 'If I don't get him out of the house, something terrible is bound to happen.' (1925 [1936], 69). Initially, she refers her son to Aichhorn because of his 'laziness and aggressive behaviour' (1925 [1936], 64), yet she also implies that he is effeminate, and stresses how 'his closet is much neater than any of his sisters [...] housework and reading are no work for a grown boy.' (1925 [1936], 66). So, rather confusingly, his waywardness is characterised both by excessive domesticity and by slovenliness, 'clear(ing) up everything around the house nicely' even though he is 'careless about his person' (1925 [1936], 69). Such contradictory accusations again seem to articulate ambivalent narratives of delinquency, imbricating class, gender and generational conflict.

We are therefore left with the impression that Aichhorn's wayward youth is out of kilter with the class and gender values of his family, that he is *illegitimately* laying claim to a realm of adolescent affect. Foreshadowing Keith Waterhouse's eponymous fantasist in *Billy Liar* (1959), Aichhorn's wayward youth is distracted by aspirational dreams, yet cannot quite leave home. Both Waterhouse's and Aichhorn's wayward youths overly identify with internal space, and so become cuckoo-like presences in the family house. Both boys take on typically bourgeois adolescent traits such as narcissistic daydreaming and immersive, indiscriminate literary consumption—'he will stand before the mirror for an hour arranging his tie and combing his hair' (Aichhorn 1925 [1936], 69), and 'He read a lot in his spare time—anything that came to hand, without discrimination' (1925 [1936], 66). Both boys daydream of other places: 'Are you really going to London, or just pretending?' (Waterhouse 1959, 183). And both boys waver on the brink of escape, drawing back from the outside world.

'WITHOUT REALLY KNOWING WHAT WE WERE DOING...'

Wayward Youth is probably most famous for the fact that Sigmund Freud wrote its foreword, and at first glance, Freud's introductory remarks seem to offer a cautious optimism about the future possibilities for combining psychoanalysis with pedagogy. Danto (2005) explores how, between 1922 and 1936, Freud supported a 'social activist' movement to establish The Vienna Ambulatorium as a free clinic and child-guidance centre. Yet in *Wayward Youth* Freud's tone is also guarded, perhaps even a little anxious, about maintaining the institutional authority of psychoanalysis, and he insists that 'educational work is *sui generis*, not to be confused with nor exchanged for psychoanalytic means of influence' (1925 [1936]: vi). With hindsight, Aichhorn's work effectively marks both a threshold and an impasse in the history of the Freudian institution, paving the way for a hybrid version of psychoanalysis that never really quite takes off. It is perhaps not surprising, then, that *Wayward Youth* resonates as a liminal text, replete with liminal subjects. And perhaps this is why Aichhorn's narrative voice often seems rather disoriented, not quite in the right place, or in the right institution, at the right time. Aichhorn self-consciously draws attention to his potential failures as a storyteller and expresses concern that his readers 'will be incredulous, that the interpolations of theory will interrupt the story, and that you may criticize me for being unscientific.' (1925 [1936], 12). As if to counter this uncertainty about his authority as a narrator, Aichhorn sometimes slips into a normative, conservative rhetoric about 'leading the dissocial back to conformity' (1925 [1936], 3), and attempting 'to fit a child for his place in society' (1925, 7). In some ways, therefore, he seems a little too keen to produce narratives of 'cure'.

Then again, Aichhorn repeatedly emphasises how he refuses to take up a position of authority with young people, and insists that 'I am not a detective nor a policeman and I don't need to know everything' (Aichhorn 1925 [1936], 96). Indeed, Aichhorn's colleagues seem to attribute his famous 'charisma' to such protestations of ignorance, 'his attitude of being "ignorant" about the subject-matter to which he has devoted his life's work, his belief in always beginning anew, in being eternally a student and pupil, not a teacher' (See Paul Federn's preface to Eissler 1949: XI). By using these strategies to efface his clinical authority, and by emphasising the 'no-man's land' qualities of his consulting room—'there is nothing to be afraid of, that this is neither a police station nor a court' (1925 [1936], 127) Aichhorn maps out a kind of heterotopic space for his delinquent subjects to inhabit, a space 'capable of juxtaposing in a single real place several spaces, several sites that are in themselves incompatible' (Foucault 1967, 6). In other words, he tries to cleave out an alternative, decentred institutional position that has the potential to meet the wayward youth's demands for 'his own special brand of reality' (1925 [1936], 40).

'Continuous Flux and Flow'

In his 1927 study of 1313 gangs in Chicago (published just two years after Aichhorn's *Wayward Youth*), Frederic Thrasher, a pioneer of The Chicago School, focuses on *collective* forms of delinquency. His young gangs are inhabitants of *outside* spaces. They are also 'lawless, godless, wild' (Thrasher 1927, 6), and we find them in the cracks and crevices of the city, beyond the reach of both private and public jurisdiction, 'almost beyond the pale of civil society' (1927, 6). Whereas Aichhorn seems to be concerned with *individual* crisis-bound subjects, whose relationship to the outside is ambivalent, or even phobic, and who often 'did not enjoy going out in the street' (Aichhorn 1925, 15), Thrasher's youths are almost always represented in terms of their positive spatial identification with the street, and he tends to use a rather giddy, libidinous vocabulary to describe the spatial dynamics of 'gangland'. According to Thrasher, for 'the gang boy who has not travelled, the great outside world is a place of mystery and magical wonders' (Thrasher 1927, 166), and 'Once a boy has tasted the thrilling street life of the gang, he finds the programs of constructive agencies unsatisfying' (1927, 79). (See also Dimitriadis 2006).

By contrast, the gang boy's home only seems to register as a point of departure—a place to be 'away' from. And yet the gang's apparent flight from domesticity is far from unequivocal, and Thrasher highlights their tendency to move 'without direction', stressing that gangs are characterised by 'locomotion for its own sake' and by 'interest in mere change and movement' (1927, 171). In other words, Thrasher seems to associate the gang with undecided forms of mobility, and with non-developmental, unresolved, narratives—'movement and change without much purpose or direction' (1927, 85). One of his case studies features a gang called 'The Bimbooms', and he describes how 'They were constantly chasing each other about the room, in and out of doors, and around the block'(1927, 85). According to Thrasher, 'This ceaseless activity without purpose or direction, this chaotic expenditure of energy, may be regarded as a form of "milling" typical of the gang.'(1927, 85). Perhaps most significantly, Thrasher defines 'ganging' itself as a 'process' of 'continuous flux and flow' (1927, 35), and he vividly articulates its non-linearity through the open-endedness of present participles—through actions such as 'prowling', 'roving', 'roaming', 'wandering', 'loafing', and of course 'milling' itself.

In Thrasher's text, both gangs and ganging are represented through a vocabulary of borderline spatiality and he specifically places the term 'interstitial'—'spaces that intervene between one thing and another' (1927, 22)—at the axis of his text, emphasising that it is 'probably the most significant concept of the study' (1927, 22). Thrasher famously portrays the gang as 'an interstitial growth [...] flowering where other institutions are failing to function efficiently...' It is a 'symptom of the disorderly life of the frontier' (1927, 495). And so, as he weaves together these botanical and medical metaphors, what emerges is a paradoxical sense that gangs both *animate* and *clog* the city's interstices. Like tidal flotsam and jetsam, Thrasher's gangs 'flux and flow', yet they also 'collect and cake in every crack and cranny' (1927, 22).

Perhaps most significantly, Thrasher seems to suggest that gangland is constituted through the imaginary transformations of play, and that 'most of the boys, like the "So-so's", the "Onions", and the "Torpedoes", lead an irregular life in the street, *which is their playground.*'(1927, 15) (my emphasis). As I have explored elsewhere (Smyth and Croft 2006), the playground conjures a space which merges the psychic with the social, action with imagination. As such, it is a heavily freighted term in Thrasher's text, not least because it draws attention to the overlap between psycho-analytic and topographical discourses. Just as Thrasher describes how 'the 'gang boy transform(s) his sordid environment through his imagination' (Thrasher 1927, 117), so Freud himself describes transference as a play-ground (Freud 1914, 154), while Winnicott nominates play as a space of borderline potentiality, 'neither inside nor outside' (Winnicott 1971, 113).

Thrasher's gangland, therefore, is defined not only as a geographical and social territory, but also as an imaginative space: as the gang-boy expe-riences the street as a playground, so the subjectivities of 'wayward youth' and 'teenage dreamer' collide. Indeed, at times, Thrasher's gang-boy con-spicuously takes on the mantle of teenage dreamer, one who:

sees in a broken sewer a sea on which sails the Spanish Armada [...] To him the piles of rubbish in the city dumps or the mud along the drainage canal are mountain fastnesses, while stretches of wasteland become prairies of the Golden West. (Thrasher 1927, 116)

Here Thrasher uses heightened literary language to represent transfor-mative relationships between environment and imagination. Moreover, his syntax suggests a distinct shift in focus *away* from the collective social identity of gangs, *towards* a singular daydreaming subject, which in turn implies that youthful imagination is inextricably bound up with both indi-viduation and literariness. At one level, therefore, Thrasher's narrative seems to open itself to the positive effects of immersive adolescent literary identification. Yet he also seems to suggest that reading can have negative, antisocial effects, and he makes clear connections between the gang-boy's literary consumption and his waywardness:

Thrilling stories of far-away places read in books and magazines are likely to have the same effect upon the boy. The Bureau of Missing Persons asks, as one of its first steps in locating runaway boys, what they have been reading. (Thrasher 1927, 165)

In a move which goes against the grain of current educational rhetoric about the benefits of 'reading for pleasure' (See for example Clark and Rumbold 2006), and which also anticipates his later work on the potentially detrimental effects of comics (1949, 1954), Thrasher argues that certain forms of reading actually stimulate delinquency. Though some of this material is excised from later editions, *The Gang* originally features chapters with headings such as 'The Quest For New Experience', 'The Role of the Romantic', 'The Movies and Dime Novels', and 'Wanderlust'. Most strikingly, Thrasher shows how the gang boy's reading apparently inspires truancy rather than excessive interiority:

> Wanderlust behaviour represents a response to a two-fold stimulus situation: it is, on the one hand, an attempt to escape or to compensate for what is dull or uninteresting; while on the other, it is a quest for novelty and adventure impelled by previous experience and further stimulated by the movies, reading and personal narratives. (Thrasher 1927, 170)

Like Aichhorn's truants and runaways, Thrasher's boys are 'impelled' in ways, which are distracted or fugue-like, and they apparently follow these wayward trajectories because they are 'stimulated' by books and films. In *Wayward Youth* Aichhorn poses the rhetorical question, 'Why should the delinquent not have his own special brand of reality too?' (Aichhorn 1936, 40), while in *The Gang* Thrasher he argues that 'the gang boy's life is fanciful [...] and many times he does not distinguish between what is real and what is not' (Thrasher 1927, 131). So, both susceptible gang boy and wayward youth read as they dream as they move. They summon up their own porous realities. They enter the terrain of the teenage dreamer.

'HE HAD NO WORDS AS HIS DREAMS SLID AND SHOOK'

Oscillating between consciousness and hallucination, the eponymous protagonist of Richard Kelly's *Donnie Darko* seems to epitomise the 'teenage dreamer', and much of the film's action plays upon this wavering dynamic between internal and external space. Of course, this film has strong subcultural resonances, generating peculiarly intense (especially adolescent) 'cult' identifications since its release in 2001. There are well over 2000 IMDB reviews of Kelly's film (Internet Movie Database 2016), many of which focus on its representation of the 'whole teenage angst thing'. Jake

Gyllenhaal (the actor who plays Donnie) introduces *The Donnie Darko Book* (2003) by speculating about the film's enigmatic, 'subversive' appeal—'Call it cult. Call it genius. Call it what you will' (Kelly 2003: viii), and he also implies that Kelly's film has the capacity to provoke meanings which are not 'conscious' (2003: vii). Subcultural responses to *Donnie Darko* seem particularly invested in how the film opens up other registers of consciousness, and comparisons between the original 'theatrical' cut and the director's cut often make much of the play between internal and external (even extra-terrestrial) spaces: with each version turning upon a slightly different topography of consciousness, the film conjures multiple configurations of inside and outside.

A number of Kelly's iconic montage sequences highlight movements between inside and outside, with tracking shots often lingering upon threshold sites such as hallways, doors, front gardens and the school entrance. Axiomatic to the film's narrative is the image of a fractured, violently penetrated domestic realm, shaken to the core and almost destroyed by an inexplicable object (a stray plane engine, without a plane) which crashes through the Darkos' roof, ending up in Donnie's bedroom. As the private space of the teenage bedroom is torn apart, and opened up to the street's public gaze, so this breach of architectural boundaries brings with it other tropes of conceptual interpenetration or oscillation which are key to my understanding of subcultural borderline subjectivity in this chapter.

But the film does not open with this moment of collision. Instead, Donnie is first pictured as a dreamer who is adrift in the outside world—'shivering, curled up in the foetal position', lying in the road in his pyjamas, 'asleep at the edge of a cliff'. He wakes up and is 'disoriented by the morning light' (Kelly 2003, 3). A few scenes later, we see Donnie stirring from sleep for a second time, as he is beckoned by a disembodied voice 'to wake up'. Apparently this is the voice of 'a grotesque 6 ft bunny figure' (2003, 10). Next, Donnie wakes again in the morning sunlight, 'dazed and confused', but this time on the seventh hole of the golf course. These opening scenes therefore establish Donnie in an excessively liminal realm—as a teenager caught on a threshold between sanity and psychic breakdown, and as a dreamer, poised between night and day, waking and sleeping, on the outskirts of the suburbs. In the film Donnie is also emphatically portrayed as a *subject who reads*: early on, we see him reading a collection of Graham Greene's short stories in his bedroom, and then performing a different kind of intense reading in the bathroom—staring at his own reflection in the medicine cabinet mirror, and scanning the words on a bottle of his anti-psychotic pills. In the opening sequence of the film, Donnie reads a note written on the fridge door which asks 'Where is Donnie?' This phrase, a question about the enigma of liminal subjective location, is a refrain that repeats throughout the film.

Of course, Donnie is not just a daydreamer, he is also a sleep walker, and Kelly makes it clear in the film that these borderline forms of consciousness are associated with Donnie's potential for psychosis. Indeed, even the golfer who wakes him on 'the seventh hole' hints at this, as he happens to be the Darkos' family doctor (an institutional figure involved in Donnie's diagnosis). The scene on the golf course also anticipates a later scene when Donnie is woken up from a hypnotic trance by his therapist: '*Donnie is now undoing his belt. He is no longer paying attention. Dr Thurman quickly claps her hands. Donnie jolts awake.*'(Kelly 2003, 32). Here, the therapist interrupts Donnie in his dream state, just as he prepares to masturbate, and this gesture of censorship reflects how Donnie tends to be *on the threshold of consciousness* when he experiences such supposedly therapeutic interventions. Melissa Gregg points out that 'Donnie's character is unavoidably implicated in an omnipresent therapeutic culture' (Gregg 2005, n.p.), and certainly these episodes indicate that Donnie comes to us with a crisis-bound history, as an adolescent whose parents 'pay someone two hundred dollars an hour to listen to all (his) thoughts…' (Kelly 2003, 5). Above all, though, Donnie is identified as a *permeable* subject who is besieged by forces from elsewhere, whether in the guise of institutional surveillance, or in the form of extraterrestrial, hallucinatory messengers.

Throughout the film, Kelly represents Donnie Darko as a protagonist with an excessive and volatile interiority. Donnie articulates an acutely adolescent position, and, crucially, reading is one of the key actions through which Donnie's psychic porosity and emotional depth is signalled in the film. Immersive literary consumption is, of course, a familiar sign of adolescent intensity (see for example Smyth and Croft 2006; Moretti 1987; Neubauer 1992), and the capacity to read 'with insight' typically allows the protagonist to accrue subjective complexity. It is no coincidence then that the scene with his English teacher, Karen Pomeroy, (played by Drew Barrymore) follows the filmic conventions of a traditional rites of passage narrative: literariness, or more specifically, literary insight, operates as a marker of separation from the group, underlined by the following implicit mantras—'I understand, but they don't', 'I have depth, but they don't'. According to the familiar patterns of such narratives, the teacher in turn apparently recognises this depth, often through a look, rather than through dialogue. By insistently portraying Donnie's 'depth' through the iconography of literary adolescence, Richard Kelly reinforces the audience's intense identification with Donnie, following the narrative logic that we can 'read' Donnie, and so are not like his classmates. The film therefore offers up peculiarly adolescent viewing pleasures, affirming the audience's cultish 'uniqueness' through a series of readerly projections: we recognise Donnie's depth as being like our own depth, our 'I' is like Donnie's 'I'.

So what is this story that Donnie understands better than his fellow pupils? What triggers such a concatenation of identifications? Donnie's class has been set the homework task of reading Greene's 1954 short story, and ironically this a text which shatters conventional literary tropes of adolescent interiority. In other words, Donnie Darko's status as a sensitive *literary* reader is shored up by his capacity to offer his teacher a knowing response to a shockingly nihilistic narrative. 'The Destructors' describes how a gang of children and teenagers painstakingly demolish an old man's house *from the inside*—'"We'd do it from the inside. I've found a way in [...] We'd be like worms, don't you see, in an apple." He said with a sort of intensity.' (Greene 1954, 12). The story's brutality is exacerbated by the gang's leader, T's, insistence that their actions should only be motivated by the desire to destroy, that 'destruction is a form of creation' (1954, 15). T also asserts that 'All this hate and love [...] "it's soft, it's hooey. There's only things"'(1954, 16). So, on T's instruction, the gang sets about meticulously destroying Old Misery's house. By taking as its target a 'beautiful' and precious building, which was supposedly designed by Christopher Wren, and which has miraculously survived the onslaughts of the Blitz, the gang is destructively mobilised not only against 'things' but also against both 'home' and 'history'.

At the heart of Graham Greene's short story there seems, almost literally, to be a black hole—a gap in representation which can only be filled by destroying the concept of home. And if 'Where is Donnie?' is Kelly's filmic refrain, for Greene the equivalent literary refrain is 'Where's my house?' (Greene 1954, 21). The figure of T (or Trevor) is probably the closest thing to a narrative focaliser in 'The Destructors', and yet where we might expect to find interior monologue, we find only a disquieting absence of adolescent introspection or uncertainty—'it was as though this plan had been with him all his life, pondered through the seasons, now in his fifteenth year crystallized with the pain of puberty.'(1954, 13). Indeed, there are striking similarities between Greene's portrayal of youth in 'The Destructors' and the 'youth without youth' of Wolfgang Borchert's unnerving manifesto, written in 1945:

> We are the generation without ties and without depth. Our depth is the abyss. We are the generation without happiness, without home, and without farewell. Our sun is narrow, our love cruel and our youth without youth. And we are the generation without limit, without restraint and without protection—thrown out of the playpen of childhood into a world made for us by those who now despise us because of it. (Borchert 1949, 39)

With this incantatory repetition of 'without', Borchert pictures his generation through a language of absolute negation, not quite eviscerated of all affect, yet almost triumphantly empty. Like Thrasher's gangs, they occupy some kind of interstitial realm, yet their space is emphatically detached from both play and home. Greene's gang, it seems, are of this same unbounded, un-housed generation. They are 'youth without youth' emerging from a 'hill of rubble' (Greene 1954, 21). And even when domestic life occasionally still impinges upon their world—when for example, we read that 'Mike had gone home to bed'—these moments only accentuate the pervasive sense that 'home' is antithetical to the gang's potency. So, as T's authority in the gang is temporarily challenged by another member who tells him to 'Run along home, Trevor' (1954, 18), we are left with the feeling that a reversal has somehow taken place, whereby the house that previously 'shelter(ed) daydreaming' (Bachelard 1958, 6) now robs the daydreamer of language, negates his capacity to dream:

> T stood with his back to the rubble like a boxer knocked groggy against the ropes. He had no words as his dreams shook and slid. (Greene 1954, 18)

So what happens when the narratives of *Donnie Darko* and 'The Destructors' cross paths? Perhaps we might argue that as Donnie identifies with the postlapsarian 'kind of imagination' (Greene 1954, 15) revealed in Greene's story, he also frees himself from the conventional discourses of adolescence. After all, it is Donnie's sensitive literary identification with Graham Greene's story which paradoxically inspires his somnambulistic vandalism ('They made me do it'). Donnie moves as a disoriented dreamer and seer between two different spatial identities—from the 'I' who reads privately but does not act, to the 'we' who acts out delinquently. Thus, when Donnie—in a dream state—attacks his school with a sledgehammer we witness a hyperbolic collision between wayward youth and teenage dreamer.

CONCLUSION: 'A BORDER RESEMBLING THE MEETING OF TWO CLOUDS'?

> Often we have no guiding principle for our absence and do not persevere once we have set out. Reverie merely takes us elsewhere, without our really being able to live the images we encounter along the way. The dreamer is set adrift. (Bachelard 1943, 3)

I began this chapter with a song about a teenage dreamer caught between bedroom and street, and have ended up with Donnie Darko: a figure on a rather different kind of threshold, who dreams his way back and forth between private and public realms, and who also somehow slips a gear in time and space. By focusing upon states of borderline consciousness rather than upon more familiar aspects of subcultural identity, I have shown how the teenage dreamer often articulates an overdetermined state of liminality, or as the psychoanalyst Andre Green puts it: 'a border resembling the meeting of two clouds' (Green 1972, 63). According to Green, 'to be a borderline [...] implies a loss of distinction between space and time' (Green 1972, 63), and in the texts that I have focused upon in this chapter, 'wayward youths', 'suggestible gang-boys' and, of course, 'teenage dreamers' all seem to experience an equivalent loss of distinction. My readings therefore illuminate those interstices which mark the divide between the exterior public domain (where youth presents a potential threat) and an interior, psychic realm (where the adolescent elaborates a highly individuated language of introspection and emotional intensity). Ranging across disciplines and historical moments, I have traced the (necessarily) rather hazy trajectories of these young subjects in states of reverie. And by seeking out those spaces in texts where imagination seems most acutely bound up with hesitant actions, I have highlighted the association between teenage dreaming and ambivalence. This is perhaps not surprising in the context of Aichhorn's psychoanalytic case studies, yet what is striking about Aichhorn's wayward youths is that they often seem to express their uncertainty through dream-like *movements*. Less predictably,

Thrasher's sociological ethnography also emphasises that gang life is shaped by imagination and play, often articulated through 'wandering' mobilities. And so it seems that both the problem, and allure, of teenage dreaming lies with its proliferating possibilities for in-between-ness: emerging from a tangle of borderlines, the teenage dreamer is 'set adrift' (Bachelard 1943, 3).

REFERENCES

Aichhorn, A. 1936/1925. *Wayward Youth*. London: Putnam.
American Psychiatric Association. 2013. *Diagnostic and Statistical Manual of Mental Disorders: DSM-5*. Washington, DC: American Psychiatric Association.
Bachelard, G. 1971/1960. *The Poetics of Reverie: Childhood, Language and The Cosmos* (Boston: Beacon Press).
Bachelard, G. 1994/1958. *The Poetics of Space*. Boston: Beacon Press.
Bachelard, G. 2011/1943. *Air and Dreams: An Essay on the Imagination of Movement*. Dallas: The Dallas Institute Publications.
Borchert, W. 1996/1949. *The Man Outside*. London: Marion Boyars Publishers.
Clark, C. and Rumbold, K. 2006. *Reading for Pleasure: A Research Overview*. National Literacy Trust.
Croft, J. 1992. *Adolescence and Writing: Locating the Borderline*. Sussex: Unpublished Phd Thesis.
Danto, E. A. 2005. *Freud's Free Clinics: Psychoanalysis & Social Justice, 1918–1938*. New York: Columbia University Press.
Dimitriadis, G. 2006. 'The Situation Complex: Revisiting Frederic Thrasher's *The Gang: A Study of 1,313 Gangs in Chicago*' in *Cultural Studies—Critical Methodologies*, 6, Issue 3: 335–353.
Eissler, K. 1949. *Searchlights on Delinquency: New Psychoanalytic Studies*. New York: International University Press.
Foucault, M. 1967. 'Of Other Spaces: Utopias and Heterotopias' in *Diacritics* 16 (Spring 1986) 22–27.
Freud, S. 1914 'Remembering, Repeating and Working Through' in vol. XII, *The Standard Edition of the Complete Works of Sigmund Freud*. London: Hogarth.
Green, André. 1996/1972. *On Private Madness*. London: Rebus.
Greene, G. 1986/1954. 'The Destructors' in *Collected Short Stories*. London: Penguin.
Gregg, M. 2005. 'Affect.' *M/C Journal 8.6*. 15 Sep. 2015 http://journal.media culture.org.au/0512/01editorial.php
Hacking, I. 1998. *Mad Travellers: Reflections on the Reality of Transient Mental Illnesses*. Cambridge, MA: Harvard University Press.

Houssier, F. and Marty, F. 2009. 'Drawing on psychoanalytic pedagogy: the influence of August Aichhorn on the psychotherapy of adolescents' *Psychoanalytic Quarterly.* 2009 Oct; 78(4): 1091–108.

Internet Movie Database 2016. Reviews & Ratings for *Donnie Darko* [online] Available at: http://www.imdb.com/title/tt0246578/reviews?ref_=ttqu_ql_op_3 [Accessed 5th November 2016]

Kelly, R. 2003. *The Donnie Darko Book.* London: Faber and Faber.

Kelly, R. 2001. *Donnie Darko: The Director's Cut* (film).

Lesko, N. 2001. *Act Your Age!: A Cultural Construction of Adolescence.* London: Routledge.

Lincoln, S. 2012. *Youth Culture and Private Space.* Basingstoke: Palgrave Macmillan.

MacInnes, C. 1985/1959. *The London Novels.* London: Allison and Busby.

Moretti, F. 1987/2000. *The Way of the World: The Bildungsroman in European Culture.* New York: Verso.

Neubauer, J. 1992. *The Fin de Siècle Culture of Adolescence.* New Haven: Yale University Press.

Roget, Peter M. 1935/1852. *Thesaurus of English Words and Phrases.* London: Longmans.

Savage, J. 2007. *Teenage: The Creation of Youth 1875–1945.* London: Chatto and Windus.

Smyth, G. and Croft, J. 2006. *Our House: The Representation of Domestic Space in Modern Culture.* Amsterdam: Rodopi Press.

The Clash. 1981. 'Should I Stay or Should I Go'. Epic Records

Thrasher, F. M. 2013/1927. *The Gang: A Study of 1,313 Gangs in Chicago.* Chicago: University of Chicago Press.

Thrasher, F. M. 1949. 'The Comics and Delinquency: Cause or Scapegoat' 23 in *J. Educ. Sociology* 195. London: University of Chicago Press.

Thrasher, F. M. 1954. 'Do the Crime Comic Books Promote Juvenile Delinquency?' in *The Congressional Digest,* 33(12), December.

The Undertones/John O'Neill. 1978. 'Teenage Kicks'. Good Vibrations/Sire.

Waterhouse, K. 1991/1959. *Billy Liar.* London: Penguin.

Winnicott, D. 1999/1971. *Playing and Reality.* London: Routledge/Tavistock

From Exaltation to Abjection: Depictions of Subculture in *Quadrophenia* and *Ill Manors*

Keely Hughes

INTRODUCTION

This chapter represents a contribution to the debate concerning the veracity and accuracy of defining and describing subculture in contemporary
society. Following Blackman (1997, 2005) and others (Blackman and
France 2001; McCulloch et al. 2006; Nayak 2006; Shildrick and
MacDonald 2006), it will be argued that the term 'subculture' should not
be so readily abandoned. Using an analysis of two films, *Quadrophenia*
(1979) by Franc Roddam and *Ill Manors* (2012) by Ben Drew, as illustration, the aim of this chapter will be to provide a critical discussion of the
construction of subcultural affiliations. In order to achieve this, an exploration of the role and representation of class relations and 'symbolic styles'
(aesthetic appearance, performative, territory and moral boundaries)
(Hebdige 1979) will be undertaken for each film. Through an analysis of
both film representations of subculture, it will be argued that there has

K. Hughes (✉)
Keele University, Newcastle-under-Lyme, UK

© The Author(s) 2018
N. Bentley et al. (eds.), *Youth Subcultures in Fiction, Film and
Other Media*, Palgrave Studies in the History of Subcultures and
Popular Music, https://doi.org/10.1007/978-3-319-73189-6_14

been a shift in the constructions of subcultural movements and affiliations from a form of self-othering in *Quadrophenia* to external-othering in *Ill Manors*. This shift, it will be suggested, occurs through changes within the capitalist system. In particular, the erosion of the paternalistic welfare state model of the post-World War Two era in Britain and the increasing desperation of the working classes to survive as an entity under contemporary neoliberal policies.

QUADROPHENIA: POST-WAR COMMUNITIES AND CLASSIC SUBCULTURE

During the years 1945 to 1970, Britain experienced a major social and economic reconstruction, establishing a forward-looking Britain in which an 'economy of society' and 'social mobility' would dominate public and political rhetoric. The social market economy born from this era, aimed to establish fair competition between the classes by maintaining a balance between a high rate of economic growth, low inflation and low levels of unemployment. This reconstruction of economic and social conditions provided youth groups with opportunities of skilled work, regular employment, stability and security. Weight (2013) acknowledges that 'the youth of post-war Britain represented a society in transition, a society where opportunity and affluence would potentially raise expectations, heighten class-consciousness and distort class boundaries' (p. 20). Succeeding these developments was the hope of a 'classless' society, achievable by providing full employment and opportunity to the working classes. Despite these developments, '*class refused to disappear*' (Hebdige 1979, 74). However, as Hebdige (1979) notes, 'the ways in which class was *lived*—the forms in which class found expression in culture—did dramatically change' (ibid.).

Quadrophiena portrays these new 'lived' experiences of culture for working-class youth in post-war Britain. The film tells the story of the 1964 Brighton riots between gangs of Mods and Rockers from the perspective of Jimmy, a young Mod. Working in a monotonous job as a postroom boy, becoming increasingly disillusioned with his parents and his incessant need to 'be somebody', Jimmy finds an outlet for his angst by popping pills, visiting all-night dance halls, hanging out with his Mod friends and battling with a rival gang of Rockers. *Quadrophenia* portrays a dichotomy of work and leisure as the new 'lived' experiences for post-war youth groups. This work/leisure dichotomy becomes essential to the subcultural identity for the group of Mods in the film.

Emerging from the portrayal of work and the characters' jobs is the maintenance of historic class structures in post-war Britain. Regardless of social, cultural and economic developments, traditional class structures continue in terms of low-status employment for the working classes. Nevertheless, employment provided working-class youth with disposable income, which they invested in their subcultural image through the process of 'stylisation':

> I've got a good job
> And I'm newly born.
> You should see me dressed up in my uniform.
> I work in a hotel all gilt and flash.
> Remember the place where the doors we smashed?
> (The Who, *Bellboy* 1973)

These lyrics pick up on the idea of youth being reborn or 'newly born' during the post-war era and emphasises the importance of work in creating the Mod identity. The juxtaposition between a subservient role in menial employment and a high-status value within the subculture is evident in *Quadrophenia*, in particular with the character 'Ace Face'. The 'Ace Face' to Jimmy is the ultimate Mod; he is the sharpest dresser, the coolest dancer and rides the best scooter. Yet, as Jimmy discovers, Ace Face has a low-status job as a bellboy, carrying the luggage for middle-class guests at the Grand Hotel in Brighton. Although he has high status within his subcultural group, his job reinforces his working-class status.

All the characters seemingly engage in relatively low-status work. Jimmy is the lowest-ranking employee at an advertising firm as a post-room boy, Dave works as a bin man, Peter at his uncle's scrap yard and Steph as a checkout girl. However, despite this engagement in low-status work, there is a positivity surrounding it. This is explicit in an exchange between Jimmy and Peter: Peter says to Jimmy, 'you don't work, you don't get money, and I like money' (*Quadrophenia* 1979). Work for Peter provides him with a disposable income which is pivotal in facilitating the communication of his subculture, as money enables him to acquire and create the commodities and signifiers of Mod identity.

The 'symbolic styles' of the Mods portrayed in *Quadrophenia* reflect the ideas promoted by the CCCS (Centre for Contemporary Cultural Studies) (Corrigan 1979; Hall and Jefferson 1976; Hebdige 1979; McRobbie 1980; Willis 1979) regarding the self-stylised construction of this subgroup's identity. The film portrays vividly the attitudes, rituals, leisure and style of the group, including the subversion of objects to reflect the symbolic use, meaning and importance of 'Mod' identity. The group forms a 'style' and creates a 'lifestyle' that separates itself from bourgeois hegemonic norms and the historically rooted traditions of the working-class parent culture. This separation manifests itself in the form of 'symbolic styles', including: aesthetic appearance, performativity, territory and moral boundaries (Hebdige 1979).

> *Aesthetic Appearance*
> *My jacket's gonna be cut slim and checked,*
> *Maybe a touch of seersucker with an open neck.*
> *I ride a GS scooter with my hair cut neat,*
> *Wear my war-time coat in the wind and sleet*
> *(Love Reign O'er Me, The Who 1973)*

In *Quadrophenia*, there is a clean aestheticism attached to the Mods. The Mod style includes expensive fashions, such as tailored suits, French crew tops, polo-shirts, brands like Levi's, Fred Perry and Ben Sherman, clean cut feathered or bouffant hair, parkas and Lambrettas/Vespas. The clean aestheticism of the Mod works to distance them from the dirty industrial image of their working-class parent culture and to challenge the materiality of their middle-class counterparts by owning a superior appearance; this is particularly the case with Jimmy and his parents/boss.

Hebdige states in *The Meaning of Mod* that 'the importance of style to the mods can never be overstressed—Mod was pure, unadulterated STYLE, the essence of style. In order to project style, it became necessary first to appropriate the commodity, then to redefine its use and value, and finally to relocate its meaning within a totally different context' (1979, 76). The Mods use of scooters and parkas provides a perfect exemplifier of the subversion of commodities. The customisation of the scooter (adding lights and mirrors), turned it from a practical means of clean, cheap transportation, an 'ultra-respectable means of transport', to a 'weapon and a symbol of solidarity' (ibid.) Subverting commodities such as the scooter, with lights and mirrors, provided the Mods with a commodity that functioned and represented the Mod style. Similarly, the parka is initially used to keep the Mods clothes clean when riding their scooters but are customised with patches and badges to convey the Mod style. The importance of these subverted commodities to the Mod identity is illuminated in a scene where a postman driving his van inadvertently crashes into Jimmy's scooter. Jimmy shouts at the postman, 'you've killed me scooter!' This scene symbolically marks the ending of Jimmy's 'Mod way of life'.

Performative
MRS COOPER. Where you been?
JIMMY. Fell asleep on the train and wound up in bloody Neasdon.
MRS COOPER. It's running around on them motorbikes most of the night ... I'm not surprised.
JIMMY. (*sighs*)
MRS COOPER. It's not normal.
JIMMY. Oh yeah ... what's normal then.
(*Quadrophenia* 1979)

The performative style of the Mods relied as much on their aesthetic appearance as on consumerism. Hebdige (1976) describes this performative element of style as 'consumer rituals'. The performative style of the Mods was to 'worship leisure and money' (Benstock and Ferris 1994, 52). Throughout *Quadrophenia*, the leisure activities constructing the performative style through consumer practices include dancing in all-night clubs, socialising (in cafés and at house parties), spending time listening to music, collecting records and maintaining the Mod aesthetic look by visiting fashion boutiques, tailors and barbers. For Mods, scooters aid in these consumption practices. The scooters allow the Mods to break with locality, to consume and engage in a wider variety of leisure activities in a range of locations and to define and enact their performative identity. The events of the bank-holiday weekend show the Mods travelling to Brighton to see and be seen in streets and public places (Brighton seafront and nightclubs).

The Mods use of 'blues' (amphentamines) are also an intrinsic part of their leisure lifestyle. The Mods in *Quadrophenia* consume 'blues' almost every time they are engaging in leisure activities. The Mods generally use amphetamines for extending their leisure time into the early hours of the morning and as a way of bridging the gap between the hostile and daunting everyday work life and the Mod lifestyle. Wilson indicates that amphetamines 'symbolised the smart on-the-ball, cool image' inviting 'stimulation, not intoxication ... greater awareness, not escape and confidence articulacy' (Wilson 2008, 5). This image counters the 'drunken rowdiness' of the working-class parent culture and previous generations. 'Blues' are an integral part of resisting prior working-class lifestyles and in creating and engaging in 'consumer rituals'.

Territory
Out of my brain on the 5:15
        (*5:15*, The Who 1973)

MR COOPER. Who do you think you are anyway?
JIMMY. Oh I don't know … you tell me.
MR COOPER. You're barmy, that's what you are. Staying out all hour's getting up to god knows what dressing up like a bloody freak … and stand still when I'm talking to ya. I wouldn't be at all surprised if you're on drugs … yeah, I know what you get up to down that club, you and your mates, your gang. You've gotta be part of a gang haven't ya ay … you gotta be a Mod or this or that. I mean haven't ya got a mind of your own.
        (*Quadrophenia* 1979)

The territorial style of the Mods portrayed in *Quadrophenia* is both cultural and spatial. Spatially the Mods are very much integrated into society and community; they are often seen gathering in public spaces such as cafés, bars, clubs and shops. They also construct their own public spaces through the development of a 'youth' consumer market. For example, the all-night dance halls are a space for the Mods. They colonise spaces to demonstrate and perform their identity as a collective group of shared values and meanings (Hebdige 1979). The change in socioeconomic conditions in the 1960/1970s provided opportunities for the Mods to define and create meanings and values as well as a style and practice that identified their distinctiveness not only in terms of a generational break but also from other youth subcultures such as the Rockers.

Working-class culture had until this point been quite stable in terms of its normative values (hard manual work, honest living, traditional marriage, family values and remembering one's roots). However, the Mod subculture unsettles this through the socioeconomic developments of affluence, opportunity and the chance of mobility through the changing attitudes of this group to money, power and status (Goldthorpe et al. 1968). This enables the Mods to create a space between two cultures: the bourgeois dominant culture and the working class parent culture. This is demonstrated throughout the film in various scenes between Jimmy and his parents, and Jimmy and his middle-class co-workers. Cohen stresses that the Mods 'attempted to realise, but in an imaginary relation, the condition of existence of the socially mobile white-collar worker […while…] their argot and ritual forms [continued to stress…] many of the traditional values of the parent culture' (1980, 98). The Mod subculture, therefore, forms in *Quadrophenia* from three sites—(1) generational difference, resulting from post-war economic and social modernisation in an emerging consumer society; (2) middle-class social forms and values, and (3) attitudes from the traditional working-class parent culture. Jimmy struggles with this three-way identity and struggles to find a space to be the 'Mod' both at home with his parents and at the advertising firm where he works. It is only within the Mod group/gang that his culture and identity appear to be whole.

Moral Boundaries

JUDGE. It seems strange to me to see this precession of miserable specimens so different from the strutting hooligans of yesterday who came here to pollute the air of this town. Yes. These longhaired, mentally unstable, petty little hoodlums [...] these sordid Caesars who can only find courage like rats by hunting in packs, came to Brighton with the profound intent of interfering with the life of its inhabitants.

(*Quadrophenia*, 1979)

The moral boundaries and behaviour of the group of Mods portrayed in *Quadrophenia* take the form of defiance, contempt, parody and sarcasm, to demonstrations of verbal and physical outbursts of rage. These are expressed and acted out as a form of resistance (particularly in the case of Jimmy) towards middle-class counterparts/co-workers, parents, the wider working-class community and towards the gangs of Rockers. This resistance is presented in both passive and aggressive forms and acts as a site for the negotiation of the Mod identity, allowing it to develop and present itself as an alternative identity.

In *Quadrophenia*, Jimmy highlights these two phases of subversive styles through behaviour. Early in the film, Jimmy's behaviour is passive as he challenges authority, mainly his parents and his boss. This can be interpreted as Jimmy resisting normative culture's attempts to socialise him. He resists this to develop the Mod identity. Later in the film Jimmy's behaviour becomes more aggressive; however, this aggressive behaviour is acted out among his fellow Mods. These two forms of behaviour enable the group of Mods to create their own acceptable models of behaviour, which challenge behaviour models existing in other cultural groups. The behaviour model of the Mods acts as meaningful attempts of negotiating the space between the emerging consumptive affluent worker and working-class status.

Irrespective of the rebellion found at its core, the Keynesian social welfare economy of post-war Britain enabled a mode of self-identification of subcultural identity. *Quadrophenia* presents a vision of society which provides stable economic opportunities, disposable income and an element of social mobility which appears inclusive, even if there is clear inequality between social groups. This is not the case with Ben Drew's *Ill Manors*, which reflects the subcultural horror of neoliberal capitalism in contemporary Britain.

ILL MANORS: A NEOLIBERAL SUBCULTURE

Ill Manors begins with the tagline '*We are all products of our environment... Some environments are just harder to survive in*'. Set in Forest Gate, London 2012, home of the 2012 London Olympic Games, the film presents a neighbourhood immersed in chains of violence, vengeance and lethal reprisals that ripple through the community of drug dealers, prostitutes, immigrants, local gangs and the poor. The film attempts to address the issues and experiences of young people who are economically and socially excluded under the post-2008 austerity period and the neoliberal social order. These economic, political and social regressions constitute what Henry Giroux describes as a 'war on youth' (Giroux 2010). This 'war' occurs through the lack of quality education, unemployment, the repression of dissent, a culture of violence and the discipline of the market (Giroux 2010). The lack of these fundamental economic, political and social goods shapes the dismal experiences of many young people. *Ill Manors* attempts to capture this 'war on youth' through the portrayal of an underclass council estate community to which the term 'Chav' has become the derogatory name for its members. 'Chav' has been defined as a culture that has evolved from previous working-class cultures and is often used in a classist manner as an attack on the poor (Jones 2011).

The neoliberal mantra replaces issues such as equality and justice with the incessant need to 'consume' and 'economise' oneself. The popular discourse under this economic and social system is that every individual is accountable for their own economic and social failings as every individual has choice and autonomy within the free market. The idea of 'choice' denotes having access to the means to engage socially and economically. However, the neoliberal order creates injustice, inequality and demonisation on the basis of 'choice' as not all individuals have equal access to social and economic goods. As Bauman highlights, failure under the neoliberal order is envisaged as 'the aggregate product of wrong individual choices; proof of the "choice incompetence" of its members' (1998, 78). Tyler (2013) refers to these choice-incompetent individuals, or 'the poor', as the 'social abject'.

In *The Powers of Horror*, Kristeva describes the abject as something that 'disturbs identity, system order, what does not respect borders, positions, rules. The in-between, the ambiguous, the composite' (Kristeva 1980, 7). The abject is 'being for the other' and it is the normalcy of the 'other' which gives the abject its identity. The 'social abject' therefore, works as a mode of governmentality of waste populations, through 'including forms of exclusion' (Tyler 2013). Ben Drew presents the 'social abject' in *Ill Manors*; he does this by showing the characters attempting to survive in their hostile and impoverished community. The characters turn the everyday rules of neoliberal capitalism aside, corrupting, misleading and taking advantage of them through the 'consumption' mechanism which lies at its core. The characters achieve this by engaging in underground economic activities, such as drug dealing, prostitution and theft. The perception and assumption by dominant cultural groups towards the underclass and 'Chav' in terms of economic activity is as Plan B sarcastically suggests: 'Kids on the street, no they never miss a beat, never miss a cheap thrill when it comes their way' (*Ill Manors*, Plan B 2012). It is this perception, that these youth groups who are part of the underclass are quick to sell their morals to make easy money rather than gain qualifications to become a hard-working and meaningful economic agent in society which evokes the reaction of 'disgust' towards them. It is the general consensus that 'Those at the bottom are there because they are stupid, lazy or otherwise morally questionable' (Jones 2011, xiii) rather than having unequal access to 'culturally valued resources' (Griffin 2011, 255) that enable them to conform to normalcy both economically and socially under the neoliberal order.

The abject is, however, useful under neoliberal forms of capitalism, as it reminds the non-abject (or the object) that they are not the abject (them). In these austere times, anybody can at once become 'economically displaced', so in a sense the abject keeps the neoliberal order active by reminding adequate consumers to remain precisely that, 'adequate'. The fear of becoming abject plays a disciplinary role: it keeps individuals (the non-abject) complicit in the regime of consumption practices and market rule. It is as Kristeva notes the 'abject has only one quality of the object and that is being opposed to "I"' (Kristeva 1980, 8.) Therefore, the 'socially abject', in some ways, reinforces the popular neoliberal discourse as the 'object' tries to further itself from the 'abject'. In terms of subcultural affiliations, in *Quadrophenia*, the Mod subculture positively self-construct their identity by resisting the traditional working-class and dominant middle-class culture. The Mods have a good self-image, despite of and perhaps even because of the mischief and bad press that they receive. Whereas in *Ill Manors*, the Chav as the 'social abject' accept an identity constructed by the dominant middle-class culture, a negative image which is internalised by the Chav subcultural group. The Chav as a 'social abject' is constructed from 'without' rather than from 'within,' giving this subcultural group a negative external identity in wider society.

Like *Quadrophenia*, 'symbolic styles' appear in *Ill Manors* in the construction of the Chav subcultural group. The 'symbolic styles' in *Ill Manors* which form the compound of the group identity of the Chav conform to classic subcultural affiliations, including subversion to normalcy through signifying practices of 'style' which differentiate this group from the dominant cultural group. Post-subcultural analysis prioritises autonomy in the consumption of goods and the construction of lifestyles and identity. What *Ill Manors* depicts is a lack of autonomy in these spheres as consumption practices and their subcultural affiliations are limited by economic necessity. Therefore, the Chav group cannot be categorised as the post-subcultural line of thought would argue, as a 'neo-tribe' (Bennett 1999) or 'Scene' (Maffesoli 1995) due to this lack of autonomy in the construction of their identity. However, emerging in the film in terms of the subcultural affiliations of the Chav in comparison to the Mod in *Quadrophenia* is an inversion connected to the 'symbolic styles' and 'forms of subversion' constructing their identity. Although the Mod subcultural group is constituted from *without* by its opposition to a purported 'mainstream', the Mods have more leverage through good social and economic conditions to create their own image, whilst the Chav subculture is more determined from *without* than *within* through social abjection and non-inclusion of this group in society (socially, culturally, politically and economically).

Aesthetic Appearance
SOCIAL WORKER. Anyway, stay outta trouble yeah … oh and erm take that hat off and maybe the old bill will leave you alone.
AARON. Yeah … doubt it.
(*Ill Manors* 2012)

In terms of aesthetic appearance, the visible 'style' of the characters in *Ill Manors* follows the branding culture of post-modern consumerism. The characters are seen in casual-wear and sportswear, which are mostly brands and designer labels, including Burberry, Ralph Lauren and Adidas. Other styles portrayed comprise of trainers, hoodies, baseball caps, chucky gold jewellery (bling) and accessories such as smartphones and flash cars, BMW's and Audi's for instance. The image is to demonstrate wealth and the ability to be an active consumer. The aesthetic appearance of the Chav reflects the dominance of consumerism and the power of the market in contemporary society whereby the owning of branded items becomes a status symbol. In this sense, the characters are effective in consumer practices as they are able to buy into high-end goods. However, there develops a disassociation by the dominant hegemonic cultural group to buy these products, as they do not want to be seen buying similar consumer goods as 'the poor'. As Haywood and Yar identify, the poor are 'often in the same moment both socially and economically *excluded* yet culturally and commercially *included*' (2006, 21). The Chav group try to include themselves but find themselves at the same time excluded. Unlike the Mod subcultural group in *Quadrophenia* who construct their own 'youth market' through self-constructions of 'style' and subverting commodities, in *Ill Manors,* this becomes inverted; it is other consumers choosing not to buy into the same brands as the Chav group through fear of being labelled a 'Chav' themselves that creates to some extent the Chav aesthetic.

Style for the Chav subcultural group also adapts itself to a function, which is concealment mainly from society and authority figures. Throughout *Ill Manors* the characters are shown wearing dark-coloured clothes, which emphasises this idea of concealment emerging through economic disassociation connected to this group. They use this style to engage in other economic endeavours, mainly underground, criminal activities. Featherstone (2013) argues that the hoodie has become a signifier of 'the capitalist other'. It embodies and is associated with criminal activity linked to the underground or black economy. The need for concealment to engage in such illegal economic activities is illustrated when Marcell stresses to Jake: 'You see why I'm always in black ... cuz people can't pick me out' (*Ill Manors* 2012). Rather than being a positively self-constructed style in the case of the Mods associated with materiality, the style is negative and becomes externally constructed, associated with social and economic exclusion. The need to hide, not to be identifiable, not to stand out to authority is a key factor in belonging to the group but also to be able to successfully engage in their activities.

Performative
Who closed down the community centre?
I killed time there, used to be a member
What will I do now until September?
School's out, rules out, get your bloody tools out.
London's burning, I predict a riot.
                              (*Ill Manors*, Plan B, 2012)

What occurs within the performative aspects of 'style' in *Ill Manors* and the Chav subculture is a move from a distinctive work/leisure dichotomy seen in *Quadrophenia* towards a blending of the two. The lack of education and work opportunities creates conditions in which for many there is no clear division between work and leisure time—they become the same. In *Ill Manors*, leisure becomes entwined with work through a lack of stable employment. The need to survive in a neoliberal capitalist society without formal economic opportunities requires a creative engagement and commitment to informal moneymaking practices to survive. Therefore, the performative element of the Chav subculture involves the characters attempting to make money wherever and whenever they can, but this is mainly tied to the underground or 'black' economy. The film shows Aaron and Ed prostituting Michelle in pubs and kebab shops and Chris, Ed and Aaron dealing drugs in the local pub. The boundaries between work and leisure are never separate. This results in 'leisure', such as hanging around on the streets, becoming associated with criminality, or as Haywood (2004) puts it 'street delinquency', which in effect is also waiting for moneymaking opportunities to arise.

Territory
Keep on believing what you read in the papers,
Council estate kids, scum of the earth...
                              (*Ill Manors*, Plan B 2012)

The territorial style of the Chav subculture is both cultural and spatial, like the Mod subculture. Spatially, unlike the Mods in *Quadrophenia*, who break boundaries of locality and colonise public space, the Chavs spatial territory is restricted. In *Ill Manors* the characters are only seen in the small geographic area of the community where they live (Forest Gate, London). This is further narrowed to abject and abandoned spaces. The group is shown occupying streets, alleyways, empty car parks, housing estates, prisons, abandoned properties and decaying industrial buildings. The characters coalesce in unused spaces and more often than not, this enables concealment of their engagement in illegal economic activities. Marcell's gang use a decaying abandoned industrial building to hold hostage their 'customers' who fail to make payment of drugs, and Michelle and Katya take refuge in abandoned properties.

Like the Mod subculture in *Quadrophenia*, cultural territory in *Ill Manors* is linked to socioeconomic conditions. The difference being, however, that the Mods construct their cultural territory by deconstructing, reconstructing and destructing spaces, whereas in *Ill Manors* cultural territory is constructed by others. Chav subcultural members are assembled through media and political discourse as 'scum', 'benefit cheats', 'scroungers', 'feral' and 'council housed and violent'. The Chav has become identified and constructed from the space it occupies: 'the council estate'; '*Made from stone, steele and iron beams, the council blocks they define the mean*' (Ben Drew, *Lost my Way*, 2012). The Chav has become identified and constructed through the negative associations attached to these sites by wider societal discourses. Therefore, the space they occupy defines their culture and the survival tactics employed by the Chav group constitutes a self-contraction of their identity through their practices and behaviours. This fuels the 'othering' done to them by proving that they are who and what society depicts them as.

Moral Boundaries
Like crimes the only way we're gonna feed off this economy.
Revert to type, live out these self-fulfilling prophecies.
Common goal, common enemy, economise.
        (*Live Once*, Plan B 2012)

The representation of moral boundaries in *Ill Manors* shows drug dealing and taking, prostitution, antisocial behaviour, murders, theft and even the selling of a baby. There is a lack of moral boundaries, in fact there appears to be no boundaries at all. In contrast to *Quadrophenia*, there is a large difference between the behaviours of the Mods and 'Chavs' that stems in large part from the economic conditions prevalent in each period. In *Quadrophenia*, economic conditions provide opportunities not only for relatively good wages but also for social mobility. The behaviour of the Mods is formed through resisting the parent culture to create new behaviours to construct their identity that is facilitated by the monetary means to do so. In current economic conditions, the working classes (such as those depicted in *Ill Manors*) have become stripped of the opportunity to make a respectable living known by the old working class (such as the Mods in *Quadrophenia*), let alone the chance of social mobility that was possible for some (MacDonald et al. 2005).

What emerges in *Ill Manors* through highlighting the past histories and present socioeconomic conditions these characters face is that the lack of moral boundaries is necessary, pragmatic and functional to survival. Katya steals a pram and a purse to save her baby and escape the sex-slave nightmare she has had to endure. Michelle prostitutes herself to feed her drug habit, which provides her with the only means of escaping her past. Aaron works for Ed selling drugs to afford the bare minimum life essentials. These examples illustrate the fluidity of moral and legal boundaries in the context of surviving at the margins of society. To survive in a neoliberal economy and with no capital to exchange, to some extent the only means by which these characters can acquire money to live is by eschewing their morality and becoming dehumanised in the process. It becomes apparent that the economic and social limitations this group endure force them to behave in this manner. Phil Cohen identifies that under neoliberal socioeconomic conditions

> There are increasing numbers of young people unable, through no fault of their own, to make the transition to the kinds of mobile individualism demanded by the new career culture, and whose sense of frustration leads to anti-social or self-destructive behaviour. (1999, 425)

Ultimately, these 'symbolic styles' are a response to the task of living and surviving in a hostile environment. They are not self-constructed and have become necessary as it is what is available to the Chav subcultural group; their style is not chosen. The 'symbolic styles' act, therefore, as a response to the challenges of living. *Ill Manors* shows that the subcultural group Chav is less a 'lifestyle' but rather a 'style of life'. That is, a 'lifestyle' is a means of forging a sense of self and creating cultural symbols that resonate with personal identity, which is what is seen in *Quadrophenia*. One can choose to be a Mod or Rocker and conform to the subcultural group 'lifestyle' or choose to be neither (Jimmy's sister is to some extent an example of the non-subcultural). However, in *Ill Manors*, the representation of the lived experience of Chav shows that not all aspects of lifestyle are voluntary. One does not choose to be a Chav, and *Ill Manors* highlights the struggle to escape from the Chav subculture in the character of Aaron. Ben Drew's overall view of the community in *Ill Manors* is as follows:

> *Look around this manor and all you'll see*
> *Is ill mannered people iller mannered*
> *Than the illest mannered person*
> *You've ever met in your manor*
> *Or are ever likely to meet*
> *In any manor, cause this manors' deep*
> *You judge them on the life that they lead*
> *But then it's not all as black and white as it seems*
> *They're all some way enslaved and their circumstances*
> *Shape the way they behave in their battle on the street.*
> (*Lost My Way*, Plan B 2012)

CONCLUSION

The analysis of the representations of subcultural identity and practice in the two films emphasises how subcultures are constructed and expressed within wider social and economic processes and experiences. *Quadrophenia* presents an exalted sense of importance for youth within the post-war social market economy. This economy provided youth with a positive community to reinforce their identity and oppose mainstream society. The film is about the 'Mod' subculture engaging in conscious self-constructions of identity, starting with the individual (or the self) and stamping this identity onto the wider social, economic and political spheres through group affiliations and activities. This is an 'inward-out' identification. In contrast, *Ill Manors* presents the opposite, a subcultural abject created under the neoliberal free-market economy. The film reflects how social, economic and political structures and processes shape physical and social environments, emphasising how this can promulgate inequality. In *Ill Manors* the environment is negative and hostile. The environment has a causal effect by stamping 'Chav' subcultural identities onto the people living within this community. The Chav subcultural group is shown as constructed from all that is 'other' and external to them. The engagement in subculture is unconscious, resulting in an 'outward-in' identification. It is not possible to become a 'Chav' or to buy into the 'Chav' subculture as post-subcultural theories (Bennett 2005; Muggleton and Weinzierl 2003) might advocate; it is embedded in class. This chapter has argued that subculture is not redundant, but has rather become inverted through changing market economies from a positive mode of self-identification in community, to a negative external identification through elite and popular discourses that perpetuate an authoritarian and negative categorisation and identification. As a result, the idea of post-subculture should perhaps be reconsidered.

REFERENCES

Bauman, Z. 1998. *Globalisation: The Human Consequences.* Cambridge: Polity.

Bennett, A. 1999 "Sub-cultures or Neo-tribes? Rethinking the Relationship between Youth Style and Musical Taste", in *Sociology.* Volume 33, Issue 3. pp. 599–617.

Bennett, A. 2005 "In Defence of Neo-Tribes: a response to Blackman and Hesmondhalgh" in *Journal of Youth Studies,* Volume 9. pp. 255–259.

Benstock, S. and Ferris, S. 1994. *On Fashion.* New Jersey, NJ: Rutgers University Press.

Blackman, S. 1997. "'Deconstructing a Giro: a critical ethnographic study of the youth "underclass".' In R, MacDonald (Ed). *Youth, the Underclass and Social Exclusion,* 113–129. London: Routledge.

———. 2005. "Youth subcultural theory: a critical engagement with the concept, its origins and politics, from Chicago school to postmodernism" in *Journal of Youth Studies.* Volume 8, Issue 1. pp. 1–20.

Blackman, S. and France, A. 2001. "Youth marginality under 'postmodernism'". In N. Stevenson (Ed.). *Culture and Citizenship* (pp.180–197). London: Sage.

Cohen, P. 1999. *Rethinking the Youth Question: Education, Labour and Cultural Studies.* Durhum, NC: Duke University Press.

Cohen, S. 1980. *Folk devils and moral panics: the creation of mods and rockers.* London: Martin Robertson.

Corrigan, P. 1979. *Schooling the Smash Street Kids.* London: Macmillan.

Featherstone, M. 2013. "'Hoodie Horror': The Capitalist Other in Postmodern Society" in *The Review of Education, Pedagogy and Cultural Studies.* Volume 35. pp. 178–196.

Giroux, H. 2010. *Youth in a Suspect Society: Democracy or Disposability?.* Basingstoke, Hants: Palgrave.

Goldthorpe, J.H., D. Lockwood, F. Bechhofer and J. Platt 1968. *The Affluent Worker: Industrial Attitudes and Behaviour.* Cambridge: Cambridge University Press.

Griffin, C.E. 2011. "The trouble with class: researching youth, class and culture beyond the 'Birmingham School'" in *Journal of Youth Studies.* Volume 14, Issue 3. pp. 245–259.

Hall, S. and Jefferson, T. (eds.) 1976. *Resistance Through Rituals*. London: Hutchinson.

Haywood, K. 2004. *City Limits: Crime, Consumer Culture and the Urban Experience*. London: Glasshouse Press.

Haywood, K. and M. Yar. 2006. "The 'chav' phenomenon: Consumption, media and the construction of a new underclass" in *Crime, Media, Culture*. Volume 2, Issue 9: 9–28.

Hebdige, D. 1976. 'The meaning of Mod'. In S. Hall and T, Jefferson (Eds.) *Resistance Through Rituals: Youth Subcultures in Post War Britain*: 9–74. London: Hutchinson.

Hebdige, D. 1979. *Subculture: the meaning of style*. London: Methuen.

Ill Manors, 2012. Directed by Ben Drew. Microwave: UK.

Jones, O. 2011. *Chavs: The Demonisation of the Working Class*. London: Verso.

Kristeva, J. 1980/1984. *Powers of Horror: An Essay on Abjection*. New York: Columbia University Press.

MacDonald, R., T. Shildrick, C. Webster and D. Simpson. 2005. 'Growing Up in Poor Neighbourhoods' in *Sociology*. Volume 39 (5): 873–891.

Maffesoli, M. 1995. *The Time of the Tribes: The Decline of Individuality in Mass Society*. London: Sage.

McCulloch, K., Stewart, A., and Lowegreen, N. 2006. "'We just hang out together': youth cultures and social class". *Journal of Youth Studies*. Volume 9, Issue 5: 539–556.

McRobbie, A. 1980. 'Settling account with subcultures: a feminist critique' in *Screen Education*, Volume 37: 37–49.

Muggleton, D. and Weinzierl, R. 2003. *The Post-Subcultural Reader*. Oxford: Berg.

Nayak, A. 2006. "Displaced Maculinities: Chavs, Youth and Class in the post-industrial City" in *Sociology*. Volume 40, Issue 5: 813–831.

Plan B, *Ill Manors*, 2012.

Quadrophenia, 1973. The Who.

Quadrophenia, 1979, Franc Rodam. The Who Films. UK.

Shildrick, T. and MacDonald, R. 2006. "In defence of subculture: young people, leisure and social divisions" in *Journal of Youth Studies*. Volume 9, Issue 2: 125–140.

Tyler, I. 2013. *Revolting Subjects: Social Abjection and Resistance in Neoliberal Britain*. London: Zed Books.

Weight, R. 2013. *Mod: A Very British Style*. London: Bodley Head.

Willis, P. 1979. *Learning to Labour: how working class kids get working class jobs*. Farnborough: Saxon House.

Wilson, A. 2008. "Mixing the Medicine: The unintended consequence of amphetamine control on the Northern Soul Scene" in *Internet Journal of Criminology*. Accessed 02-01-2014.

INDEX[1]

[1] Note: Page numbers followed by 'n' refer to notes.

© The Author(s) 2018
N. Bentley et al. (eds.), *Youth Subcultures in Fiction, Film and
Other Media*, Palgrave Studies in the History of Subcultures and
Popular Music, https://doi.org/10.1007/978-3-319-73189-6

255

Printed by Printforce, the Netherlands